AWAKENING
THE WARRIOR

AWAKENING
THE WARRIOR

BY

RICHARD CHARLES LAWRENCE

To Peter,
I hope you enjoy this book
and find it)) useful in your life!

Yours

Richard Charles Lawrence

First published in 2018

Illustrations by Andrew Chiu
Designed in Great Britain
Printed by CreateSpace

Discover more about Richard's work at:
www.counterstrikeuk.com

ACKNOWLEDGEMENTS

The concept and content of this book would not have been possible without the understanding that my father gave to me via his example on a daily basis. The production of this book would not have been possible without my mother whose practical support and ingenuity have been indispensable.

For the understanding of ancient philosophy and for his example of intellectual rigour, Professor Stephen RL Clark has been a constant inspiration.

For the understanding of fighting I have to thank Justo Dieguez (who created the 'Keysi' fighting method) for his creativity, insights and training. The comprehensive and scientific approach to fighting of my friend Martyn Cahill (a Brazilian jiu-jitsu black belt, amongst other things) has given me a new perspective and broadened my horizons both on and off the mats. I also have to thank Fernando Gomez, whose training has helped me greatly over the years.

Samuel Eccleston has been an inexhaustible resource for excellent book recommendations which became my required reading.

My thanks go to Cathryn Boyd and John Lansdowne for continued practical support throughout this project.

This book is dedicated to all those I have served with and in particular, James Roddis and Andrew Husband.

CONTENTS

————

PROLOGUE

This book was written in order to help the individual reach their true potential.

I was fortunate enough to grow up living next to my father's jewellery workshop, where craftsmen and women would endeavour to make objects of the very highest quality out of precious things that had come out of the ground; gold, platinum and silver, sapphires, emeralds and diamonds. These materials were transformed by the craftsman into extraordinary objects that seemed to have a life of their own.

As a boy I was fascinated by the numerous processes that were needed to make these beautiful things; the sight of the roaring blue flames of the soldering torches and the sound of the red hot metal as it was quenched in the acid bath, and the smell of the waxy rouge that was used to polish these objects to perfection.

I remember too, the fury of the craftsmen who had just made an error and had to then compose themselves and start all over again, countless hours of work wasted with a momentary lapse in concentration. It was clear that producing these miniature works of art involved incredible skill, hard work and determination, not just in a single moment but hour after hour.

We come into the world with our own raw materials; our body, our heart and our mind. It is up to us to make something out of them.

The first step in this process is to AWAKEN THE WARRIOR. Reaching our potential is a battle and if we are going to fight this battle then we need to build our warrior first. Eventually we will need to add much more besides, but to even begin the process we need to be able to put up a fight.

Imagine that I have the potential to be the greatest actor the world has ever known. My understanding of drama is unsurpassed, I am blessed with an expressive face and my voice is perfect for the theatre. But no-one will ever know how good I could be because I am too scared to get up on stage or even go for an audition. I need The Warrior.

Imagine that I am living my life quite happily, I have a good job, nice house, a nice car and marriage. An economic downturn leaves me suddenly redundant. The pressures of my new situation comes as a shock and the arguments that follow put strain on my marriage. I need The Warrior.

Imagine that I am walking through the city to meet my partner when everything goes black as a terrorist bomb detonates. When at last my eyes open I realise I am still alive. I need The Warrior.

Our ability to fight is the key in all these examples and at all times when we face obstacles and challenges in life, from the seemingly trivial to the seemingly overwhelming. The Warrior is needed so badly because it is his nature to fight and The Warrior relishes the challenge. With The Warrior awakened, we need not muddle through life's difficulties but rather view them as opportunities for growth. Every crisis is now a creative opportunity.

This book lays down the roadmap, the journey, that is needed to awaken The Warrior. The introduction gives The Warriors' specifications to show you what you need to build.

Chapter 1 (Something Missing in the Golden Age) describes the mission so that you can be aware of the nature of the terrain that you will encounter on your journey. Like any good 'ground briefing', it will pick out the areas where progress may be slowed and where opportunities for fast travel may exist.

Chapter 2 (Becoming Domesticated) describes the current cultural and societal situation. This chapter is designed to tell you in the most honest and frank way where your starting point may be. Far from being the super-slick, bad-ass of your dreams you may find that you are starting from a fairly low base. But knowing where you are is the only way to begin a journey. Beginning the journey is the only way to get to your destination. Many people would simply rather not know the truth. If you get this far, you are clearly not one of them.

Chapter 3 (The Will To Act) uses historical context to describe how learning a physical skill to a high level is a secret of successful and innovative people from a broad range of disciplines. It shows how the "will to act", is generated by the discipline of learning a physical skill and facing danger in particular. The old practise of duelling is used as an example here. And Oscar Wilde makes an appearance too.

Chapter 4 (The Will Of The Warrior) will put you in the right mental state to begin. This is where you orientate yourself to the mission and start to appreciate the reality of what it is that you need to achieve. This chapter is where you 'gird your loins'. In this chapter you will discover how to develop the correct attitude - which is the difference between failure and success.

Chapter 5 (Training Your Will) starts the journey and equips you with the knowledge you need to get up to full speed. This chapter goes into detail about how training begins to create a single will out of the normal fractious desires of our divided self. By the end of this chapter you will understand what happens to you with the correct training and what correct training should therefore consist of. This is the process of developing the 'discerning eye' that can tell something true and useful from something false and useless.

Chapter 6 (Myth and Mystery) uses the vehicle of the art of fighting to demonstrate how we must find the truth and dispose of fantasy. In this chapter you will learn some shocking realities of what the samurai were really like and how mystical nonsense came to be associated with the practical art of fighting.

Chapter 7 (The Essence of Fighting) lays down the principles of fighting. Our vehicle is used as an example for how we must boil down the components of any activity to see right through to its essence. When we see to the essence of a thing, we take it beyond the boundaries of its apparent immediate purpose and turn knowledge into genuine wisdom. Into this chapter I put all my experience of training and teaching others in this field over the years and of the wisdom I have learnt from many teachers. This chapter exists as a resource that you can continue to draw on throughout your development, or if you need to understand how principles connect across many areas of life.

Chapter 8 (**Training the Principles**) explores how to train to make the principles live within you. Using music as a metaphor, you will learn how learning to apply knowledge is not a simple case of knowing what to do, more a case of allowing the body to learn in the right environment. This is the missing link in the practical understanding of how skills are learnt and is of vital importance. Included at the end is a roadmap of awakening The Warrior which summarises all the steps along the way. Like any journey, the route you take is not set, but is up to you.

The Epilogue (Beyond The Warrior) gives a glimpse of the journey that is required when The Warrior is awakened.

INTRODUCTION
DEFINITION OF THE WARRIOR

TITLE: WARRIOR

MOTTO: BATTLE READY

BEHAVIOUR: ACTION

NATURE: TO FIGHT

ATTITUDE: THE WILL TO ACT

ENVIRONMENT: CRISIS

CHARACTERISTICS: RESILIENCE, ROBUSTNESS, RESOURCEFULNESS, RELENTLESSNESS, RUTHLESSNESS

MISSION: SELECTION AND MAINTENANCE OF THE AIM

INSTRUCTIONS FOR USE: BREAK GLASS IN CASE OF EMERGENCY

Deploy The Warrior whenever you face crisis, obstacles or hardship and it seems that the world is against you. The Warrior will never surrender and never give up. The Warrior is resolved from the beginning and achieves the mission by any means necessary.

The Warrior is in you already, but is sleeping. The Warrior will be the best ally you will ever have. With The Warrior fighting for you, you can defeat incredible odds and achieve things you can only dream about. But The Warrior needs to be woken up.

CHAPTER 1
SOMETHING MISSING
IN THE GOLDEN AGE

This is a Golden Age. There is an old photograph in Liverpool Library that shows a group of very young Edwardian children. They are gathered around the fountain near the Walker Art Gallery. Many of them have no shoes on. *They have no shoes on.*

My grandmother was alive at this time, when in this country, there were families so poor they could not afford shoes. Any shoes. How many children do you see now wearing no shoes? Thank God the answer is none.

In this Golden Age, our views about poverty have changed immeasurably. Now we talk about the 'extreme' poverty of some in our country. But everything is relative. How many die of hunger? In fact, it is more likely that those in disadvantaged areas are overweight. Diseases from eating too much food, like type 2 diabetes, have replaced diseases from eating too little, like rickets and marasmus.

To read accounts of poverty in Victorian times is to enter an unimaginable hell. The way, for example, that Irish immigrants had to live in the urban sprawl of Manchester is staggering to the mind.

It is important to appreciate how far we have come since then, despite the ravages of two World Wars. Right now, in relative terms, to be alive in an advanced Western economy, is to be among the richest and healthiest people in the whole world. It may not always seem like this because we are surrounded by other relatively wealthy people. What twists our view is that we look at millionaires and billionaires and then think we are poor! If you own a car in global terms you are wealthy.

The world that we live in in the West has so many benefits and comforts. Our cheap and plentiful food. Our healthcare. Our education. It's not perfect of course but it is amongst the very best in the world. So what's the problem? The problem is this:

We are individually less prepared for crisis than ever before, growing soft and decadent on the bloated carcass of modern living.

If history tells us anything, it is that times of plenty are fleeting and hard times are just around the corner. In the past we have at least had many great men and women ready to stand up and act. But in our Golden Age, in all areas of our lives, ease and luxury have flooded in and *we don't even realise it.*

This is a Universal Law of human society: good times produce soft and decadent people.

By 'soft' I don't mean caring or emotional or any of these good things. I mean unable to function in hard times, easy to manipulate and fragile. By decadent I make no *moral* judgement, I mean it in its true sense: the decline of certain skills.

These skills are specifically those which we traditionally associate with warriors: *the ability to prevail in the most difficult circumstances.*

Our society contains people like this of course, but their number is getting fewer and fewer as our society becomes more affluent and our culture becomes less conducive to their development. I do not imagine that this is a deliberate effect. It is merely the Universal Law at work.

OUR CULTURE

The chief observation I made when I came back from the war in Afghanistan was that people in normal life in this country operate way, way below their true potential. They have no real idea of what they are actually capable of and they are satisfied with so little from themselves. Anything for an easy life. I contrasted this with the amazing things I had seen normal human beings achieving in the crucible of conflict.

Our generation has seen incredible technological advancement at the cost of physicality and robustness amongst the general populace. Ever increasing urbanisation and urban focus has seen us divorced from the land and nature like never before. We have become so soft in this country that we won't even do unpleasant jobs and need people coming in from poorer countries to do them for us.

This is an unpleasant truth but it is true none the less. We see migrant workers coming over, working hard and doing well. The only difference is that they are hungry and come from a culture that lacks our comfort and laziness.

But we have paid a high price for this. We have abdicated responsibility for our lives to others. This is particularly true in our urbanised existence in the UK. We have abdicated responsibility for our personal security to the police. Our right to defend ourselves have been ever more and more eroded away and we have accepted our role as helpless citizens.

We abdicate responsibility for our health to the state. We have an expectation now that they will look after us, however we pollute our bodies and deny them exercise. We expect the state, rather than our own family, to financially support us if we cannot support ourselves. And we expect that support to allow us to continue living the quality of life we have come to demand as our right. We even expect the TV to entertain us.

We expect others to invent increasingly more sophisticated technological devices to make our lives easier. We click a few buttons and luxurious goods are delivered to our door within a day! These are collectively our ENTITLEMENTS. Just for being born! There comes a change point in every society where it goes from being enhanced by good conditions to becoming reliant on them. We have reached that point. We risk losing our ability to overcome the odds. The alternative is to become BATTLE READY.

BEING BATTLE READY

Being BATTLE READY means having the resources, willpower and freedom to act. It means going into a situation knowing that you can decide the outcome. No longer are you a slave to events, you are the director of them. Who would not want this in their life if they are prepared to work for it? But working for it means having the courage to try at each stage and over many years. We face failure at every step. Failure to live up to our untested opinion of ourselves for example.

There is no doubt that taking this path will teach you some humility, whether you like it or not. The alternative path though is too horrifying to consider. You live a life never testing failure nor genuine achievement. You work in your office in your mind-numbing job doing little for humanity or yourself other than taking a salary. You want to leave your job but you are scared of giving up the money, status and lifestyle. You are in fact a simple coward. And, worse than that, just another *consumer*.

It is all too easy and comfortable to be like this. If your conscience is tweaked a little, you might go a do something for charity or go and do a parachute jump or something. So what? You then go back to your normal life.

You may choose to be a bit more conscientious, to think about the things you are buying and the activities you are doing. So you become a 'hipster', drinking organic mocha-chocka skinny lattes but in fact you are just fetishising consumerism in a different way. The overwhelming *zeitgeist* of our time is glorification of the self through materialism.

SEVEN DEADLY SINS

There have been times in the past when people have been in danger of becoming 'indecently soft' as Plato put it. Indeed, in the end, the ancient Greek civilisation fell into decadence and the Romans who were keen and hungry took over. What is true on the scale of civilisations is true individually as well. Having achieved 'security' the individual is then prone to corruption. His manner of corruption is well described as 'the seven deadly sins'.

Think of our modern lives for the vast majority of us - sloth, lust, greed, envy, gluttony, wrath and pride is an accurate description. Take gluttony for example. When you look at old film footage from the 1970s in the UK you wonder where all the fat people are. You then compare this with contemporary footage and everyone looks like they have been inflated.

Take lust and sloth together and you have our modern addiction to internet pornography. And we can't get enough. We lust after pixels on a screen not even flesh and blood. We demand instant gratification. Our pride is seen at the frankly incredible attendances at weekly football matches where we take pride in acts that we had no part in.

The language of the fan - the 'non-combatant' is all about 'we'. "We beat such and such at the weekend". Often the fan isn't even from that town and none of the players are even English yet he still proudly states 'we' as if it has any meaning.

The seven deadly sins are corruptions of desire. You will not find me so censorious or prudish as to suggest that lust by itself is a bad thing. Correctly channelled it has a great creative force as 'sex energy'. Likewise wrath can provide the energy to protect ourselves and our families, as well as the ability to ensure our freedom.

Every soldier knows that you need certain forms of pride to ensure the highest standards: pride in your appearance, in your skills, in the effectiveness of your unit and so on. When these things become about glorification of yourself however they become poisonous.

If I am sitting on a beach in Hawaii doing nothing all day because I need the time to recuperate my physical body, still my chaotic mind and take the time to enjoy being alive then my 'sloth' is positive. If I stay at home watching TV all day because I can't be bothered to do anything else then my will is being destroyed.

It may seem like all this work on yourself to become Battle Ready is selfish in itself. But what we are doing is making ourselves useful and able to serve others. The leader must develop his abilities in order to lead. For him, that is how he serves the team. Likewise, the firefighter goes through his training in order to rescue people from fires and so forth.

Many people have the desire to serve. But they are typically like the gap year student who goes to Africa to help build a school with other gap year students which promptly falls down within a year as none of them learnt to build properly before they went.

If you really want to build schools in Africa, go and learn the art of bricklaying first. It will take you time and effort to learn how to do it and to do it well enough to go fast. But then you will be able to help people.

In previous times, aristocrats from Plato to Lord Byron to Churchill recognised that the privilege of their comfortable lives could lead to making them useless in times of trouble. Their antidote was learning wrestling, hunting, fencing and serving in the army for example. The common man's life was hard enough but men of aspiration also learnt to fight as a means of protection and also to improve themselves. Life is a constant battle of trying to master the mechanical dolls inside us all.

In this country, most of our lives are aristocratic by ancient standards. We have all the food we can eat and that most aristocratic of things - 'leisure time' to fill. But we have not yet realised that without the physical work that kept us honest, we are rotting from the inside.

This book is about making yourself ready. The fact that it is needed is due to the circumstances of our age. Every age has challenges of its own. Our strength as a civilisation is also our weakness. There are many reasons to love being alive at this time. The prime reason that I am pleased to live in this era is because of how plentiful and easy it is to get hold of *knowledge*.

It seems bizarre to us now that books used to be expensive objects of desire. To be able to have such a wealth of knowledge at our fingertips is beyond the wildest dreams of the ancient philosophers like Pythagoras who spent decades in Egypt and then Babylon in order to learn as much as he could. Our danger is that we don't value this knowledge enough to do anything with it. To translate that knowledge into wisdom is the aim we should be aspiring to.

OUR LATENT ABILITY

Within us all, real potential lurks. Our comfortable and safe up-bringings have kept it largely hidden, its latency proof of our failure to explore our potential. It needs to be activated, to be reclaimed. Forget about needing talent. Most people never put in the hard work for their 'talent' to make a difference anyway. Hard work will suffice for now.

When we truly understand this, it will benefit every area of our lives. Imagine how resourceful and how powerful you will become when you can deal with ANYTHING that is thrown at you.

An old army friend of mine is fond of saying 'how will YOU cope when the zombie apocalypse comes?' It's a joke but it means 'are you ready?' Little apocalypses come to all of us in our lives, from burglaries, assaults, break ups, car accidents, losing our jobs and even finding out that our loved ones are dying of terminal illnesses. We always have two choices. We can curl up into a ball and hope it goes away or we can get busy and become Battle Ready.

In the UK and in many other countries, the solution to public safety is to disarm and defang the populous in order to prevent them from harming each other. We have some of the strictest laws on the carriage of weapons for self-defence in the whole world. Basically anything you carry with the *intention* of using it in self-defence is regarded as an offensive weapon and is thus illegal.

That means not just mace and pepper spray but any object at all, modified or not. If I carry a D-Cell Maglite torch and the police believe that I am doing so to use it in self-defence then I am outside the law. If I carry an umbrella (essential in the UK) which has been strengthened to use as a weapon *in extremis* I am outside the law.

The authorities are saying 'do not defend yourself - that's our job as we do not trust you to do it yourself'. That is all well and good but it is a broken promise. For the individual, there is no way that the authorities can protect them at every turn. Neither is that the case with our seemingly random modern terrorist attacks.

In previous decades, everyone in the UK lived with the threat of an IRA bomb attack. In these attacks, which require a high level of technical sophistication on behalf of the bombers, the individual citizen can do little. One thing the IRA never had though was an explicit desire for martyrdom when carrying out attacks.

Several factors came together to thwart the IRA's offensive capability, chiefly the fact that the intelligence services were all over them and they were riddled with informants. Add to that the fact that they were stifled in their transport of weapons and people by the observation towers in South Armagh. Add to that also their own internal politics and the fact that many key IRA individuals began to make a great deal of money from their illegal activities in drugs, prostitution, racketeering, smuggling and so forth that their ideology began to soften and they became weak and greedy.

Rather than turn to suicide attacks in desperation, the IRA turned increasingly to political methods, its former commanders receiving a wage on the state and drinking tea and eating scones in government buildings. They became soft and decadent.

Compare this with the Islamic extremist. He has no cosy relationships with the government he is seeking to bring down. He does not have pre-arranged warning codes prior to his attacks. Neither does he need to consider his own safety, in fact he actively seeks martyrdom for his cause. This means that 'lone wolf' attacks are possible as little sophistication or complicated planning is required.

In any attack, 'getting away with it' needs serious amounts of detailed planning. If no credible solution can be found, the operation will be aborted. Your Islamic extremist has no need to do any of this. He will not be calling off an attack if his escape route is blocked. He has no escape route. The degree to which this makes him more dangerous is exponential. These kind of attacks cause a level of death and damage that we simply have never seen before.

I am not suggesting we should arm our citizens with weapons. We know the problems that this brings of its own. But we do need to arm ourselves with an attitude of the WILL TO ACT - becoming BATTLE READY. Such a person we can call a WARRIOR. And the nature of the warrior is to be BATTLE READY at all times and in all areas of life.

OUR METHOD

Miyamoto Musashi, the legendary Japanese swordsman said:

"We must develop a discerning eye in all things". [1]

This is a deceptively simple remark that contains exactly what we seek to learn from becoming a warrior. When we understand the deep principles of performing in a chaotic and high pressure environment we learn how to tell truth from fiction and this is where the gold is.

This is Musashi's 'discerning eye' and it is PRICELESS. It cannot be given. It has to be earned. Like everything of real value we will pay for it in one way or another. You have already made a small investment - in money to pay for this book and in time in order to read it. If you have no money and you stole this book, I salute your determination but send me a few quid when you get back on your feet mate, as I paid for this information with my blood, sweat and tears!

You cannot get this fighting spirit and will to act though from just reading this book, anymore than a reading a book on how to play the guitar will magically make you Jimi Hendrix. But it will tell you what to do to develop it. Then it's over to you.

The vast majority of people will read a book, intellectualise it and then assume they know it all and understand it all. This is dangerous. When we think we know something but don't, it is far worse than when we know we don't know which is the first necessary stage in genuine learning.

You will know someone who spouts off all kinds of stuff he has read in books - and has no real understanding from doing. This is a total dead end.

There is a secret that the most successful and innovative people have - they all have a physical ability to a high level in some or other area. This may come as a surprise but it's true.

Plato was a wrestler and a good one too. Pythagoras won the boxing tournament at the 48th Olympiad. Einstein was a professional standard violinist. The pioneering female scientist Cecilia Payne-Ga-poschkin was also known for being an 'inspired seamstress'. Niels Bohr, who formulated the 'Copenhagen Interpretation' of quantum mechanics played in goal for a professional Danish football team. Alan Turing was an Olympic standard marathon runner. Edward de Bono, who coined the term 'lateral thinking' set canoeing records at Oxford. James Dyson was a successful long distance runner. Neil de-Grasse Tyson captained his school wrestling team. Mark Zuckerburg, founder of Facebook, was captain of his school fencing team.

Speaking of fencers, we can add Shakespeare, Voltaire, Churchill, Emilie du Chatelet, Hogarth and Descartes to name a few. Descartes even wrote a book called *The Art of Fencing*. Vladimir Putin, who seems to outwit other world leaders at will is a judo black belt and wrote a book called *The Art of Judo*.

Larry Page, founder of Google is a saxophonist and studied musical composition. What he said about the development of Google is important:

> *'In music you're very cognisant of time. Time is like the primary thing...it's amazing to the extent I think that modern operating systems are terrible at being real time.....if you think about it from a music point of view, if you're a percussionist, you hit something, it's got to happen in milliseconds, fractions of a second'.*[2]

This understanding that Larry Page learnt from playing music was the bedrock of his solution to how to make a successful search engine. The revelation made him develop algorithms that had speed as the primary concern. And the rest is history.

Steve Jobs got his inspiration for the typefaces and fonts that have become the worldwide aesthetic of personal computers from doing calligraphy. Once again, the physical expression, the doing of something is how we uncover the PRINCIPLE. The PRINCIPLE then leads us to the solution.

We will explore this in detail in later chapters but for now we need only acknowledge that a wholly academic approach - an approach based on theory and thinking alone will never give us the solutions and results we are looking for.

It is fascinating that the ancient Greeks used to educate their young men by teaching them wrestling and music. This approach was explicitly designed to develop character. Later, a group called the Sophists began to teach these young men in how to develop intellect, but via the use of rhetoric so that they could be clever with words and get into politics. It is these men that Socrates criticises for their emptiness of character. They are not interested in truth, but only the appearance of truth. The person who develops character is interested in *virtue* - doing the right things based on truth.

Our body is our most direct way of experiencing the world and the simplest way to uncover truth.

The physical skill most suited to the problems of the modern world is in learning to fight. The art of self-defence is perfect for our needs because in addition to learning essential principles, we can develop the ability to take responsibility, withstand pressure and use aggression properly - all things that are sadly lacking in our society. We lack an individual fighting spirit. This is the way to get it back.

Learning the physical skill of fighting is our method of developing the integration of will that we require to build The Warrior.

YOUR PERSONAL DEVELOPMENT

If you are reading this book, I will assume you are interested in self-development. Because you have taken the time to read a book about it, rather than just watch a two minute video on the internet, I will assume your interest is genuine and serious. What I have attempted to do with this book is just that - to produce something genuine and serious.

I received many suggestions about what to call this book. My mother said 'why not just call it 'how to beat the shit out of people?' I laughed at first but then realised that in a way this was the book I was writing. But not just how to beat enemies, but to beat the odds and beat the circumstances however stacked against you they are. This is what it is to be The Warrior.

When my mother came out with this, it reminded me of an occasion years ago when I was very young. I had been taken to the cinema with my parents and sister.

The film must have been quite popular as we could not sit together on the same row, rather my parents sat in the row in front with my sister and I directly behind them. In the row in front of my parents were a noisy gang of teenage youths, full of aggression and nervous energy.

During the film showing, my mother lent forward and told them to settle down as they were ruining the film. Several times she had to do this. My mother is not much over 5" 1". She was an active member of the local church, sang in the choir and often did the flowers. Not exactly what you would call a hooligan or hard-nut. At the end of the film when the lights came on, this gang towered over my mother and offered all kinds of physical threats.

Sitting behind, I had the view of these aggressive creatures threatening my mother. The girls with them had scraped back hair and cheap gold coloured jewellery. They looked ready for violence. My mother fixed them with a stare and laughed in their faces. It wasn't even a full laugh. More like the kind of dismissive expulsion of air French people make when they say "bof" to deride a stupid comment.

I looked at my father, who was by no means young and he was fixing them with the same stare without saying a word. The gang seemed to physically shrink back and, almost embarrassed by their own retreat, withdrew out of the cinema in double quick time. It was like the will had been sucked out of them.

My parents clearly thought nothing of this at all, never mentioned a thing and our evening continued as normal. I was fascinated by this and years later understood that my parent's generation were the ones that had lived through the war as little children. My mother was born when the war began in 1939 and all of her most formative years were spent in its shadow.

Living in Watford, she had spent a great deal of time in air raid shelters with bombs dropping around her. On one particular occasion, the bombing was so bad that her mother informed her that they were all going to die as they could hear a V2 'buzzbomb' overhead. 'Buzzbombs' were unmanned aircraft that the Germans directed at targets in England. They dropped to the ground when they ran out of fuel - and the engine could be heard cutting out by those below. As fate would have it, that bomb exploded in the next street.

My father was five years old when war broke out and also lived near enough to London to be in danger from the blitz leading to his evacuation. This was a generation, like the one before them, that had lived through the worst war that there has ever been. It is easy to come up with all kinds of clever sounding psychological theories but compared to these experiences, a gang of narky youths were not the scariest thing they had ever seen. It was like my parents knew that they were all talk and noise and not really up for fight.

It's funny but as little children we don't imagine our parents had all kinds of life experiences before we were born. As kids we are self-absorbed to the extent that it is difficult to imagine a time before we existed. As we grow older though, we learn to appreciate our parent's experiences more and perhaps understand them better.

Often I would hear my parents discussing the relative merits of one individual or another. The ultimate test was always 'would you want them standing next to you in the trenches?' This has become my test too, not only of others but for myself. It's really the only test that counts. Think about the people you know and apply that test. It may be that some of those that you decide you would want next to you in the trenches are not the people you like best or whose morals and behaviour you admire most. Now apply that test to yourself - would others chose to have you next to them in battle?

I count myself very lucky to have been in situations where you can observe people for real when the shit hits the fan. This is the real moment of truth when you see into their soul and past all the masks and smoke that we build around us and call our 'personality'.

The spirit of this book is greatly inspired by all occasions where, like during the war, our backs are against the wall and things do not look good. In these situations, the time for gentleness and diplomacy is gone. We need something of an altogether more fundamental nature.

It's that thing that the gang saw in the eyes of my parents. We cannot go back to the circumstances of their youth (and I'm sure would not want to). But, nevertheless we need to know how to generate and develop that spirit. It's the spirit that our leaders need and the only thing that can take us through the toughest times. Only this can help us adapt and improvise under real pressure.

If you want to function well in crisis you need a roadmap on how to achieve this and you need a vehicle to help you get there. This book is the roadmap and the vehicle is learning how to fight. Nothing is more immediate, more primal and more appropriate in our modern era. It's what we have lost and what we need to regain.

HOW TO USE THIS BOOK

To get the best out of this book read it once straight through like a novel. This will place the work you have to do in context. The next stage is to re-read Chapter 7 - *The Essence of Fighting* and Chapter 8 - *Training the Principles* in more detail to support your training.

CHAPTER 2
BECOMING DOMESTICATED

My father remembers little from the moment the butcher's knife went through his hand to waking up in the hospital. It is an amusing detail that the nurse he saw when he first opened his eyes was a former girlfriend. For a second, he believed he had died and entered heaven after all, so strange was the coincidence.

Pain brought him shooting back into the present. The knife had indeed gone all the way through his hand and out of the other side. Amazingly, it had missed every single tendon and through pure luck not wrecked his hand forever. That was not even the biggest stroke of luck he had had that day.

The year was 1956 and my father was a manager at a bacon smoking factory in the East End of London. This is hard, physical work and the junior managers like my father had to do just as much of the manual work as the men. A bacon smoking factory takes whole sides of bacon - basically the side of one whole pig minus the head and trotters and hangs them up in a smokehouse; a room with burning wood chips over the floor.

The process of smoking food in this way was developed thousands of years ago to preserve the meat as well as adding flavour.

A standard work team is six men. The first opens the bales of bacon and sticks a big metal hook through the end of the bacon side. The second man lifts the side onto his shoulders and takes it to a table where the third man covers the meat in meal. The fourth man lifts the side off the table and hooks it onto the rope, and the fifth man, up on a balcony, winches the side up to the ceiling. The six man is used as a runner.

This can be unpleasant work as well as hard graft and not only for the men. Stories are told of freezing winters with horses slipping and sliding their hooves over the icy cobbles. On many occasions, whole cartloads of goods were spilled over the roads as horses smacked into the unforgiving stone surfaces.

This was still a time before the clean air act in London and the fog of pollution hung over and around the River Thames, often engulfing the docks and the warehouses of the East End and all across London Town. The basic pay was poor and the kind of men that did this work were mainly Irish immigrants, uneducated and unable to read or write even. On Friday after work, the wives of the men would wait outside, ready to take their wages off them before they could drink the money in the pub.

Fights were common, at least occurring every few days. The standard procedure was that the other men would separate the fight as soon as humanly possible, as when these men fought, they fought to kill rather than disable their opponent. In an environment with meat hooks and butcher's knives easily to hand, this outcome was made a distinct possibility.

These were men that had grown up in a time that was very different to kids today. Although in terms of human history it was not so very long ago, it is rare indeed in this country nowadays to find groups of men that can neither read or write and whose only possibility for making a living is via their ability to physically haul produce around.

Doing this kind of muscular labour all day gives you a strength of body that cannot be easily replicated, even by going into a gym regularly and lifting weights. For these men, this was their lives until they were too old to continue.

One of these men, a big man with dark eyes had been left by his wife. The rumour amongst the workers was that his wife had 'gone off with a black man'. It needs to be remembered that the post-war period in Britain was a time when there was a large influx of people from the Caribbean and it was not uncommon for boarding houses to have signs in the windows stating 'No Coloureds' or 'No West Indians'.

In the prevailing attitudes of that time and place, to be cuckolded was one thing, but to be cuckolded by a black man was another. The experience had turned this man's state of mind inside out. His anger was directed to everyone and he insisted that he kept hearing his co-workers chanting "spade, spade, spade" *sotto voce* as he walked past.

A fragile state of mind in a man already prone to violence and with the strength of life long physical work is not a good mix. Inevitably, this man's rage became directed at the nearest authority figure, in this case, my father. Waiting for my father to turn his back, this man ran towards him with a long butcher's knife in his hand, with the clear intention of plunging it into his back and dispatching him into the afterlife.

The stroke of luck my father had was that he had turned his back in order to check the weight of a parcel of bacon that was being prepared for delivery. The scales that were used for this were not digital instruments but rather had large, highly polished analogue dials.

At the last second, my father had seen the approach of this murderous man reflected in the glass of the dial. Turning around and moving on instinct, he had put up his hands to protect himself. The knife, rather than going through his back had gone clean through his hand. The other men had rushed in and restrained the man, who had been disarmed by virtue of the fact that his knife had remained stuck in my father's hand. Their method of restraint was basically a massive 'pile-on' with the bear-like man unable to move through sheer weight of bodies.

What is striking to me about this story is how it presents such a sharp contrast to the working lives we have today in this country. Even though this was only sixty years ago, it was a time when hard manual labour was still an everyday reality for thousands of men. This was a time still of miners, dockers, millworkers, hod-carriers and so on. To make a living from the sweat of your brow was common.

The 'language' of physicality and hard graft was the common tongue in many communities, from the docks of the East End of London to the mines of St Helens and Wigan. My father's attempted murder did not even make the news, not even the local paper.

The truth is that nowadays, we have never had it so soft. For people in the developed world, we have never had it as easy. Even the ancient Greeks, with their slaves and leisure time had the constant threat of war hanging over them. This is not to mention the rudimentary state of healthcare.

Some would call this progress. And it is. Would we really want to go back to a time like the Victorian era, where if you lived in an impoverished slum area in Liverpool, the infant mortality rate might be more than five hundred deaths per thousand? More likely to die than live![3] No thank you, I'll stay in my own time if it's all the same to you. I'll stay with my free medical care, my life expectancy of over eighty, my cheap and plentiful food.

We have no need to work ourselves into early graves through hard labour. The need to be physical has reduced rapidly, as the industries that demanded it have either declined or been automated. The last coal mines have closed in the UK and many other physical occupations are done by robots.

According to the 'Flynn Effect', as a result of less manual labour and more jobs requiring cognitive ability, the average cognitive ability of the populace has increased. Put simply, we are smarter than we used to be and this is to be celebrated. BUT - our average manual and physical skills have decreased with all the good things that come with them.

The good things that come with them are a kind of understanding that can only come from 'doing' something; only from being in *action*. And one of the Warrior's essential characteristics is to be a 'man of action'.

Because we are exposed to hardship, violence and difficulties much less, we have never been worse prepared for it when it happens. Our violence is confined in the main to inner city gangs rather than being a cultural norm. The shock of violence in this era is overwhelming precisely because of its everyday absence.

The problem is, it's those moments of hardship, difficulty and violence that become the key events in individual's lives and the defining moments in history. Moments that we are now less and less ready for and able to deal with. We have fallen into a state of bovine conformity and luxurious apathy.

OUR SPECIAL KIND OF DYSTOPIA

As a child, I remember reading books of science fiction that told stories of nightmarish dystopian futures where every citizen was forced to wear a tracking device. The citizens of that future were under constant surveillance and could be eavesdropped at anytime. I remember thinking that if anyone tried to put a tracking device in me, I would fight them to my last breath.

The horrible truth of the present day is that we have all collectively agreed to carry a tracking device on us at all times. The same device can be used to eavesdrop on our conversations. No-one forced us to carry a mobile phone. In the end, modern life seemed to make them essential. Funny that we got on just fine without them before.

Nobody should be naive enough to think that our mobile phones cannot be listened in to at anytime. I know that some have suggested that with all the mobile phones in the country, only very few could be monitored. But this technology has gone the same way as manual labour - it's now done by machines.

The Government Communications Headquarters in Cheltenham (GCHQ) has five ACRES of computers in their lower floor. Imagine how small and powerful a laptop computer is and then imagine the most sophisticated computer technology. And imagine five acres of it. We Brits are so good at this form of spying that the Americans pay us millions and millions of pounds every year to do it for them as well.

Our governments in this country of late, whatever their political colour, have been relatively benign. But let us pray that they never turn against the people. We would be crushed. With our Facebook profiles and Twitter accounts we have compiled a file of information on ourselves that would be beyond the wildest dreams of a KGB officer.

In this high technology world, everything we do is traced,

everything recorded. If we live or work in a city or town, we cannot avoid being caught on CCTV many times every single day. Our internet use can be recorded, our calls are logged by our own mobile phones. Every time we visit a cash machine we are caught on CCTV and a record is made of the visit. We are fixed in location not just by our mobile phones but every time we use our credit card.

More personal information is available about us online than ever before. You can meet a person at random through work, google them and immediately find pictures of them drunk with their mates, or in a bikini at the beach. This is so common that it's not even weird anymore. But it *is* weird. Our lives are open books like never before. Not even in the regimes of the Stasi and KGB were normal citizens so heavily monitored - and we have done it to ourselves.

Even when my father was young, many people lived entirely 'off the grid' but in plain sight in our biggest cities. They had no passports, no credit cards, no identity documents of any kind and worked in all cash businesses. They paid no tax. If they needed healthcare, they went to a doctor and paid in cash. This was, in any case, normal as this was before the establishment of the National Health Service.

Many of these people were not 'criminals' in the true sense. They just liked freedom. They asked nothing of the state and gave nothing back. They looked after their family and friends and got on with living life. No one in authority tried to pin these people down. It was accepted and they were more or less left alone. It is more or less impossible to live like this anymore.

Surely we have benefits now of the way we live however? Surely our conformity and surrender to surveillance has some reward? It certainly does. We have never lived in safer times. Our average life expectancy is longer than it ever has been. Risk has been enormously reduced. Our roads are amongst the safest in the world, with the lowest mortality rates. Health and Safety regulations mean that fewer industrial accidents occur now than ever, despite a growing population. Our gun ownership laws in the UK are more or less the most restrictive in the world.

We may not appreciate that our times are super safe because

of the way our media is able to report every incident. This gives us an impression that we are living in times of high crime and high violence, but this is not the case. Even the attacks we occasionally have from terrorist groups do not make these times more violent than in our history. Many forget that in the UK, the early 1970's were a time of constant violence in Northern Ireland, with casualties in the many hundreds.

As we go back through history, we reveal how the people of that time had a closer relationship to violence than now. For example, in the early Victorian era, one need only to look at what was considered to be normal, healthy entertainment. People of all social classes mixed together to bet on dog-fights, badger-baiting, rat-baiting and all manner of ingenious blood sports.

It is interesting that the fighting spirit of the English is often referred to as the 'bulldog' spirit. This is a direct reference to the dog's ability to bite and hold onto the snout of a bull during bull-baiting. These dogs were bred especially for their courage in attacking a much, much larger and more dangerous animal. These animals were not pets. Baiting of the larger animals was not banned until 1835, although the practice was hundreds of years old back then. Rat-baiting continued legally for decades after, giving us some of our favourite dog breeds.

The issue of 'blood sports' is an interesting one, given that we in the UK have all but banned them. I was present at the last ever 'Waterloo Cup', a hare coursing event near Liverpool. This event ran from 1836 until it was banned, along with all hare-coursing on the UK mainland in 2005.

The reason I had gone there was because I knew it would be the last one and I try never to miss an opportunity to experience something and perhaps learn a thing or two.

Hare-coursing involves the 'beating' (driving) of a hare onto a course where a man waits holding onto the leads of two greyhounds. The man is known as the "Slipper' and the dogs are referred to as being 'in the slips'. This man is usually big and strong, as when the hare arrives from behind him and runs onto the course, the dogs strain like fury at the leashes.

The Slipper has to judge how much head start to give the hare before releasing the dogs at exactly the same time. The greyhounds chase after the hare and the winner is the dog that gets closest to the hare. Occasionally, one of the dogs catches and kills the hare.

The contest is between the fast speed in a straight line of the dogs and the ability to change direction of the hare. Often I saw the hare slow down in order to bring the dogs closer before changing direction. This causes the dogs to get in each other's way and hampers their progress. The drama in each race is created by the fact that you are witnessing the hare's life-and-death struggle - it is literally running for its life.

Let us not shy away from the fact that hare-coursing involves, in essence, the creation of a situation in which an animal is put in mortal danger. That danger and the uncertainty of the outcome is what's compelling and ultimately, entertaining. You can understand too the objection of those who believe that animals should not be endangered and killed for entertainment.

Wildlife programmes are fabulously popular worldwide, particularly ones that involve predators chasing prey. This allows us all to be entertained by the life and death struggle of animals. The narrator such as Sir David Attenborough reads a script that anthropomorphises the animals involved, increasing the sense of jeopardy the animals are in and our identification with them.

We usually see the young of that animal and their struggle to survive. If the programme is from the predator's point of view then we are made to feel anxious for them if their mother has been unable to hunt some food. Sometimes we watch as they starve, until the mother gets a kill.

If from the prey's point of view, we focus on the danger to the young from the predators. Never once have I seen a wildlife programme that balances the fact that life for one means death for the other. Always the intent of the story is to manipulate your feelings towards one or the other. Neither have I ever heard any animal rights supporter complain that watching these programmes is tantamount to being entertained by the real life and death struggle of living creatures.

Perhaps that is because these programmes are presented as

being educational, merely reporting on what is naturally occurring. But if this is truly the case, why do they not take a neutral view of the struggle for life and death? Why present whatever animal is the focus of the episode to be one you empathise with? Because by doing this, we are entertained as well as feeling righteous and good about ourselves for 'caring' about animals.

The main difference I felt about watching the Waterloo Cup for real and watching wildlife documentaries on television was the distinct lack of the feeling of being manipulated watching the blood sport for real. It was all there - for good or bad. I was free to make up my own mind without a saccharine voiceover talking about young animals as if they are human babies.

Part of what makes the anthropomorphising of animals possible is our increasing separation from the land. Fewer and fewer of us know what it is to grow up surrounded by wildlife and by the daily life and death struggle that goes on around us. I count myself lucky to have been brought up in Cumbria, where I was able to experience first hand the fact that nature is the continual interplay between life and death.

The essence of life is found in death. As a young child I spent a great deal of time in the woods. I watched stoats dance around injured birds. I watched owls swoop at mice and heron snatch fish out of the stream. This was the beginning of a fascination with hunting that continues to this day. As a child, I did not think myself any different to those animals, but rather part of that cycle. When we ate a pheasant that had been shot locally, or ate a fish that had been caught in the salmon traps on the River Eden, that place as part of the cycle of life and death seemed obvious.

It wasn't until I went to university that I first came into contact with people who thought it was wrong to kill animals. My first reaction was bafflement. How can it be wrong to kill animals when the whole of nature is the dance of life and death, of one animal killing another? Did they think they were outside this process? We had been brought up to respect animals, to acknowledge that life was possible because of their death.

To suggest that animals should not be killed seemed to be a

rejection of the natural process of life and, in some way a misunder-standing of animals themselves. Had they watched a kingfisher dive for its food? Or how a barn owl scoops up a vole? The hunting of one animal by another is as natural as it can be.

But more than that, it is the struggle for survival that creates the beauty in nature. None of this was appreciated by those who condemned the killing of animals. I discovered that those with this view were exclusively from urban or suburban backgrounds.

These townies were divorced from the land yet talking as if they had a superior understanding to those who had grown up around it. But they had no experience of it, only through wildlife programmes and their own domestic pets. They kept saying to me 'how would you like it if you were an animal?'. But then they took their pet dog to the vets to have its testicles removed.

Domestic pets are a case in point. They have chosen a life of ease and pampering away from the uncertainties and risks of the wild. The price they have paid for this is their freedom. The process of domestication is an interesting one. It seems to happen almost without design initially and then, before you know it, you cannot return to the wild. Sound familiar? We are doing this to ourselves - we humans are becoming domestic pets.

There is a feature of domestic animals known as limited rever-sion and domesticated animals lose the brain mass that their wild forebears had. This brain mass cannot be regained. The area of greatest brain reduction is in the limbic system, the part responsible for controlling hormones that in turn control aggression and aware-ness of threat.

They forfeit their ability to adapt and lose their true independ-ent fighting spirit, only doing what they are told to. A dog can bite but a dog is NOT a wolf. A cat can scratch but a cat is NOT a tiger.

This is what we are increasingly becoming - domesticated. It means that we are more easily manipulated, more likely to go with social pressures and less likely to fight back. Because we are squeam-ish about getting our hands dirty and reticent to engage in genuine confrontation we are much more easily manipulated.

THE PASSIVE-AGGRESSIVE TRAP

Think of the viper-pit that the modern workplace has become. This can be a place where people lie in wait to ambush you with their latest passive-aggressive trap. It's a place where rivals can spread false gossip about you but if you challenge them face to face, you are sanctioned for being 'too confrontational'.

You may even be reported for 'inappropriate' comments for exercising some much needed bluntness. Heaven forbid you have the courage to be honest with people.

The modern way is to be false and sneaky and write up reports in code, talking about people as if they are not real and damning with faint praise. How often have I had to suppress a roar of frustration in meetings that go on for too long with phrases like 'reaching out', car parking, going forward, offsite chat. It takes 2 hours to say something that should take twenty minutes. It is indirect and opaque, rather than direct and crystal clear.

All the while, colleagues climb over each other to ingratiate themselves with superiors whilst making anyone who could be a potential rival look bad. We are like pigs in a trough. An example from a team meeting I attended with our manager:

Team Member to Manager: "I'm so pleased that you have decided to get behind my idea 100% and roll it out for the whole team to comply with. I know some team members had problems supporting this when I originally suggested it.

(Team Member turns to address me) "Richard, do you have any more concerns now that our manager is fully on board?"

This kind of shenanigans was a real shock to me when I first encountered it in the workplace, after leaving the army. I couldn't believe that this was an accepted way of going on. People seemed content to play these games despite that fact that everyone felt anxious and stressed at work.

The attitude was that as long as I get my pay cheque and can go home at the end of the day, I accept that I spend most of my waking hours in a passive-aggressive snake-pit. It is now in the culture that any subtle form of attack is accepted as par for the course, but any open and honest confrontation is evil. Even straight-talking is a threat. Long is the list of things that make people feel 'uncomfortable'.

Before we get too caught up in the negative effects of this, it needs balancing with the fact that we have greater opportunity for all and much more consideration often for the individual. People generally do not face physical or outrightly aggressive confrontations at work. Nor does everybody have this experience! It is, however, a feature of the times we live in. And it is no good for producing warriors.

During my time in this environment, the only thing that kept me sane was going training in the evening and weekends. During this training, I would grapple and with my training partner, pour with sweat and feel the release of the day's frustrations.   Occasionally, I would come into meetings with abrasions on my face as a result of grappling. At a big national meeting in London, a manager took me to one side:

Him: "Richard, can I er.... can I have a word?"

Me: "Yes, of course."

Him: "You have been doing that fighting recently haven't you? You know, that cage fighting?"

Me: "Er, no, I've been doing some grappling"

Him: "Oh, well, the thing is.....how do you, er, think this might be perceived by customers?"

Me: "Well, normally it provokes a conversation, in fact I was talking to Mr Johnson the other day, did you know he used to box for Cambridge? He asked me to come and see him again next week so I thought I would....."

Him: (interrupting) Well, the thing is Richard, you know, it can, er, make some people feel, er........uncomfortable"

Me: "Nah, they're not that uncomfortable, in fact, I hardly noticed when it happened, I think it was just the rough jacket my training partner had on".

Him: "No that's not what I meant, I mean some team members might feel uncomfortable."

Me: "Eh? Why would team members feel uncomfortable when they are on my face? I don't understand".

Him: "It's just that, with you cage fighting..."

Me: "Grappling"

Him: "...it can make them feel uncomfortable having you in meetings with marks on your face".

Me: "What? Really? Who feels like that?"

Him: "Well, it has been mentioned to me."

Me: "By whom?"

Him: "Well, I don't want to get into specifics."

Me: (laughing) "Why, in case I grapple them?"

Him: (not laughing) "It's important to make sure everybody has a safe working environment".

Me: (baffled, as I realise he is not joking) "Oh, ok then, I will make sure I protect my face".

Him: "Thank you Richard, please do that going forward".

Me "Going forward where?"

Him: "I mean in future".

Me: "OK".

I was so confused after this exchange that I ran it over a few times in my head. I even thought that maybe this was the same across all civilian industries and maybe this was a good point in this new world I found myself in. Then, later the same day, the Welsh sales teams arrived. Three of them had marks on their faces, one of these also had a cauliflower ear and a black eye, now going yellow.

After having said hello to everyone, the very same manager shook their hands and joked with them about how the rugby was going!

But there is a very different perception of a game like rugby, where aggression seems incidental, and a combat sport where aggression seems to be the requirement. I can only think that this is the reason for such different treatment. Marks from actual fighting, albeit sport fighting present a challenge in an environment where aggression is frowned upon.

But humans don't suddenly stop being competitive and aggressive, the aggression merely becomes passive rather than active and now this is a game where women can play equally as well. Now we have an 'arms race' of passive-aggression! Covering your back is paramount.

The sheer man hours spent in ensuring no-one can drop you in it or avoiding responsibility is staggering. On so many projects I was involved in, the primary concern was not how to drive the business forward, but how not to look bad or get caught out.

It's enough to make you run home, slam the door and play a Slipknot album at cosmos-shaking volume.

And this problem is getting worse not better. The young graduates working in finance, insurance, IT, data analytics, retail and all sorts of other office jobs tell me the same stories.

WORDS BETWEEN WARRIORS

It doesn't have to be this way. In the army, for example, it happened that two individuals would come into conflict. The culture in this organisation was to get it out and get it done with. This often involves a frank and honest exchange.

The reason this can happen in this organisation is because it's based on respect. It's a respect born of shared, honest and challenging experiences. This begins with a shared experience of rigorous training and is developed through good and bad times on operations.

During these times, you see what your comrades are made of and they see you. No spin or varnish, you see them warts and all. If you have ever been in a tiny, covert observation post, living with comrades for days on end in a small hole and holding clingfilm tight for them to defecate into, there can be few secrets between you.

Don't get me wrong, the army and organisations like it are far from perfect. When they get it wrong, bullying and intimidation are the result. But it's a kind of bullying and intimidation that is in the open and can be seen and cut out, with the individual commanders held responsible and disciplined. The kind of bullying and intimidation that goes on every day in some of our biggest business is less easy to see and eradicate.

Neither is this to say that the army is always right and business is somehow wrong. There is much in modern business practice that the army and armed forces desperately need to learn. But on this point, it's something business used to have, but has lost.

In many cases, it's a systemic infection, part of the culture. It seeps into every part of working life, poisoning as it goes. It's subtle, but ever present. Far from being founded on respect and trust, it's founded on disrespect and distrust. This corporate culture assumes that anything you say bluntly must be a personal attack on the very values of the individual you say it to. It allows for no benefit of the doubt, it allows for no trust that you are saying it in the interests of the team.

To have a genuine culture of respect and trust, we need to be robust enough to risk being offended. We need to be secure enough in ourselves that we can listen to the bald truth without crumbling like Wile E. Coyote after hitting a wall. How powerful and resourceful would you be when you can deal with anything that is thrown at you?

We all already have that strength within us. I refer to activation of this fighting spirit as being "Battle Ready". Being Battle Ready allows you to suffer the slings and arrows of outrageous fortune. Being Battle Ready will make overwhelming problems seem manageable.

THE DEPERSONALISATION OF THE WORKPLACE

When I spoke of my experiences in the modern workplace, can you see how all the passive-aggressive games are designed to do just that - to manipulate you. This is why any signs of aggression or confrontation are rooted out; because they counteract manipulation.

The evidence of fighting in the marks on my face suggested

an individual that enjoyed confrontation and was prepared to resist. This is why that kind of corporate culture is so threatened by it, as **violence is the ultimate expression of resistance to oppression and manipulation.** Employees that do well in this culture allow themselves to be manipulated by superiors whilst being the best at manipulating fellow team members and those under them.

In this kind of corporate culture, men are emasculated and engage in gossip and petty one-upmanship that should be beneath them. Women become devious and spiky. All are paranoid with good reason. Things like 'morality' and 'honour' are words to fling about, being dispensed with when they become a nuisance.

The ultimate aim of modern corporate management is to create conformity and domestication. Working in the pharmaceutical industry I was often faced with the fact that highly tenuous claims were made from clinical data in order to make products look more effective.

The culture claimed to encourage individuals to speak out if they thought a claim was exaggerated or not entirely honest. In reality such individuals were marked as disloyal or troublemakers. Any course of action, regardless of how underhand was justified as being in the interests of 'The Shareholders'.

These totally anonymous and faceless people were apparently the ones driving all this sharp practice. It just became an excepted fact that we were all working for them. Who we could neither see nor talk to. It seemed that the raison d'être of the whole corporate machine was purely to provide a dividend for Messrs unknown.

I am no anti-capitalist. In fact, it's trade and trading that has always been the prime mover in developing civilisation, from the exchange of goods and the ideas and relationships that go with it. But when this process becomes impersonal, it allows individuals to drop moral responsibility.

Suddenly we are working for a machine rather than an accountable and moral individual. This is why there is now such a stark contrast between public corporations and family run companies. Faceless masters produce an unchallengeable culture of conformity, manipulation and expectation. A known and accountable master feels a personal responsibility - especially if he carries the honour of his family.

The modern corporate worker is enslaved by expectation. There is a dream that has been sold - the dream of more stuff. When you think about it, there is nothing more ridiculous than working like a slave for a car that is more expensive than your neighbours and friends car. There is nothing wrong with the pleasure that can be taken from nice things, but when the acquisition of them becomes your motivation, you have become a puppet rather than a free individual.

We can be further manipulated by our horror of getting old and dying. There is nothing more natural in life than death and yet we are more scared of it than ever. We now have an expectation of long life, rather than an awareness that any moment could be our last.

This has a stupefying effect that pushes us away from being alive in the present moment. We do everything we can do stop looking older in a totally futile attempt to prevent our own deaths. We see death as an evil, rather than as an inevitable consequence of existence. **Death is the price of living and it always gets paid.**

When we examine the attitudes to death of previous ages we see a much closer relationship than now. We seek to push it away, to not talk about it, to make it taboo. The Victorian's embraced it. The Elizabethan's wrote fabulous poems and plays about it. We try to not think about it.

We talk about someones death 'not being fair' as if the concept of fairness has anything to do with it. The expectation of fairness can come only from a privileged background. By this I do not mean 'being born with a silver spoon in your mouth'. I mean the privileged background that we all enjoy in this country.

You compare even our poorest people with those in parts of India, The Philippines, Mexico, Nigeria, China, Somalia, Brazil and so on, you find that there is no comparison. Nobody in our country is poor. There is something obscene in the way that some people talk about people in the UK living in 'absolute poverty'. This is a sick joke.

There are children in the world that literally cannot afford to be fed and clothed, but they are not in this country. In our language, a 'deprived' child is one that does not own a smartphone. Street kids there do not expect 'fairness', they must fight for whatever they can get. The problem with expecting fairness as a right is that you are not prepared for crisis.

DISLOCATION OF EXPECTATION

I found that the fastest way to test someones character when I was teaching officer cadets leadership skills, was by something I called 'dislocation of expectation'. For example, let us imagine that you are deployed on an exercise into a woodland area. The weather is below freezing. You are sent on various missions with each cadet taking turns to lead. These missions are physically arduous and demand fast thinking and good control of the group.

For rest, you hole up in the woods in bivouacs, with a camouflage sheet slung low between trees as your only cover. You eat either cold food or boil in the bag rations. You have only a few hours sleep each night, the rest being spent either on missions or on sentry duty. On the fifth day you have been told that you will return to camp for a central debrief, there you will spend the night in a heated barrack block with hot showers and a proper meal.

The fifth day is very hard, but you get through it knowing that blissful warmth and comfort is only hours away - so what if you are being made to work extra hard for the last few hours remaining?

On the last mission, you are given a grid reference ten kilometres away to meet your transport to the camp. Working out the distance and timings, you realise that you will need to move fast to make it, so as a group you put all your efforts into getting there in time. Exhausted, you make it, just as the sun is going down. You don't mind your discomfort and the cold, as a beautiful, wondrous, hot shower is coming.

But the transport isn't there. Instead, you are met by your directing staff (me), who is dressed in full kit ready for a march. I hand the group leader some written orders. Rather than going back to camp, you have been re-tasked. An enemy position has been discovered fifteen kilometres away. The team is tasked with destroying this position. This will involve an overnight route march over difficult terrain in order to achieve surprise. The time for the attack is dawn, with H-Hr set as 0600hrs.

This is a fixed time that you must make, as fire support has been co-ordinated to suppress the enemy position at H-Hr minus five minutes. After this mission is completed, you will re-organise and wait for orders. This mission requires the cadet leader to immediately plan how to achieve this and get the team motivated and ready to go.

I look across the cadet's faces. They cannot afford to waste time sulking about things 'not being fair'. But some are crushed. It seems like all that stored up tiredness hits them all at once. Yet had they been on the transport back to camp now, they would be laughing and cracking jokes, having found some energy from somewhere. Nothing has physically changed, only their expectation.

Some of them listen intently to the change of plan and then get stuck in immediately to the job in hand. A good cadet leader in this situation tasks someone to get a hot brew on, tells the guys to sort their feet and kit out and reads through the new mission again. He or she spends no time brooding or sulking.

These are the kind of people that you want in a crisis - The Warriors. Because whatever that crisis is, be it combat or a flood or a street fight or bankruptcy or whatever, it is never 'fair'. Such a thing has no real existence. Yet some of those cadets stopped being effective human beings just with a manipulation of their expectation. They were putty in my hands. Not so for the more robust cadets.

At Sandhurst when I myself was a cadet I experienced the 'Escape from Moscow'. This is without doubt one of the hardest physical trials I have ever done. It's a lesson in expectation management under physical stress.

In the 'Escape from Moscow' an empty troop transport vehicle travels in front of the platoon at a pace just fast enough to keep it 100 metres or so in front while the platoon runs behind. In our case, the road it drove up was a steep gradient on a hillside in Brecon in Wales. For those of you who don't know the Brecon training area, it's basically what I imagine the Earth was like 100 million years ago. Its bleakness is matched in severity only by its weather. Horizontal rain is the normal state of play. We had already been deployed onto this area for many days before we started this run. We were wearing normal battle dress, with full webbing and carrying rifles.

In the cab of the transport vehicle was a Gurkha driver, keeping the pace just right. The transport looked like it was just in reach if we could run a little faster. The driver pushed his pace a little as we got faster to remain 100 metres in front. With this increase in speed, the platoon became strung out, with the best endurance runners in front and the rest just trying to hold on.

At an appointed signal, the transport stopped, and the back came down ready to receive the troops. Cue thirty men racing at sprinting speed to get on it. Being not the fastest bloke running uphill, I had slipped down the extended line of men and was towards the back. Being something of a sprinter though and seeing the transport stop, I went flat out to get on. I quickly began reeling in the guys ahead of me. I was tantalisingly close to the vehicle and could see a handful of blokes had already got on. Just as I was about to jump on and with the blood pounding in my ears, the back of the truck was flipped up again and the vehicle resumed its journey up the hill.

I had not only completely wasted my effort but was now exhausted and faced the daunting prospect of chasing the damn thing up the hill again. It would have been better if I had ignored this first opportunity to get on the back and just allowed the best runners their victory and continued at an even pace, ready for the next. There is something horrible about chasing a vehicle you can never quite reach.

Now I had to try and forget about this and just keep going. But my lungs were screaming and my legs felt like they belonged to someone else. It's common to have dreams about trying to run away from an unseen menace but you feel like you are running through treacle. This was the reality of the nightmare.

Due to the effort I had made, all my gains were quickly lost as I slipped down the pack again. In fact, it felt like I was going backwards with the speed with which I was being overtaken by those I had just sprinted past. In the distance, impossibly far now, I could see the truck stop again. Those nearest sprinted forward and got on whilst the rest continued up the painful hill.

Eventually I flopped into the truck on its third stop in genuine physical distress, feeling like I might soil myself or vomit at any moment. The truck carried on, collected the remainder of the platoon and drove over the hill to a live firing training area. We all got off the truck in a pretty poor state and we looked it too.

I could see the live ammunition all ready and waiting to be loaded into our rifles. A live firing platoon attack over difficult terrain is no laughing matter and requires a whole host of safety staff. The training colonel took one look at us before going looking for our platoon commander. When he found him, we could see them in the distance, the colonel tearing a strip of our commander.

What had upset him was not the fact that he had us do the 'Escape from Moscow', more that we arrived in insufficient time to recover before doing the live firing attack. The last thing the colonel wanted was someone getting shot by an exhausted and inattentive officer cadet. We were given a few extra minutes to recover before cracking on. I don't remember much about that attack except the fact that no-one died.

Reflecting on this later, I could see that our distress was caused not just by the physical effort (which we were used to) but by the emotional stress of following the just out of reach. You have an expectation of fairness and fair behaviour. When that illusion is shattered, the effect can be devastating in both body and mind. When we give up this expectation, we free ourselves from it and become more resilient and robust, better to cope with 'unfairness' and get on with it.

I am not talking here about people who work towards making society fairer, often they themselves do not expect fairness, hence why they work hard to achieve it. It's a fine desire to see better conditions for all. What I am talking about is the state of mind that expects fairness as a right. When fairness does not come, as it won't in moments of crisis, they are rendered ineffective by complaint and the overwhelming feeling that 'this shouldn't be happening'.

One of my favourite examples of this portrayed in popular culture is Private Hudson's meltdown in the film *Aliens*. The contrast between his 'Oh dear Lord Jesus, this ain't happening man,' and 'This ain't fair man' and the heroine Ripley's stoicism is stark. Ripley would never say 'This ain't fair'. because it has no relevance to the situation. It's not fair - so what?

Ripley faces each crisis with no expectation. She has no idealism at all, she is totally pragmatic. When an appeal is made to her that she cannot be responsible for the destruction of an entire race, her simple reply is 'wrong!'. Her strength is her determination and resolution. In dealing with a merciless uber predator, she relies on herself, without expecting to be helped by 'the system' or 'authority' which she has seen for what it is - a self-serving sham.

Ripley proves herself to be the real warrior, despite being surrounded by the official 'warriors' of the Colonial Marine Corps.

It is fascinating to see how many movies in popular culture have the heroes working against a malevolent system. In the *Alien* movies, that system is represented by an amoral big corporation. So too in the *Terminator* films and in a similar vein in *RoboCop* too. *Fight Club* makes a car firm the symbol of oppression and the evil machines do the same job in *The Matrix*.

We have a real appetite for watching these lonely symbols of humanity fighting against the impossible odds of the power of evil authority. In reality, the powers against us are rarely so evil and rarely so obvious as in the movies. Rather, these movies are an allegory of us fighting against ourselves. We fight against our own materialism, selfishness and laziness.

The remarkable thing about modern Western government is not how corrupt it is but how relatively benign it is. Note I used the word relatively. In the UK, we make a national sport of complaining about the government, of whatever political flavour. In reality however, our country is lead well enough to produce the best conditions we have ever had. No wonder migrants and refugees risk death to try and get here.

Much vitriol directed at our politicians is a displacement for our own failings as human beings. We may want to rage against the machine but instead our rage should be directed inwards towards our own personal corruption. The big question should be "Why do we seem powerless to control ourselves and our lives?"

TAKING RESPONSIBILITY

We can start by holding ourselves responsible for everything we do. Such an approach can be summed up by the maxim "it's my fault, even if it's not my fault". In other words, my own responsibility for what happens to me is total.

This is the 'Age of Entitlement' where we expect to be looked after by the state. We expect everyone to be treated the same, we expect this and we expect that - we expect that every child should get a prize: why? Because it's our RIGHT! This focus on 'rights' and our 'entitlements' is so damaging because we abdicate responsibility for ourselves when we focus our expectations on what should be given to us by others.

If you want to hear a beaten man speak, listen to the news when an anti-austerity or anti-capitalist protest march is on. In the interviews with protestors you can hear the same language of 'rights' and what others should be doing for us. I'm not trying to make a political point here, it's just that these causes attract people with this disease.

I describe people like this as 'beaten' precisely because they have given up the idea that they are wholly responsible for themselves, politicians and governments be damned. The 'Battle Ready' man or woman always finds a way to survive.

In this country, in particular, children at school are taught to resolve bullying and disputes without violence. This is sensible and represents a 'civilised' way of dealing with matters. But this approach has spun out of control into 'anything is better than violence' mentality. So a child being bullied is meant to report it to teachers after it has happened. When those teachers fail to stop it the child is given strategies to help avoid it, such as being even with words and not rising to the bait. When the child gets kicked in again, the teachers look at moving the child to another school. Anything to avoid preparing a child properly to face violence.

This teaches the child that being passive is the right way. That violence must always be avoided at all costs. That they are to let themselves be abused and then rely on others to sort it out. This develops a passive and submissive mindset. We are hardly building warriors for the future.

This trend has developed alongside others, such as not bringing children to funerals and not allowing them to play unsupervised for fear of hurting themselves. Every effort is made to avoid children feeling any discomfort, hardship or pain. This sounds like a good thing, and in the main it is - thank God that no children are forced into the mines now or up chimney stacks.

But this approach has got way out of hand to the extent that children are deprived of the learning experiences gained by over-coming obstacles and occasionally getting hurt. These are experi-ences that are vital if we are looking to develop brave, bold and capa-ble individuals rather than compliant low risk taking herd animals.

It is common now for parents in restaurants to re-order food for children if they say they don't like it. In some cases food goes back three times before the child is satisfied. This is a revealing modern tendency. It reveals how we are being poisoned by our afflu-ence and comfort, stupefied by the opium of our luxurious lifestyles. Unless we have discipline to stop us, the natural human urge is to suck every available tit dry. Selfishness and greed are a legacy of our evolved need to survive.

But because we are beasts by nature it does not follow that we need act like them. Humans have been given the gift of self-aware-ness and the possibility of will to control their actions. But will can only be developed through facing hardships of one kind or another.

In our schools, there is a growing move to restrict physical hardships and challenge. Never was this more obvious than in the schools of this nation that have stopped encouraging competitive sport. Competitive sport is off the menu for many educators as it provides an obvious and overt theatre for controlled aggression with clear winners and losers.

Contact sports like rugby are coming under increasing pressure.

A large cadre of 'experts' are suggesting that only 'tag' versions of rugby are played in schools and full contact is prohibited. Sport for many of us is increasingly a thing to be watched rather than played, with the elite players of these sports looking less and less like an average human being.

In fact, a casual observer from another planet may think that these professional elite sports people are becoming a separate race of individuals altogether. Perhaps this is the beginning of H.G Wells's 'Eloi' and 'Morlock' race separation!

The move in education as well as in the corporate world is to the passive-aggressive, with direct confrontation being seen as a threat to conformity. The selfishness and self-interest that brings bullying and intimidation are not reduced by this shift however, they just take different forms. They go from open to hidden.

KEYBOARD WARRIORS

The way people are interacting on social media reflects this cowardly modern approach to things: hide behind a computer and issue all kinds of heinous threats, without ever having to face up to the consequences. Social media is now a very large part of the daily communication of the vast majority of us. Because it is now so common, we are in danger of losing the outrage that we should be feeling to the way we are typically interacting with each other. This is particularly true when it involves people we do not know personally and don't imagine we will have to meet.

I remember a time before the internet and it was a time before we knew for certain that if people had a chance to say something anonymously to someone they didn't know, it would be threat or insult. Thank you, internet, for this revelation!

We are at the time when people are now asking the question about whether the internet is a 'good' thing or a 'bad' thing. Few things are all good or all bad. The internet means we can communicate with more people than ever before, but face-to-face interaction is a smaller proportion of our everyday social dealings.

It is very interesting what employers and recruiters are saying about the young people coming into the jobs market, people who have only ever known a time with social media as a dominant part of their lives. What they see is a generation that is super tech savvy, well motivated and full of phrases from reality TV such as "this is my dream" "this would mean the world to me" and "I am following my passion". This can seem a bit strange when the job they are applying for is an entry level admin role at an insurance firm. But at least there is some enthusiasm.

Where these applicants seem to really struggle is in their interpersonal skills, particularly with different types of people. I watched this as a salesman when one of the young recruits fresh out of university had to deal with a fifty year old male client. It was fairly cringe-worthy to see how the recruit floundered by trying to talk to him as he would one of his mates, or someone of his own age and experience.

I have found generally, that people who come from close communities, such as exist in some geographical, rural or church communities do not have this problem. I live in the north west of England, where we still have some of these, what you might call 'old-fashioned' communities, often from mining or mill towns. These have always been based on straight-forward, face-to-face communication.

Some of this community feel remains even in cities in the region, like Liverpool. It remains common for young and old to strike up conversations between them at bus stops and so forth. When I attended the University of Liverpool as a mature student, one of the most common observations of undergraduates moving here from other parts of the UK was how friendly the older people were at bus stops, talking to them with no suspicion or fear. This had been a real surprise to them and it took them some time to adjust.

With people being ever more mobile and the population being far more transient than ever before, these communities are getting less and less. It amazes me how many people do not even know the names of their neighbours.

Our lives are becoming ever more compartmentalised around

a small clique of people that we deal with personally, and a large amount of people we deal with impersonally via the web. This itself brings amazing exchanges of information and wonderful opportunities for developing more cognitive ability. But again, it's at the expense of developing people of action.

Look at the faces of the people around you on public transport or in cafes or any other place where human beings congregate - and look at us all staring into our phones, hypnotised by whatever we are currently sending or receiving. The bovine conformity phrase comes to mind again, or as a friend of mine calls it 'zombie nation'. We risk becoming cattle, domesticated by stealth and apathy, stupefied by technology and luxury.

If we feel like we want to assert our individuality, to do something 'radical' we go and sit passively and indulge ourself with self-glorifying tattoos that 'mean something' to us. Our lazy way of self-expression is to have someone else draw on us to satisfy our vanity. Something else that we just go out and consume.

RITES OF PASSAGE

The modern obsession with tattoos is a kind of misplaced faint echo of the old tribal rites of passage. Almost like a hankering after something without the understanding of what it was for. If we examine the kind of rituals that tribal societies developed to mark the point between a boy becoming a man and a warrior and leaving his childhood behind, we can see exactly what it is that we have lost and need to regain.

The tribal tattoos of the Maori, the Ta Moko, are an example of a rite that marks a change into adulthood. When the boy gets the markings, he takes on the face of The Warrior and leaves his childhood behind.

Joseph Campbell relates a story of a tribe in Papua New Guinea that brings up the boys to fear the masks that are worn at ceremonies by the men in representation of the Gods. When a boy reaches a stage when he is ready, the masked men enter his hut and kidnap the boy. The boy is forced to fight a masked man.[4]

When he has shown himself brave the man allows him to win, takes off the mask, revealing his true identity, and then places the mask on the boy.

If we look at the Satere Mawe tribe of Brazil and their bullet ant ritual we will see an example of this. The bullet ant is an incredible creature. Due to the intensity of competition in the Amazon rainforest, it has become supersized and evolved a sting that hurts like being shot! No doubt the bullet ant is a 'warrior' ant!

As a way of transforming boys into warriors, the shaman collects bullet ants from the jungle. He sedates them first so they can be handled, then inserts them into specially made gloves fashioned out of leaves. The boys place their hands into these gloves as the ants regain their wits and begin to sting them. The warriors of the tribe hold onto the boys and dance with them as they undergo the ritual.

The boys have to take the ritual many times before they are regarded as warriors. This is an immensely strong and profound experience for the boys and creates a special change in them. As one boy said after enduring the ritual for the first time "I feel like the jungle lives inside me". These rituals are ways in which The Warrior is awakened. And what a way to awaken him!

The key element to these rituals is death and rebirth. There is a death of the infantile ego, the dependant ego that is reliant on the care of others. The boy is reborn as an adult who has responsibility and authority. From being a ward of the tribe he is now a representative of the tribe and as a warrior he will guard and defend the others with his life.

The death of the infantile ego is a necessary step to becoming a warrior that is often missing in our modern culture. It is common now for young adults to continue living with parents for a long time and to stay in education for a long time as well. Whilst receiving education you stay in that state of dependence, without responsibility. Only by striding out alone do we break the shackles of our dependence.

This can be seen as a 'cutting of the apron strings'. An example of declining power of these rituals can be seen in the Jewish 'Bar' and 'Bat' Mitzah rituals where young Jewish boys and girls come of age and take on the responsibilities of an adult. But in many cases, particularly in America, these have become unbelievably lavish parties that instead are displays of materialism.

One of the mechanisms that became a way of taking up adulthood was entering an apprenticeship, which would take the individual from dependence in a skill, through to a journeyman level where he could be employed and then later apply for membership of a guild through the creation of a 'masterpiece' which, if successful, would qualify him as a master craftsman able to work on his own and establish his own workshop.

Again we can see with this the essential component of the death of the infantile, dependant ego and the rebirth of the adult, responsible ego. It is fair to say that one of the great problems with our present culture as regards creating warriors is concerned is that more and more people never leave the phase of the infantile ego. Their warrior remains fast asleep.

AN ANTI-WARRIOR CULTURE

I have taken the example of these tribes because, in their so-called 'primitive' state of development, their warrior culture is still alive. The warrior is honoured and respected as the defender of the tribe, the one who allows the tribe to stay free and alive. His part of the bargain is to be prepared to fight to the death to defend them. If he is up to this task, then he is worthy of the honour and respect afforded to him.

It is almost a cliche in our society and in Western society in general for those returning from combat to feel like a fish out of water. The state, rather than society is expected to look after returning soldiers. But the state is not society, it is a series of imperfect and unwieldy organisations, far too big to operate effectively. Particularly when the soldier leaves his immediate family (and by that I mean his regiment) he feels disconnected. Is it any wonder those returning can experience mental difficulties?

The mental problems come, not when you are in combat but when you come back. The reason for this, the reason for the depression, the PTSD, the anxiousness, the hyper-vigilance is the because of the difference between the theatre of combat and the reality of our everyday existence.

I do not claim to have experienced problems like some of my comrades have. After all, many of them were throwing grenades into compounds whilst I was coordinating the battlespace in the operations room in Helmand. But I did have one experience which is an example of what happens.

Afghanistan is only a six and a half hour flight from Brize Norton in leafy Oxfordshire. That means that you can get on a plane in Kandahar with the heat, dust and sand of Afghanistan, having been immersed in a combat zone and less than half a day later be walking out of that plane into the lush greenness and safety of England.

My abiding memory was of the smell of England when I returned. I don't notice it now but when I had been away for many months at a time, you can truly smell your own country when you come back. It smells of grass. Sweet and rich grass.

The day I returned I went into a large supermarket to buy some food and maybe a bottle of wine to reacquaint myself with alcohol. I had only got to the second aisle when I heard a man furiously shouting down his mobile phone to what I assumed was his wife. They were arguing about what beans to buy. What beans to buy. I couldn't believe that I had come back to a place where people argue about what beans to buy. Do they not know what is going on in the world?

This made me feel so weird I had a kind of mini-panic attack and ran out of the store. There were guys on my tour that had fought battle after battle and seen the worst of that type of combat. How must they have been feeling?

In our society, we send in counsellors to talk to children when one of their classmates has died. It's almost like 'society' has given up and handed these quite normal jobs of support over to so-called professionals. The truth is that our society can no longer deal with it as traumatic events have become rare and unwelcome. We do not prepare for them at all, it has become a specialisation rather than something everybody is capable of dealing with.

Have you seen what happens when you heat up a test tube and then put it under cold water? I am sure that this is something most schoolchildren have done in chemistry class. The test tube breaks from the sudden and huge change in environment. Is it any wonder that soldiers suffer problems from being placed from one into the other?

For some troops, a week of 'decompression' was granted where they went to Cyprus for a week to unwind before returning home. This is a great idea but......home is still home and a week is not long. We must understand that if anything, our current society is anti-warriors. This should not discourage us, but it should focus our attention to the fact that we are no longer good at producing the skills the warrior needs by default in our culture. We need to take a definite path with a definite aim to achieve our goal. It will NOT happen by itself.

GOING THE WRONG WAY

We can see some of the ways in which the energy present in young people can get misdirected without the presence of a definite aim. Some young people get caught up in criminal gangs which seem to promise a way of becoming a warrior. The fact that this is attractive is because they are given status and respect amongst their peers. This is a reaction to the safeness of our culture.

They get excitement and a sense of tribal identity from their association, in lieu of a better and more available alternative. But the reality of these gangs is not that they are modern day 'Robin Hoods' looking out for and taking care of their communities. In fact, they run from responsibility and are parasites living off their communities. Add to the fact that many do not work for a living and are dependant on the state and you have a sorry state of affairs.

We see a similar pointless self-indulgent activity in football hooliganism. You take a group of disaffected men, who feel bored by the banality of everyday life and go looking to simplify everything into red versus blue or whatever and go looking for an authentic buzz of genuine emotion. Genuine fear and genuine excitement.

Part of that feeling of excitement comes from the group experience, the comradeship of facing things together.

It is undeniable that this can be exhilarating in a way that our normal lives no longer give us. But it's channelled in a way that is ultimately pointless and negative.

I witnessed first hand the kind of buzz that people enjoy in riots when I was stationed in Belfast as part of the Public Order Battalion. Our daily routine was training to separate rival factions of Loyalists and Republicans on the streets of the Ardoyne and Limestone - Hallidays.

Deploying onto the ground with your helmet, shield and baton was exciting, but tempered by the responsibility you had and the job you had to do. Being a company second-in-command (also called company operations officer in Northern Ireland) at the time, I had the job of reporting and receiving reports on everything that was going on and making sure that everybody was kept informed. This is the mainly the 'Control' function of 'Command and Control'.

Command and Control is particularly difficult in public order situations as there are often many moving parts, the volume level of the crowd is usually deafening and your helmet and visor make face to face communication more difficult. You have to be proactive with your fight to get the information you need and to make sure everyone who needs to know, knows what's happening.

The situation can change very quickly when the mood of the crowd changes from excited but contained to all out violent. Looking at the angry and violent crowd in front of me I quickly realised one thing; they were having a whale of a time.

With the average age of the rioters being fifteen or sixteen, the look of joyous hatred on their faces as they threw rocks and petrol bombs was clear. They were loving it. You imagine being a fifteen year old boy being raised to hate the soldiers and having a respected local IRA commander sanction the use of acid attacks against another human being.

Never mind that the person you are throwing acid in the face of is a nineteen year old soldier born in Fiji. But the fact that you can commit acts of violence with impunity and even receive praise for doing so is a dream come true.

You could feel the energy and excitement coming off them. When I use the phrase 'turned on' to describe their state, it's exactly the impression I have always got when seeing violent crowds in the streets or outside sports events. There is a sexual energy that is palpable.

It appears to be caused by the crowds desire to get their kicks through violence and as such, is an ugly form of mis-placed sexual energy. As it's mis-placed, it's an impotent rage that fuels a pointless activity. This is not the solution and these people are not warriors. The rage, the energy, the desire for something better must be channelled into improving yourself first. Only then can you expect to be a more capable human being.

CHAPTER 3
THE WILL TO ACT

_____

"In order for man to succeed in life, God provided him with two means, education and physical activity. Not separately, one for the soul and the other for the body, but for the two together. With these means, man can attain perfection."

"Excessive emphasis on athletics produces an uncivilised type, while a purely literary training leaves men indecently soft".

Plato, The Republic.

Not only was Plato a wrestler but it is said he was well known in this capacity and competed in tournaments. What 'education' did he feel that this type of physical challenge provided that other types of learning could not? What in fact is wrong with people being 'indecently soft'?

Let us try to understand what it is that makes us capable human beings. By 'capable' I mean people with the ability to select and achieve an aim. If we take Plato's aim of 'attaining perfection' we can start to unpick what qualities we need to develop to do this.

In every undertaking, we have a battle. That battle we can call 'the battle between yes and no'.

Once we have stated our aim and begin to follow that path, we put our forces of 'yes' in motion. These forces are everything we can muster together to achieve that aim. The forces of 'no' are everything that stands in the way of us achieving that aim. The higher the aim, the more obstacles we will face in achieving that aim. Ultimately, success means that our 'yes' has defeated the 'no'.

I may have decided that my aim is to lose 10 pounds in weight. My 'yes' is driven by my desire to look more attractive, to be healthier and feel more energetic. This should be a very simple task indeed. Having examined my diet, I resolve to eradicate alcohol and sugary drinks until I have lost the weight. I decide that five weeks should be an adequate amount of time to achieve this task. I also decide to start immediately. Later that day, an old friend of mine calls and says he is in town. That old friend and I served together and his friendship is highly valued. He asks if I want to meet for a drink. I resolve to start my new diet tomorrow.

A simple example such as this illustrates why our human situation is the constant fight to achieve aims within the context of an ongoing battle between yes and no. Weight loss provides a simple example as in fact, I can completely control all the food and drink that goes into my mouth and yet I still have a fight on my hands to achieve my aim. How much more difficult is it to achieve an aim when we do not control all of the factors?

At the other end of the scale, let us imagine that I am a general and my aim is to win a war against a capable and determined enemy. The tactical situation suggests that I should not commit more forces to reinforce one of my besieged defensive positions situated in a small town. If however, I decide not to send a relief force, the troops and civilians in that town will almost certainly be killed by the enemy.

Having desperately searched for an alternative, I find there is no other course of action that makes as much tactical sense as abandoning the town to its fate. How strong is my 'yes' to win this war? Strange thoughts come into my mind - what if I send a relief force and get lucky? What if I lose the war but console myself with the fact that I never left anyone behind?

In the end I remind myself that only by defeating the enemy will my people be able to live in freedom. No relief force is sent and the memory of it haunts me till my dying day despite my ultimate victory.

It is said that all wars are won in the will and it is the force of your will that is the subject of this chapter.

SELECTION AND MAINTENANCE OF THE AIM

All army cadets learn that the master principle of war is 'selection and maintenance of the aim'. This is remarkable in a way as it's identifying that THE most important principle in warfare is merely working out what you need to do and sticking to it. This should underline how difficult this process is, in any area of life.

Look at the anatomy of success in any field and you will find that the force of will of the protagonist is the unifying feature. This is what you cannot get from 'literary learning'. Without this we can be truly called 'indecently soft'.

We need not think that what we are talking about here is simple brute force and ignorance. Rather, it is the ability to suffer defeats, face obstacles and disappointments and yet still push on toward the aim.

We can see all of these qualities exemplified in the historical figure of Winston Churchill. What is so striking about his leadership is not his talents or natural gifts but more his ability to endure in the most difficult circumstances.

It is remarkable that Churchill even stayed in politics after the debacle of Gallipoli in the First World War for which he was responsible. To come back and lead a country in the greatest of all wars is one thing, but to lead the forces of Great Britain and the Commonwealth when they stood alone against the might of Nazi Germany is astonishing and represents the ideal of the indomitable will. Many of the quotes attributed to this man reflect his tenacity and willpower:

> "If this long island story of ours is to end at last, let it end only when each of us lies, choking in his own blood upon the ground".

> "Never give in, never give in, never, never, never, never - in nothing, great or small, large or petty - never give in except to convictions of honour and good sense".

Perhaps Churchill does not fit our ideal of what the warrior leader *par excellence* should look like. He cannot be said to have been of heroic countenance or bearing; and yet, he was all those things and what's more, he was all those things when it mattered most.

In the naval tradition of Britain, sailors would often have 'HOLD FAST' tattooed across their fingers in order to maintain their grip on the wheel during the worst storms. How often can we live to fight another day if we just 'hold fast' in the present moment?

From my own experience of being an operations officer during difficult situations in Afghanistan, this principle is the key. If things get bad we live hour to hour. If really bad we live minute to minute. If desperate we just aim to get through the next second, and then the next. It never failed to amaze me that despite how tense situations were, they seemed to be better when the new dawn came. What had at times seemed almost overwhelming now seemed a fraction more manageable. Still appalling, but with hope.

In his excellent book on Churchill, Boris Johnson makes the case that Churchill knew that the eventual success of the war depended on the involvement of the United States of America. He turned his considerable efforts into Britain surviving long enough for that to happen. Holding on until the industrial and fighting might of the USA could be brought to bear. Churchill said later that after the tragedy of Pearl Harbor, he slept well again for the first time since the start of the war.[5]

This is no cold blooded lack of empathy on Churchill's part. After all, this was a man who had seen and taken part in bloody conflict at first hand, had been a prisoner of war even and knew the cost of war as well as any. But everything was subordinate to his unshakeable will to achieve his aim.

Another notorious incident demonstrates this fact. When France had fallen under the control of Germany and an armistice signed between the two countries, the French had a squadron of ships moored at Mers-el-Kebir in Algeria.

Knowing that there was a possibility that the French would hand over these ships to the German Navy, Churchill issued the French with an ultimatum to join the British or to deny the use of the ships to the enemy by sinking them. The French squadron included an aircraft carrier and a number of battleships and Destroyers that would have greatly enhanced the capabilities of the German Navy.

Churchill's ultimatum made it clear that if the outlined courses of action were not taken, the British would use 'whatever force was necessary' to deny the enemy use of the ships.

Whether or not the French really believed that their British allies would do this is not known. However, with negotiations terminated the British fleet attacked the French ships with the resultant loss of almost thirteen hundred French lives.

Understandably, this was a highly controversial action then and still to this day. But what an expression of will. I imagine there were some characters in Berlin who felt something of a cold chill down their spine on the realisation that they were now facing an opponent that would deliberately kill their own allies in order to deny them an advantage. When we think that at this time in the war, the German forces had rolled up Europe and only Britain and the Commonwealth were left in opposition. Perhaps it would be safe to assume that the Germans believed it was only a matter of time before Britain capitulated. Perhaps also, the Americans who had yet to enter the war questioned the resolution of the British forces against the might of the Third Reich.

What a message Churchill sent with this action, both to his enemy and to the people whose involvement he saw as being the key to winning the war. It is said that ultimately ALL battles are won in the will, often by the side that is the least exhausted. At this crucial moment, with backs to the wall and facing the end of the nation of Britain as we know it, Churchill showed what his will was made of.

A HISTORY OF VIOLENCE

It has become somewhat unfashionable in our modern era to celebrate the character and tenacity of Winston Churchill. In times of peace we fall out of love for warriors. We do not know what challenges will come, we think peace will be forever. It seems easy to regard these old heroes as being old hat and unnecessary, to think of praising them as being jingoistic and flag waving. We have the luxury to able to criticise Churchill only due to the fact that he lead the country to victory.

This is how it always goes with fighting men: they are the heroes of the day during war and then embarrassing reminders of violence during peace. From the comfort of our armchairs and the lifestyles they died to protect, we are able to pick apart their actions in super slow time and issue meaningless statements about what they should have done. There are scores of academics whose entire living is based on doing this.

This habit of expressing our disgust at violence and killing whilst simultaneously being fascinated by it tells us a lot about our relationship to violence. Whether we like it or not, the simple fact is that we would not have survived as a species, as a tribe, as a country without being able to be extraordinary violent when we needed to be.

In fact, if we take Britain as an example, we have been extraordinarily violent not only when we needed to be, but also when we have not needed to be. The fact that we remain a wealthy country has been built on it. America too, is a nation built on extraordinary violence, from the wars against the native peoples to the War of Independence to the American Civil War and so on. In fact, if we look at every stable and prosperous nation state we will find a similar history of violence.

It is tempting to see violence as being more apparent in Western civilisation than in any other, due to the aggressive conquests that have shaped our modern world. The colonisation of Africa, the Americas, the Antipodes and many other areas around the world by European powers seems to prove this fact.

But this phenomenon is due to the technological advancement of Western civilisation, rather than any genetic or racial factors. Firstly, the Spartans laid the blueprint for Western military discipline, cooperation and martial focus. The Romans built further upon this and created systems that still have a resonance in modern Western armies. The complex system of trade that developed allowed technology to advance, making best use of natural resources.

Technology begets more technology as science and knowledge develop and you then have nation states with much more power than less developed nations.[6]

This allows the Western nations to defeat the Native Americans, the Mayans, the Incas, the African tribes, the Maori and so on. We have a ridiculous notion that before the white man came along, the Native Americans were all living in harmony together, passing round a peace pipe and getting on famously, tribe among tribe.

The reality is that the tribes fought each other savagely - the practice of scalping was not invented when the white man came along! In some cases, entire tribes were decimated by inter-tribal wars. So too the Maori enslaved and cannibalised the Moriori people, of whom no pure blood individual survives. The violent human sacrifices of the Mayans are well known. The violent expansion and conquest of the Bantu people in Africa is less well known.

The point here is to understand that violence is a human trait across all nations. This nation state violence is merely a macrocosm of the individual human evolution within the context of the natural world. In order to succeed, everything living thing has to fight for survival. This is one of the great truths of our existence. One of the great lies is that 'violence solves nothing'. Ultimately it is ONLY violence or the threat of violence that ensures our survival.

Something as important as this then needs to be understood if we are to have any real understanding of life at all. The fact that this is unpalatable to some does not make it any less true. If we wish we can place ourselves in an imagined moral high ground, looking down on those that practice it whilst failing to acknowledge that the freedom and security we enjoy is down to these people.

It is a common trait amongst humans to do this. When I was stationed as part of a company of men from my regiment in Basra Palace, Iraq, I had a very clear example of this. The job we had been given was to provide security to Basra Palace. The palace was one of Saddam Hussein residencies and perhaps once it had been luxurious. But now it was dilapidated and tawdry, with soldiers shoe horned into every available space.

Basra Palace was home to many agencies and units from many

different countries, UK, USA, Romania and so on. One of the key departments there was the British Foreign and Commonwealth Office - your classic civil servants.

From a UK plc perspective the political effort in Basra was paramount and so the FCO represented the UK's means of influencing the politics of the region. To do this of course, they needed security in which to operate. The daily tasks of our company were to patrol the local area in order to prevent rocket and missile attacks on the palace and to reassure the local population.

This was a summer tour so the temperatures on occasion went above fifty degrees celsius. When you are wearing a helmet and body armour and carrying a rifle and equipment, that's reasonably warm. This is particularly the case when you are in an armoured vehicle with broken air con. How our army chefs managed to cook in these temperatures I will never know!

I had come back into the palace from a patrol up to brigade headquarters at the airport. As we were driving back in, I had a message via the radio to report to the Foreign and Commonwealth Office to pick up a package to bring back. As our drivers parked up our vehicles, we unloaded our rifles and I went into the building. Finding no-one there, I went into their main office area.

I stood there waiting for somebody to speak to. And kept waiting. There must have been fifty people in there. I was stood there in full patrol uniform, with my helmet strapped to my webbing and a rifle in my hands and every single one of these dudes that we were protecting studiously ignored me. In fact, worse than that some looked at me and turned their noses up in distain. I could feel my tenuous hold on my own temper starting to give way.

Just as I was about to explode I saw a navy liaison officer come running over to grab me. Fair play to him, he had just walked in and seen that I was about to go bang so grabbed me and ushered me out. His first words to me were 'Don't worry about this lot, they send emails to the person sitting next to them rather than risk actual face to face contact'. That saved the situation but I never forgot the feeling of being hated by those we were protecting. There was no doubt that we were viewed as unspeakable thuggish scum by the pen pushers doing their best to make a mess of the country.

It is an observable truth that the more peace and luxury we live in, the more we move away from respect for those who train for violence and danger. If, in our daily lives, we are not exposed to violence or danger we seek to push it ever further from our minds. Out of sight, out of mind. How shocking is it then when it arrives uninvited?

This is the great problem of our age, not that we live in dangerous times - our streets our safer than ever, but that our daily lives are so far removed from danger that we are unprepared when it happens. We have lost the WILL TO ACT. What Churchill represents, what fighting men represent, what we need violent men and women for is that these people can actually DO SOMETHING when it matters.

The rest of the herd, the vegetable eating peace loving cattle can only freeze and try and hide until it goes away. If we continue to try and push violence and hardship away, we are creating more and more of these people. And as our lives continue to be softer and more luxurious, this will become more and more of a problem. What happens when our circumstances change? Will we still have people ready to step up and face the music?

Our capacity to forget history is astonishing. We imagine everything through the filter of our experience of modern life. We think that everything then was like everything now. Nowhere is this more amusingly wrong than in our perception of what men like Plato or Socrates or Aristotle must have been like.

Think of a 'philosopher' and we perhaps think of a dry and dusty academic surrounded by books. His skin is pasty from never seeing the sun and his physical frame is reed thin, a legacy of him forgetting to eat whilst enraptured with cosmic thoughts and musings. He gets no exercise and neglects his health as his mind is constantly on higher things. His mind juggles the Platonic dialogues, the meditations of Marcus Aurelius, The Enneads of Plotinus and so forth.

When we get to the actual people who wrote them what do we find? The same kind of dusty, emaciated geeks? Far from it! We find a famous wrestler, a Roman warrior emperor and a man who joined the army of Gordian as it marched on Persia. These were fine examples of men of action. Socrates was well known for his courage and conduct in battle, drawing the admiration of his peers for his strength in crisis. These were not 'soft' men who only had a literary learning.

This perception of 'philosophers' extends to 'artists' as well. Think of your stereotypical artist. A delicate soul flouncing about in a floppy hat, living the bohemian lifestyle, alternatively intoxicated with beauty and narcotics in a dreamlike fugue state. But when we examine the lives of Leonardo Da Vinci and Michelangelo we find something altogether different.

Leonardo was a practical man *par excellence*. He was a military engineer, a map maker, a designer of arms and military vehicles and he painted a bit too. Michelangelo was said to be more proud of his ability to straighten out horseshoes with his bare hands than he was of his skill in painting.

Perhaps the world's greatest goldsmith, Benvenuto Cellini was a celebrated soldier and also famous for his street fights and confrontations, having to flee on several occasions to escape the authorities. One cannot think of murderous artists without mentioning the painter Caravaggio. This is a man who has been credited with the invention of modern painting yet was almost equally famous for his fighting and was another who had to flee to avoid the law due to the consequences of his street battles.

Least we think that this martial spirit was confined to painters and craftsmen, we should remember that the playwright and poet Christopher Marlowe was killed in a street fight. Ben Jonson, another hugely influential playwright and poet fought a duel with swords against an actor called Gabriel Spencer and killed him. Shakespeare was an accomplished fencer and was arrested for affray for fighting in the street. [7]

We should never think that artistic and creative ability is somehow opposed to fighting spirit. If you read Ben Jonson's "On my first Sonne", written in mourning of his boy that died at the age of seven, you will realise that this same man that fought and killed a man in a duel was a sensitive and sophisticated soul with true humanity.

You can get this feeling also by looking at the ink drawings of the aforementioned Miyamoto Musashi, who was not only Japan's greatest swordsman dueller, but also one of its greatest painters with ink. His *Shrike on a Withered Branch* is a masterpiece of composition and simplicity.

To me, that kind of composition and simplicity is reflected also in the work of the French surrealist painter Yves Tanguy, the son of a navy captain who served in the army before he began to paint.

It is possible to take from this that creativity and violence are not mutually exclusive. Whilst this is obviously true, we need to go much, much further. What is clear to me is that their co-existence in these men was the very reason their artistic fruits were so rare. Look at the state of modern art today. It's mostly shit. And not just a bit shit, but totally, awfully 'you are having a laugh' shit. Conceptual art is the emperor's new clothes on a grand scale. Of course, there is some good stuff amongst the dross but it's low in number. Look at the artists that produce this stuff. Where is the conflict, the drama, the life lived, the spirit? This has disappeared from the mainstream world of fine art.

If you want quality, you need to look at the fantasy and commercial art being produced by the likes of Brom and others. This kind of art is, ironically looked down upon by the art crowd.

This is what happens when the spirit leaves a thing. It does not go away, rather it enters another field. We need to recognise this, as we can get caught up in the trap of thinking that 'everything was better in the old days'. What happens in reality is that a civilisation, organisation or a movement will have a period of energy where good quality is produced before that thing corrupts and ultimately declines.

This can be seen clearly in the history of the Greek civilisation before it was superseded by the Romans. Having had a time of amazing productivity, innovation and energy, ultimately the Greek civilisation declined as it fell into corruption and easy living. This was enough for the new energy and will of the Romans to be able to take over as the dominant culture.

This is the universal truth of empires, be they Greek, Roman, Persian, Ottoman or British. There is only ever enough energy to sustain them for a limited period, depending on the opposing forces. We see this too in, for example, organisations like the Church of England which have had enough energy to be a major force for a few hundred years but are now in terminal decline, the spirit and energy having left. Think of the modern soft Anglican Vicar. Is this a man of conviction, a man of action?

My mother, a lifelong Anglican is greatly saddened by the transition of these Churchmen from strong, steadfast and robust leaders to the flabby caretakers many have become. The WILL TO ACT has fizzled out.

DUELLING

The WILL TO ACT is the essence of being Battle Ready. Imagine if you will, the existence of a culture where at any time you can be challenged to fight to the death for an insult you have given. How would that change your attitude to life?

Duelling and challenges have existed as a cultural norm and only relatively recently been eliminated.

Think back to my example of the modern workplace. How might individuals conduct differ if they could be held accountable for their actions through being challenged to a duel? How might it change the actions of our generation of internet trolls if they knew they could be asked to fight to the death for what they say?

This attitude of accountability and responsibility for what you say and do is a characteristic of the martial way of life. It is perhaps natural that so many of the men that fought duels in times past were military officers, but most were not, except during the Napoleonic wars.[8]

It is a good indication of the attitude of the time in the eighteenth and nineteenth century that results of disputes between gentleman were published in the papers so all could see that the matter was done with and resolved.

Duelling as a phenomenon tells us a great deal about the development of our culture in this country. Although the later practice of duelling with swords may have come from Italy, it has its roots in the jousts of the medieval period and, perhaps even further back than that in the 'trial by combat' of the Norman conquest period. The idea that a duel of arms can achieve 'satisfaction' is an idea that needs close scrutiny as it gets to the essence of how shared risk between opponents for a higher ideal can bring humans to a resolution of differences.

There is an undeniable intimacy that exists between two individuals engaged in combat. This is very obvious too even in the modern day 'professional duels' of mixed martial arts. Your opponent is in physical contact with you, you can smell his sweat and smell his breath, his sweat is on your body and yours on his.

This is an intimacy of a kind that is normally experienced only in a sexual context. When that context changes to be one of doing violence do each other the physical proximity may be similar, but the emotional content is changed. One is of love and lust, the other of aggression and violence.

Many of my psychologist friends (particularly the ones influenced by Freud) may have fun with the premise that they are one in the same thing, but anyone who has ever fought like this knows the context is not sexual. In fact, a man's body instinctively reacts to fighting by protectively withdrawing the genitals as close to the body as possible! To think sexual thought whilst being hit in the face is not common, except for those with fairly niche desires!

You will have seen in fighting sports like boxing or mixed martial arts how opponents embrace after the fight is finished. Having been joined together in the contest and sharing risk and facing danger together, there is an unmistakable bond that is created between the protagonists. This does not mean that animosity disappears, but respect is earned.

This then, is fundamentally a 'bringing together' of opponents in order to force an outcome of resolution, one way or another. For the modern MMA fighters this is for sport, but this principle was used to resolve all manner of grievances where honour is concerned. The matter was not left to fester and become poisonous by inaction.

There is also something much more significant about the practice of duelling in that it demonstrates within a culture that there are things more important than death. That honour and courage are worth risking life for. There is within this idea that if you are not willing to die for your principles, then you have no principles.

Certainly it is very easy to speak in a principled way, but to stand before an opponent and feel the unmistakeable spread of fear in your stomach makes you suddenly accountable for what you have said.

Before we get too carried away with the romance of this, it is worth acknowledging that these men who duelled could afford principles. At least, they were not so poor that all their energy was taken up just to stay alive and feed themselves and their families. If for example, a man found himself in this position, it would be selfish and reckless indeed to risk his life for an insult when he had dependents that literally might die should he be killed.

However, as has been previously stated, no-one in our modern society lives in the kind of abject poverty that means that they would die of starvation. Being in this constant state of poverty means that you cannot do other than just survive. No real progress is possible while your every waking moment is taken up by staying alive.

Duelling is intrinsically linked to the aristocracy; gentleman and those that would seek to be gentlemen. This can be seen quite clearly when we look at those that duelled in history. They were men of titles such as the Duke of Wellington who fought a duel while he was the serving prime minister of Great Britain[9], military officers and latterly, lawyers and doctors who were seeking the status of gentlemen and so took on their customs.

Men are strikingly similar when stripped of titles, fine clothes, ceremony and the trappings of wealth, so what then distinguishes a 'gentleman' from one of base breeding but his conduct in matters of consequence?

This idea allowed the men of the upper classes to live a life of assumed superiority of character over their fellow men. They were not just expected to have principles but to prove it as well and duelling was among other things, a mechanism to demonstrate that they practiced what they preached. It was in effect, a way for all to see that a gentleman had substance and hence, was civilised rather than having only an animalistic existence of doing anything to survive.

It may seem bizarre to use the word 'civilised' in relation to the practice of two men fighting to resolve a dispute but when the modern duel was created in Renaissance Italy, it was done so to replace the *vendetta*.

The *vendetta* was a particularly nasty cultural phenomenon, given that it could last for an indefinite period, over many generations, often with the original reason for the feud forgotten.

This kind of historical blood feud became rightly viewed as a destructive aberration that perpetuated, rather than resolved the dispute. In duelling, a man fought his own battle and the issue was resolved there and then.

We have to bear in mind that often law enforcement was sporadic in these times and the legal process was often corrupt and not to be trusted. The legal status of duelling is an interesting one and it shows a certain pragmatism on the side of the courts. Although generally, duelling was illegal, if it could be shown that the correct duelling procedure had been followed, then more likely than not, no further action would be taken. There was a kind of indulgence toward duelling which is unlikely had the protagonists not been gentlemen.

Most duels of the pistol period did not end in fatalities and a great many ended with no injuries at all yet with honour satisfied. The key component in the duel was the role of the 'seconds'. Perhaps this can tell us something about we how we ought to be resolving disputes in our own time.

No duel could be fought without a challenge. A challenge should only be issued once an apology has been refused. Once that challenge is issued and accepted, seconds are appointed and from then on, it is their job to try and resolve the dispute before weapons are drawn. This takes the heat out of the argument by the use of intermediaries in a formally recognised process. It acknowledges fundamentally that insults have consequences and that reputation and honour are of paramount importance.

If the matter is not resolved and the matter has to be settled with arms, this is deemed a failure on the part of the seconds. In fairness however, there are some instances where the grievance is so great that they may never have stood a chance!

The move from swords to pistols is an important one in the history of duelling in this country. With swords, the difference in skill between the duellists may be enough to decide the outcome. It also potentially gives an advantage to a younger and more vigorous man should there be a big age difference between the duellists.

With pistols, not only is the relative skill level not as important, but the seconds can agree a larger or smaller distance depending on the animosity of the protagonists. For example, twelve paces was about normal, but twenty paces could be decided upon to lessen the chances of death, or six paces if there was a great desire on both sides to kill or seriously injure the other.[10]

The seconds were further required to procure the weapons and arrange for a surgeon to be present. During the duel, the seconds were on hand to ensure that no foul play occurred and that neither of the parties had an advantage.

British duelling pistols, of the like made by the genius Joseph Manton or Durs Egg are not just items of exceptional beauty. They originally had no aiming sights or rifling as it as considered ungentlemanly to take aim at an opponent. Rather the weapon should be brought up and fired with no delay. Under some duelling conditions, the duellers took turns to fire but again, it was considered poor form to stand and take careful aim.

Over time, aiming sights became more accepted and some pistols had subtle rifling grooves as attitudes towards aiming softened. Manton 'blued' his barrels to reduce glare into the firer's face. The pistols were designed and made as pairs so as to give no advantage to either firer.

Duels were, counter to popular belief, held at any time of the day but the practice of holding them at dawn reflects the fact that they were illegal and hence better held when no-one was around. Additionally, the seconds were responsible for arranging a time when the duellists would be sober especially if the quarrel had been fuelled by drink, as so many were.

In that time, gentleman drank far more and far more often than in modern times with port being a particular favourite. This made it all the more important that they be formally allowed time to sober up and apologise if something rash had been said.

The position of the state and the church towards duelling is interesting, chiefly because it reveals that duelling was seen as a challenge to the power structure. After all, these gentleman were following a code that was regarded as being above the law of the state and above 'God's law' as decreed by the Church of England. As such, it was a direct challenge to the power base of both church and state.

The state as represented by the courts found a more pragmatic accommodation to duelling. After all, if the prime ministers, lords and aristocrats who ran the state were duelling despite its illegality what could they do but fudge a kind of acceptance, lest they put themselves in the dock?

For the church, duelling was more problematic. Even though some clergyman were famous duellers (one suspects they were gentlemen first and clergymen second) to have a code of honour that was not authorised by them was anathema to those that would seek to control the hearts of men as well as their minds and bodies.

The church as an established institution has always sought to control the heart. This has been the source of its power right from the beginning when Constantine decided that he would have 'one empire, one religion'. Through centuries of running an empire, the Romans could see that the growing religion of Christianity would challenge their authority if they stood against it. So, from throwing Christians to the lions they came to adopt it as the authorised imperial religion. In doing so, they allowed the aristocratic Italian elite to continue to hold power - which remarkably they still do in large part to this day with that cabal known as the Vatican.

This was the power structure of control that Henry VIII broke off from to be replaced in this country by the 'reformed' Church of England. It is hard for us today to imagine the power that the church had in previous times. Even when my parents were children, the church had a level of influence far beyond the current times.

A great part of that influence came from their ability to control an individual's attitudes to death. In particular this meant creating a fear of going to hell to be tormented for eternity. It was a great trick on the part of the church to simultaneously present an all loving God of forgiveness who was also a merciless judge, sentencing you to never ending and unimaginable torture for not believing in Him!

The men who duelled did not fear death and damnation above all things. That is not to say that they did not fear death or injury. Only the very stupid have no fear. But they were driven by a greater fear of breaking their own, not the church's, code.

The history of duelling clearly shows that men who are willing to fight in this way are outside of external control. At the moment of their contest, they were free men, bound only by their self-imposed code of honour for which they would die. They made the rules, not the state or the church or anyone else.

Ultimately, public opinion turned against duelling and greater punishments for military officers caught duelling sounded the death knell for the practice as it was. A significant factor in the demise of duelling was the increase of the middle class, particularly in the industrial cities, to whom duelling was an impediment to the practice of making money. Of course, the fact that duelling had become abused, with arguments over laughably trivial matters ending in death did not help either.

If we think of how duelling originated, as a more civilised way of ending a dispute than a *vendetta*, we can see how it became corrupted over time as all things are. It was replaced in this country by boxing and the Marquess of Queensbury, the aristocrat that he was, had rules designed particularly for 'amateur boxers'.

In those days, that could only mean gentlemen resolving disputes as sporting leisure time of this kind was not a privilege of the working man. The working man could box of course, but as a money earning prize fighter. He would not have the time or energy to spend on an activity that did not bring financial reward. Before the Marquess of Queensbury's aristocratic influence and activities took hold, his rules were viewed with distain by the prize fighters as being 'soft' and 'for toffs', and seen as being 'effete.'"[11]

But boxing and duelling with pistols are not the same thing. It may seem more 'civilised' to have less risk to life but what you are putting on the line is reduced. It also re-introduces the advantage to the skilled participant without the equality of pistol shooting. Later, the idea of resolving disputes this way fell completely out of favour and the courts became the primary means of gaining 'satisfaction'.

There is something to be learned here in the example of the Marquess of Queensberry. On the face of it, he and the Victorian gentleman boxers were harking back to a more classical understanding of how a gentleman should be educated both in body and in mind. The Marquess of Queensbury was one of a number of aristocrats that promoted boxing for its supposed ideals of promoting 'manliness' and courage and other such things. Likely they too, as I do, take great inspiration from Plato's words concerning a purely literary education making a man soft. But the aristos' of this era such as the Marquess had a massive blind spot in their development which can be seen most clearly in the spat the Marquess of Queensbury had with Oscar Wilde.

It is typical of the kind of brutish type that the Marquess of Queensbury was that he would leave a card for Oscar Wilde accusing him of being a 'posing sodomite'. In actual fact, he misspelled 'sodomite' as 'somdomite'. Bear in mind that in the early era of duelling, this kind of insult would undoubtably have led to a challenge. At this point Oscar Wilde was already very successful and famous. He was also romantically involved with the Marquess' son, Alfred, known as 'Bosie'.

It would be easy to posit this case as a simple 'aristocratic brutish villain versus artistic sensitive man in love' but the reality is more complicated than that, more tragic and more seedy. Oscar Wilde had involved Bosie in the practice of purloining working class male prostitutes for purely sexual purposes, rather than, for example same sex relations in the way that Plato would have known. The practice of homosexuality was a serious criminal offence in those days and for whatever reason, Wilde decided to sue the Marquess for libel.

The trouble was, he WAS a posing sodomite. In fact, he was an actual sodomite as well. So if the Marquess' legal team could demonstrate that this was the case then not only would the libel case fall apart, but it was likely that Wilde would be charged with a criminal offence.

Which is exactly what happened. All they had to do was prepare the male prostitutes to testify. This was not difficult given the bribes and threats the Marquess could bring to bear on them. After all, they had the threat of being criminally charged too and were also desperate for money. This is useful if you are trying to force their hands to testify. In the end, they didn't have to, as the threat of their testimony was enough for Wilde to call off the litigation. This left him with the costs which promptly bankrupted him. Then he was charged with 'gross indecency' found guilty and sentenced to two years hard labour which perhaps contributed to his early death.

Here we have two very different men - the Marquess of Queensbury; a physical man, who knew nothing of the arts, was an atheist and blunt instrument and Oscar Wilde, the leader of the literary movement know as 'Aestheticism' , a celebrated wit and playwright.

The route that Wilde took of going through the courts to receive 'satisfaction' was ruinous to him - perhaps it was his hubris that was his downfall. But in the development of the animosity between the Marquess of Queensbury and Wilde, can we speculate that a duel would have been the more civilised course of action?

It is ironic that when the Marquess of Queensbury turned up on Oscar Wilde's doorstep unannounced, threatening him with physical violence. Wilde replied "I don't know what the Queensbury rules are, but the Oscar Wilde rule is to shoot on sight".

The benefit of the English emphasis on pistols in the duel is that despite their inequality in physical prowess, the pistol provides a more level playing field. It is interesting to wonder at an alternative history where Wilde and Queensbury duel, honour is satisfied and Wilde goes on to live a full life with many more creative works of art being produced. We will never know.

CARRYING A BIG STICK

By then the duelling period in England was effectively over, consigned to a time when law enforcement was uncertain and there was no police force, and the gentlemen was 'Battle Ready' at all times, ready to defend his honour or his person. This aspect, of not being able to rely on the police or the courts made the individual more immediately responsible for himself. This is made very obvious in the carrying of personal weapons. If we again look at the fabulous work of the pistol maker Joseph Manton, we can see the exquisite arms he produced for personal protection, from double barrelled pistols for drivers of carriages to gentleman's pocket pistols, easy to conceal in his garments.

Psychologically, a big change occurs when we carry a weapon capable of causing death. This is very obvious when carrying a rifle around say in Afghanistan or Iraq, but I found that the biggest change of mindset was closer to home - carrying a concealed pistol in Northern Ireland.

To be in civilian dress, looking like everyone else and mingling among them yet with the destructive power of a firearm in the back of your jeans creates a mental state of alertness that is hard to replicate. I remember well walking down the street of a town in Northern Ireland when a gang of youths started heckling me, presumably out of boredom. The knowledge that I had the power of life and death with me was an almost overwhelming feeling. The word to describe the feeling is not 'confidence', it's more a total awareness of the potential you have to destroy. I felt that the last thing I wanted to do would be to get into a pointless argument.

My father told me an interesting story of some of the time he spent with the manager of a large manufacturing plant in the States. This manager had a problem in that he was prone to losing his temper and saying things that he later regretted. He was not a violent man but his outbursts were causing harm to his reputation. His novel solution was to at all times carry a powerful concealed .38 Magnum revolver under his jacket. The weight and feel of this man-stopper was enough to constantly remind him to keep his anger in check - or face the dire consequences of his actions.

The men who duelled had a constant awareness of the fact that their actions had serious consequences. They could not go about speaking insults with impunity.

ETHOS

The phenomenon of duelling was the embodiment of an ethos. The unwritten ethos of this elite group of gentlemen was an agreed code of conduct. The code is that there are things worth dying for such as honour and reputation. In being prepared to die for these things, the gentlemen intended to place himself above the base behaviours of the common man who was viewed as being only out for himself.

The gentleman's code is focused on others, after all, the gentleman's reputation is a measure of how much he values the thoughts of his fellow men. To be noble is to be mindful of others - the very basis of manners. To be common and base is to only regard oneself. The fact that many of the duellers were military men should not surprise us either as what is the process of becoming a soldier other than a way of becoming a member of a group of individuals that place each other before themselves?

I will discuss ethos in much more detail later but as the law and lawyers took over, the letter of the law overtook the unwritten gentleman's ethos and that ethos began to be rarer. The growing number of industrialists and middle class had no need for duelling as it got in the way of the pursuit of money and material wealth.

It is not fair to say that all duellists were noble and of good mind of course. There were some shocking abuses of the practice and many out and out murders disguised as duelling. We are well aware also of the abuses of power that were carried out in the name of being a 'gentleman'. This occurs when the gentleman starts to believe that he is superior to a common man in value irrespective of content of character. But duelling was designed to demonstrate that a man had 'bottom'. That he was a solid man of integrity.

The word comes from nautical terminology and means keeping

your head in a crisis, with the necessary qualities of stability, courage and resolve. The boat with 'bottom' can withstand the storm without 'keeling over'. The man who is good in a crisis does not run off, leaving others to take the consequences but rather steps up and accepts his responsibilities. Such a man as this is to be admired and emulated. This is a man who stands for something beyond himself and beyond his own ego.

CHAPTER 4
THE WILL OF THE WARRIOR

MOYERS: What are some of the other rituals that are important to society today?

CAMPBELL: Joining the army, putting on a uniform, is another. You're giving up your personal life and accepting a society determined manner of life in the service of the society of which you are a member. This is why I think it is obscene to judge people in terms of civil law for performances they rendered in time of war. They were acting not as individuals, they were acting as agents of something above them and to which they had by dedication given themselves. To judge them as though they were individual human beings is totally improper.

Extract from *The Power of Myth* by Joseph Campbell

Joseph Campbell also relates a story of a samurai who had the duty to avenge the murder of his overlord. When he finally caught up with the man who had murdered his master, after many weeks of search, he had him cornered and was about to dispatch him with his sword when, out of fear and panic, the man spat in his face. The warrior sheathed his sword and walked away.[12]

Joseph Campbell explains that the reason he walks away is that in that moment he was made angry and to kill the man in anger would have made it a personal act, rather than the impersonal act that he had come to fulfil.

This is the man again that stands for something bigger than himself beyond his own ego. It is possible for us to go into all kinds of avenues of spiritual development and talk of why it is that we need to connect to that which is beyond our individuality. But that itself is beyond the scope of this book. This book is about how we become Battle Ready by developing FREEWILL (winning the battle between YES and NO). To develop freewill, we need to be able to think and act beyond our own immediate individual self-concern and apathy.

When we think of the warrior or military man, we should understand that this is what he or she embodies. The warrior exemplifies the adherence to the 'code' of the warrior. Over the course of history, warriors have held codes as their philosophy of life, different in different times and geographical locations but always being that factor that unifies them.

It is possible to take inspiration from the samurai, from the Spartans, from the Romans, the Mongols and so on. But for this example, I wish to start closer to home and look at the Royal Navy at the time of Admiral Lord Nelson.

Nelson, like Churchill, embodies the will and cunning of our exemplary 'Battle Ready' man. Again, like Churchill he does not fit our idea of the square jawed muscular hero, Nelson was small and weak. He reached the level of admiral on pure merit and was everything the Royal Navy was at that time, cunning, innovative and above all, ruthlessly aggressive.

In those times, a man of ability and hard work could make good money in the navy via the 'prize' system. Under these arrangements, the value of any ships and ship's cargo that was captured by a vessel was shared out throughout the whole crew. The man that worked out who would get what was the ship's 'prize officer'. Naturally a bigger individual portion went to the ship's captain who was, after all, chiefly responsible for the capture of any booty. As an admiral, Nelson would also have been entitled to a share of any prizes that any of the ships under his command took.

In these times, there was no conflict between being patriotic and serving ones country and also earning good money by taking prizes. It was a much later idea that a man should serve one's country without hope of reward. To professionals like Nelson, this was part of the contract of being a naval commander. Not only that, but this system helped to generate and maintain that attitude of opportunism and aggression that made the Royal Navy the most feared in the world.

This opportunism is being 'Battle Ready' and the aggression is our WILL TO ACT. It also helped that the Articles of War for the Royal Navy had been updated to include capital punishment for any officer that 'failed to do their utmost against the enemy, either in battle or pursuit'. In other words, if you don't act, you get shot. This is a perfect example of the 'carrot and stick' method of motivation!

Before the modern era, it was much more tolerated for a naval officer to be a gambler and womaniser. After all, these men did not go to sea for a luxury cruise. They were men that faced death and disease in harsh conditions. They deserved their 'vices' to keep them sane and in good spirits. To expect men to be effective and efficient warriors and conform to an arbitrary 'moral' code is to ignore what the business of fighting is about.

Morals change over time and by geographic location. Often these changes happen quite quickly. To be an unmarried mother in my parent's youth was totally 'morally' unacceptable. In the present day, it's the norm and is 'morally' fine. The so called 'morals' of society are a joke, something to be used against people when it suits. This is particularly true in the UK where we make a national pastime of taking the moral high ground. Our ability to do this in such a variety of different ways is truly amazing. It also explains how the class system manages to survive well beyond its literal reality.

For example, when someone says "I come from a working class background" in an argument, the subtext is often "I know what hardship and hard work is and I am more authentic than you. This gives me not only moral licence to talk about any issue of hardship but also negates any experience you have from your privileged upbringing - you had it easy". The ultimate satirical expression of this is found in Monty Python's *Four Yorkshiremen* sketch. Here, four self-made millionaires drink champagne and attempt to out do each other in who had the toughest childhood.

To rely on your privileged upbringing as if it gives you some greater right or cultural understanding is equally as bad. If we assume a moral superiority because we have had the luck to be born and raised in a certain class or geographic location we commit the same error.

Even tramps in this country take the moral high ground. I was once walking past a wino in Liverpool, heading home from a days work. I happened to be wearing a business suit. The wino, cradling a bottle of Buckfast screamed at me "Eh lad, nice suit mate but at least I don't werk for the fuckkkkhhhhhhhhing man ya sell out bastard".

Yep that's right I thought. I had indeed 'sold out' by getting a job and paying taxes. The tramp on the other hand with his booze and piss-stained trousers was living a free and authentic life! Except of course, he was in the ultimate slavery - that of addiction. But just because of this, it would be dangerous for me to assume my own moral superiority over him. I knew nothing about the circumstances that had brought this unfortunate soul to his current state. There but for the grace of God...

The reason it is necessary for us to examine the arbitrary nature of our own cultural morality is because we need to be free from it. That is not to say we should have no morality - far from it, but we should recognise the traps and problems we get into if we mistake the cultural morality of the times we happen to live in for actual objective virtue.

The sub-text of moral superiority is no less prevalent in those who view themselves as higher up the chain but often the means are more subtle. The way you speak is a huge one in this country and often people have judged your class the moment you open your mouth. It may seem ridiculous if you happen to be reading this book in Australia or in the United States of America. But it is true. Take my own background for example. Many of my direct forebears were clergymen. Others were craftsmen and coach builders. My own father was a manager, a business consultant and a jewellery designer and goldsmith. On my other side and further back were naval officers and educators. Look a bit further around the family background and you will find gardeners, farmers, miners and all sorts. So what? Much more relevant to the way I am perceived and treated by my fellow countrymen is the way I speak, regardless of my ancestors and actual background. This is a trap as well. To start assuming any moral superiority over someone else due to the way they speak is a red herring that does not get at the truth of the matter. Fundamentally, we need to be able to 'develop a discerning eye in all things' as Musashi said. We need to be able to see the golden nugget of truth that can help us develop amongst the many masks that people wear and amid the fog created by the times we happen to live in.

WILL AND FREEWILL

To understand why the warrior develops willpower beyond the average person we need to first understand a little of the human condition. Remember that the master principle of war is 'Selection and Maintenance of the Aim' - choosing what you need to do and sticking to it. It should tell us a hell of a lot about people that the most important principle of all is simply staying on course.

Can you remember those quotes from Churchill? They are all about perseverance and holding fast. He understood this more than anyone. The human being is capable of extraordinary things only when he can develop and exercise his will.

In order to develop our will and therefore our ability to achieve our goals we need to understand one stark reality first. We have no FREEWILL. The normal response to this statement is disbelief. After all, haven't you made a free and open choice over all the aspects that impact upon your life? Don't you DO exactly what you want to do from the job you do to the way you spend your leisure time? Aren't you in fact the master of your future, in total control of yourself and others? Absolutely not. And yet it is typical of us as human beings to assume that we have the personal power and detachment to make genuinely FREE choices about anything we wish.

The problem is, we have many, many WILLS, plural. All of

them are selfish and want their own way. The one that shouts the loudest in any moment is the one that wins.

The warrior has created a leader for his many and unruly wills - when they are given a mission, all of them dance to the same tune, or else. The warrior is RESOLVED to achieve his mission, even if death is the price. Consider these quotes from the samurai text *The Hagakure*:

> "There is something to be learned from a rainstorm.
> When meeting with a sudden shower, you try not to get
> wet and run quickly along the road. But doing such things
> as passing under the eaves of houses, you still get wet.
> When you are resolved from the beginning, you will not be
> perplexed, though you still get the same soaking. This under-
> standing extends to everything."

> "If by setting one's heart right every morning and
> evening, one is able to live as though his body were already
> dead, he gains freedom in the Way."[13]

Imagine how powerful you become when you are truly resolved. What if you found out you had one day to live? This may seem extreme but we all face this possibility every day. Maybe today is the day of your death. Far from being a morbid thought, this realisation should liberate you. What do you really have to lose? Much of the mentality of a warrior revolves around death - for obvious reasons, but it applies to us all.

MEMENTO MORI

Today the fashion is to want to live forever and refuse to think about dying. But death is the one thing in life you can guarantee. Look at the desks of educated men in paintings from the renaissance period and you will often see human skulls on them. These 'memento mori' were powerful reminders to be resolved and act now as time is ever ticking away. By embracing death we embrace life and we begin to truly live.

The warrior has a head start on us here as the nature of his occupation forces him to consider his death and those around him. My own experiences in the army, dealing with the death of comrades had this profound effect on me. What really do we risk in life knowing that we all end up dead? Is it really a risk to set up your own business or to leave a job you hate to do something else? What is the fear of failure when few will care anyway when we are gone? This should not be a depressing thought, but an exciting one. The theme of embracing life by embracing death is an ancient and powerful one - can you think of a more powerful image of this in Western art than Christ on the cross?

We see loads of so called motivational memes on the internet about seizing the day and all those vapid banalities about how you can achieve whatever you want to. None of them say that to do this you need to embrace the reality of your own existence - you will die.

This is the first realisation that the warrior needs in order to be resolved from the beginning. *The Hagakure* even tells us how to do this:

> *"Meditation on inevitable death should be performed daily. Every day when one's body and mind are at peace, one should meditate upon being ripped apart by arrows, rifles, spears and swords, being carried away by surging waves, being thrown into the midst of a great fire, being struck by lightning, being shaken to death by a great earthquake, falling from thousand-foot cliffs, dying of disease...And every day without fail one should consider himself as dead."* [13]

This is not to wallow in self-pity but to wake us up and focus on what really matters in life. A word of caution with this though - this does not mean that we should go around reminding other people of their own mortality! They may not thank you for this. Work of this kind is only for those on the path to being Battle Ready.

Fear is always an accompanying emotion when considering

death and dying. Most people do not want to be frightened. As a young platoon commander of 23 years old I was stationed in Northern Ireland with my platoon, with the job of patrolling the rural areas at night. Looking back, this was a great foundation as it involved jumping on and off helicopters, navigation, vehicle drills and other essential soldiering skills in a real operational environment.

One of my responsibilities with the other commanders was to command 'CMVs', or civilian military vehicles. These were basically normal looking civilian transit vans that could be used to covertly drop off or pick up troops from the ground. We used to do them up to look like working vehicles - newspapers on the dash, takeaway wrappers and so on. The driver and the commander in the cab needed to look the part too, tracksuits and jumpers were the normal rig. One of the nightmare scenarios when commanding these vehicles was to drive into an IRA illegal vehicle checkpoint.

In the past, the IRA had set up these checkpoints on roads echoing the way our forces would do the same. The basic intention was to show the population who was boss and that they could operate with impunity. When manning these checkpoints they would wear balaclavas and carry rifles.

In reality during my era, the threat of these happening was pretty low but we trained for them and of course - you never know.

Whenever it was my turn to command the vehicle I would always run through the drills of what to do if we drove into one of these with the driver. Basically, it's not great. We carried pistols but the thought of getting into a firefight with or without troops in the back was not a reassuring one. The enemy is in a much stronger position than you. All you have on your side is the element of surprise and once that's gone you are outnumbered and outgunned.

Writing this now, I can feel my heart beat faster, remembering the drills. You have one chance and that's it. Even with troops in the back, they can't see and in any case would all have to deploy out of the same small door - hardly ideal if under fire.

Every time I was on this job I would run the driver through the drills, even though he knew them, just in case. On about my fourth time of doing this duty I suddenly noticed that my driver's hands were shaking. The driver knew the drills back to front but I was needlessly scaring the shit out of him by going over it again and again. As his driving suffered from him being wound up I used to go through the drills once with each new driver to make sure he knew what to do then left it at that. Not everyone wants to be on this path.

For us though it creates the right frame of mind to begin. It starts with seriously visualising your own death and a time after you have gone. This will centre you in the present and allow you to focus on what counts and what is important to you. There is a clue to how this should be done from the sources we looked at. It needs to be done daily as the mind of the human being will quickly forget. This is why the renaissance men had a human skull on the desk. Only this kind of shock tactic kept them mindful. To be mindful of your own death must become a habit.

THE STOIC APPROACH TO LIFE AND DEATH

It's not just the samurai that meditated on death as a practical tool to live properly. If we look at the philosophy of the Stoic school, we can see the same thing. It is important for us to make a study of the Stoic school of philosophy a priority if we wish to become Battle Ready. The importance of the Stoics is that they developed practical methods to know and understand themselves and life. We are only interested in practical methods. Everything else is merely interesting at best or pointless and a waste of time at worst.

It says a great deal for the practical exercises of the Stoics that the Roman Emperor, Marcus Aurelius, was a student of these methods. The exercise that the Stoics developed for meditation on death was called *praemeditatio malorum* - meditation on poverty, suffering and death. By meeting these head on and directly engaging with the possibility of them happening we can begin to build a resource for encountering their reality. A simple way of thinking about this is that they become a known rather than an unknown.

The Stoics were particularly concerned with being indifferent in attitude to normal and natural things in life (like death) that we cannot control. For us in the modern world, a mere meditation is not enough. This is because we do not have anymore the closeness to death that they had in ancient Greece and indeed any period up until the present times. For example, the sacrifice of animals was routine in these times. If we wish to be able to have sufficient material for our meditations on death we need to have some practical experience if we do not already.

If you are very much the urban individual, who buys meat from the supermarket then you need to go and kill and butcher an animal or at least witness it being done. Watching a video on YouTube is not enough. It is a relatively simple thing to arrange to go and hunt a rabbit for example and then learn how to properly butcher and prepare it for eating. You can still do this even in the UK. You can go fishing too.

If you have never seen real poverty, take a trip to a country where people struggle to eat to open your eyes. To see this first hand is a powerful experience that you will not forget. This again will make your meditations real and your understanding based on experience.

The other effect that this first hand experience should give us is liberation from the idea of FAIRNESS. I have mentioned previously how the expectation of fairness makes us prone to crumble. Seeing first hand real poverty and disease makes a mockery of our cosy Western views on what is fair. We need to absorb the reality that there is no 'fairness' in this life and nor could there be.

Some children are born into the most desperate poverty from which they will never recover and die early. The resolve of the warrior cannot be diverted by expecting fairness. On the contrary, the warrior expects the unexpected effects of chance and puts plans in place to deal with them.

RUTHLESSNESS

I was lucky enough as a boy to get a scholarship to a school in west Cumbria that had a good reputation. This reputation was based largely on its emphasis on drama and sport, both areas that became very important for me. One of the weaknesses of the friendly and caring atmosphere that the school engendered was the fact that it did not prepare us fully for life outside. The area that they did not properly teach was RUTHLESSNESS.

This might seem strange but let me give you an example. We sometimes played the local comprehensive schools at rugby. Most of us were pretty physically fit as the school had games or physical education nearly every day and being a boarding school, we had plenty of mates to practice with after school and who were always available. The school had a policy that if you were sent off during a game, you immediately were sent to the headmaster to be disciplined. We were left in no doubt that any foul or aggressive play was forbidden and the worst thing you could do. To lose the game was preferable to having to resort to violence.

When we played these comprehensive schools it is no surprise that they set out to intimidate us. Despite us being often more physical and fitter, we were hand tied by the policy of not fighting back. This is all very well if you have an able referee and linesman who can spot foul play, but in a school game of rugby in atrocious conditions and poor visibility a hell of a lot goes unnoticed. Often we lost these games by being physically dominated when there was no need to be.

When I started playing rugby league for a local team I was shown a very different way. I was a half-back in rugby league, responsible for co-ordinating the attack. Typically half-backs are on the smaller side and are often targeted by the bigger players on the opposing team as a way of shutting down your ability to score points. On the first game I played I had just passed the ball out wide when I was hit late from behind with a shoulder charge that sent me slamming into the turf. As I went to stand up I could see a real punch up going on with limbs going everywhere and a referee desperately trying to regain control.

My own team-mates, who I had known less than a week had immediately leapt to my defence without concern over being polite or playing the game fairly. As far as they were concerned this aggression could not go unchallenged - and the referee was not to be trusted in dishing out the correct punishment. The law was immediately taken into their hands.

With so many people fighting, the referee was unable to single anyone out individually so instead awarded me a penalty and gave everybody a 'serious talking to'. I was able to play the rest of the game without being illegally targeted and having won the 'arm-wrestle', we went on to win the game.

The final nail in the coffin for any idealistic notions of 'fairness' came when I took my promotional exams from lieutenant to captain in the army. Back then, to qualify for promotion you needed to pass an exam which consisted of a series of practical and written tests - on map reading, how to assemble a radio, other basic skills and finally a TEWT - a Tactical Exercise Without Troops. This is basically how to put together a plan of how to attack an enemy position with the resources you are given and then deliver that plan to an invigilating officer - normally a major from the infantry or cavalry.

You were expected of course to pass this exam and it was a considerable black mark against you if you didn't. To fail was often seen as letting the other officers in your battalion down and making the unit look bad. This was the last thing I wanted to do, I had joined an excellent battalion with exceptional officers and men.

I had been informed at short notice of when mine was to be held. I went down there and stayed in group accommodation - basically a big dormitory with the other officers about to take the test. It became quickly apparent that I did not have a lot of the equipment I should have had and therefore was totally unprepared.

For whatever reason, the message had not got through that I needed to have a certain map ready, marked up and prepared for the next day. I needed to be familiar with the ground depicted covered by the map as the test would be particularly hard. It was already 2300hrs when I found this out. Did anybody have any spare maps? No, they didn't. OK, what else was in the test that I didn't know about? Why did everyone know what was in it but me?

It turned out I also needed a reference book I didn't have and needed to assemble a radio I hadn't trained much on. Marvellous. There wasn't much I could do right then so I decided to get some sleep after rushing around trying and failing to find a map.

It was 0200hrs before I got to sleep and I got up at 0600hrs ready for a long day and to catch the coach to the exam location. I hadn't had much sleep at all worrying about how I was going to pull off passing this exam.

As I was sitting on the coach being taken to my almost certain failure I began to feel furious. This was totally 'unfair'. Some idiot had forgotten to pass vital information to me meaning that I would fail this exam and forever have this question mark over my ability. No one would give credence to a sob story of 'I never had the right map' and all that stuff. This was to be a bad day at the office.

The madder I got though, the more determined I became to not let this happen. Imagine not being able to be promoted due to failing the exam! I would be a laughing stock amongst my peers. Not just that but these men would again be serving with me on operations and relying on me as I relied on them. The last thing I wanted was for them to think I was a weak link. The men under my command too would begin to raise a few eyebrows. Not something that instils confidence in your soldiers. But just because I had been served a shit sandwich didn't mean I was going to eat it. Not knowing what I was going to do I resolved to pass the exam by whatever means necessary.

To play by the rules seemed stupid when the odds had been so stacked against me through no fault of my own. I thought back to those days of playing rugby. Any means necessary. My attitude for the day was to be one of ruthlessness.

Having made this decision out of desperation and fury we were herded into the briefing outlining how the day would work - a series of stands, done in rotation with us divided into smaller groups each with their own order of stands so a group was always at one stand or another but doing them in a different order. At the end of the briefing there was a long and dire warning about those caught cheating with some very grave threats indeed. There was some talk about 'integrity' and all of that. They fell on deaf ears in my case as I was already resolved.

The first stand for us was signals - assembling this radio I had hardly trained on. To examine and mark our progress we had each been assigned a signalman - a private soldier from the Royal Signals. I looked hard at my guy. Was he an understanding guy? Could he be bribed? Could he be intimidated? My intuition told me it was far better to play the 'nice but dim' officer stereotype and hope he had some compassion.

As I started to piece together the unfamiliar equipment, he could quickly see that I was in trouble. I mumbled 'er, um, right, er ok ya, this goes.....er here I think sort of...' and waited for his help. He didn't let me down bless him. 'Not exactly sir, keep trying' 'Right you are, oh it's here isn't it, of course it is, I knew that' and so on. At one point he said 'we're not supposed to help in any way sir' I replied 'Oh gosh, yes of course totally, where does this go, here?' He just nodded then rolled his eyes in typical soldier fashion when confronted with a nice but thick officer. On to the next one.

This was a written test which was open book so no problems, except it was from the book I didn't have. Bollocks. I sat around under a tree to complete this test and saw a mate of mine who also didn't have the book. Not just me then. I gave him a look to say 'what are we gonna do?' and he pointed to a female officer he used to date. When I say 'used to date' they had got drunk together at a party when he was dressed as Dolly Parton and she was dressed as Catwoman.

In a whisper he said 'Lend us your book will you? Go on. Go on. Go on. Please. Go on. Go on.' The relationship can't have ended that badly as as soon as she was finished she threw it at him. To be fair though she threw it at him pretty hard. Without much time left he scribbled out his answers and then threw the book at me. Five minutes of a half-hour test is not a long time to complete the whole thing. I reckon I managed about 80% by furiously writing up until the last minute.

The next stand was map reading. The stand that you needed a pre-marked up map for. I didn't even have a map. What the hell was I supposed to do? There was no way my map reading was good enough to do a test like that cold. No way. When I got to the stand location the group before was just finishing. I saw some mates of mine in that group all of whom were in the Army Air Corp and flew helicopters. One of them saw me and said 'are you ok, mate?'

I replied 'No mate I haven't even got a map, someone cocked up and I wasn't told.'

'Do you want to borrow mine? We're finished.'

'Thanks mate you're a life saver.'

'No dramas, see you at the finish'. This was strictly illegal but he didn't hesitate to help me out with a map.

This was good but I still had the problem that I had done absolutely no preparation and had never even seen the ground before. I was pretty certain this one would get away from me and I would fail. I looked at the question sheet. My worst nightmare - but with time passing I needed to make a start. I looked down at the map that my Army Air Corps mate had given me.

Not only was it all beautifully marked up in a way consistent with being a helicopter navigator but..... all his workings out were on it too which totally negated the fact that I hadn't been able to prepare. All I needed to do now was work out the answers and now I had an even chance I could do that well enough. My friend had known this when he lent me his map of course and never even made a big deal of it.

I learnt another valuable lesson then. Time after time during the most difficult moments we are helped out by the strong personal relationships we have made. It is incredible what people will do for people they know well. The cultivation of close personal relationships of mutual trust and support is essential for the Warrior.

With that stand dealt with I was ready for the big finish - the TEWT. This one was the most important of all. It was also the one for which, as an infantry officer, I needed no help with. This was our bread and butter and I felt very relaxed going in as, for the first time that day, I felt prepared and ready to go. My battalion had regular and thorough training for the junior officers on this and that training stood me in good stead. My own company commander had personally taken me through many different tactical situations in training to bring out the key principles.

Having briefed my plan to the invigilating officer I made my way to the finish where you wait for the results. I was exhausted from the lack of sleep and the nervous energy. It seemed like a very long time before they came to read out the results.

As per the custom in the British Army and I am sure armies across the world they are read out in the full presence of everybody else. I not only passed but came in the top five due to a strong performance in the TEWT. However, if I had failed anyone of the stands I would have failed overall.

I felt a number of things: pleasure in being able to pull off what had not seemed likely, relief in not having to carry the shame of failure but the strongest emotion was fury at those that had failed to do their job by giving me the necessary information to prepare. I felt absolutely no moral qualms about having bent the rules. If I had, I wouldn't have done it. I knew exactly what I was doing and why. Playing by the rules is fine as long as the system works, but when it doesn't we need to take the initiative. Had I been given the list of things I needed to bring with me and prepare for in the first place I may well have come much nearer the top.

As fate would have it, in any case the army later introduced a new promotional course that I had to retake anyway, but I didn't know that at the time.

This experience made me never trust the 'system' again and it did me a great favour. It taught me that you do what you have to to get a thing done. It taught me that you need to expect someone to have not done their job and prepare for that. Although I didn't know it then, that lesson would be a vital one on operations that I would later serve on in Afghanistan. It also taught me that close personal relationships are much, much stronger than rules. The resolve I felt going in gave me a sense of power. I felt a great freedom, liberated from constraints such as the need to 'play fair'.

Without doubt I also felt the danger in this. I understood now how people can get addicted to operating without restraint - Nick Leeson was in the press at the time, the man who had broken the oldest merchant bank in the world with his runaway trading. One also thinks of unrestrained commanders during war, or for example, the CIA. From little acorns, big trees can grow if we are not careful.

It's potentially a slippery slope.

Before this happened, I would have been very squeamish about taking such a radical course of action. Now I saw it as being necessary in certain circumstances.

When you decide to step outside of the rules, be it in an exam, on the trading floor or in life, you need to be sure about what the reason for it is. I was sure and learnt that to be RESOLVED meant accepting that all courses of action are open.

BEING RESOLVED

If we think of the Spartan boys that were taken at the age of seven and put into a training regime, known as the *agoge,* we can see that what it taught in essence was to be resolved. They were encouraged to steal to supplement their meagre rations during extended training exercises but were flogged if they were caught, not for the act of stealing but for not doing it without being detected.

There has always been this theme of not limiting yourself to arbitrary rules within military mythology. Perhaps we can also think of how Alexander the Great solved the Gordian knot. In this story, a people called the Phrygians had a sacred ox-cart that was tied to a post by a fabulously complicated knot in a rope. The legend was that whoever could untie the knot would rule all of Asia. When Alexander attempted this he could not find the ends of the rope to untie it so instead cut the rope in half with a single sword stroke to make two ends that could then be untied.

Military 'tricks' have often been employed to confound an enemy. You may have heard the phrase that 'necessity is the mother of invention'. Often in the military, 'desperation' is the mother of invention. When we are truly resolved the solution HAS to be found and this sometimes leads to doing something that has never been done before.

The received wisdom in Hannibal's time was that an army could not cross the Alps in order to get into the Roman Republic. Because of this, the route was not heavily guarded by the Romans. Not only did Hannibal manage to cross this way but he did it with elephants. The key difference with Hannibal was that he was resolved from the beginning and therefore able to take the extremely high cost in men and *matériel* that the mission involved. If Hannibal had extraordinary vision, then he also had extraordinary skill in execution as well. Here is what Machiavelli has to say about how he did it:

> "...although (Hannibal) led a huge army, made up of countless different races, on foreign campaigns, there was never any discussion, either among the troops themselves or against their leader, whether things were going well or badly. For this, his inhuman cruelty was wholly responsible. It was this, along with his countless other qualities, which made him feared and respected by his soldiers. If it had not been for his cruelty, his other qualities would not have been enough."[15]

Desperation means by any means necessary. It is fair to say that the whole concept of 'guerilla' tactics came out of desperation. This is case where the last thing you want to do is engage the enemy in a 'fair fight'.

There is a mindset that develops when we become aware that there is always a solution and the accepted wisdom can always be challenged.

THERE ARE NO DRAMAS, ONLY DISCUSSIONS

During my own officer training, I once had the responsibility of making sure that all necessary supplies of ammunition were loaded onto vehicles in order to be taken to a major exercise. There were strict rules laid down in the administration order over how long it was needed to order the ammunition from the store and so on. When I made the final check before loading I realised there was not enough machine gun ammunition. In fact, we were thousands of rounds down and we had only two hours before the ammunition needed to be loaded. On the face of it, nothing could be done - 24 hours at least were needed to get the ammunition ordered. It may not have been my fault but it was my responsibility.

With some trepidation I went to report to the company sergeant major, a very experienced Irishman from the Irish Guards. Knocking on his door and coming to attention, I asked for permission to enter his immaculate office which smelt, as all guardsman's offices do, of boot polish. As I entered I prepared myself mentally for a real bollocking, possibly even some immediate punishment such as being sent to the Sandhurst jail.

He could see that I was flapping as I said to him "Sir, I've got a drama". A 'drama' is British Army slang for a serious problem. He took a drag on his cigarette, leaned back in his chair and said with a measured tone "There are no dramas' sir, only discussions. Take a seat". I sat down next to his desk. He regarded me for a moment and said "Now, what is it?". I did my best to keep it concise and to the point expecting him to go into full 'screaming skull' mode. Instead he nodded and reached for his telephone. He made one call and spoke only a few words. As he put the phone down he looked at me again "Sorted. Anything else?" "No sir'. "Happy?" "Yes sir, thank you". Coming to attention again I asked for his 'leave to carry on'. He smiled at me and said "See you later".

This was an almost archetypal encounter between an inexperienced officer cadet and an experienced and worldly wise company sergeant major. I suspect that is why he had smiled at me as I left. There was an almost paternal tenderness with which he had educated me, the master of his environment passing on some wisdom.

He knew that there are always ways of overcoming the 'rules' if we talk to people. This is true in any system where people are involved. Think of the times people have got into 'invitation only' parties with a bit of resolve and discussion! This is the spirit that we need. I cannot count the amount of times his words have rung through my head in every situation where things look bad. 'There are no dramas, only discussions'.

This is true from small dramas to big dramas. Years later as the Brigade Operations Officer of Task Force Helmand in Afghanistan we had a situation where ten of our troops had been isolated on the ground and surrounded by a reported one hundred Taliban. They had been isolated due to the company of Afghan Army they were mentoring withdrawing without communicating that fact to them! This is what you might call a bit of a drama. But there are no dramas, only discussions.

That day many discussions were had in a very short space of time, between myself and the Americans who immediately offered any support we needed and between the air, aviation and artillery guys who kept fire support going to suppress the enemy. The callsign was extracted by a Viking armoured vehicle with no casualties having liaised with the battlegroup operations team who co-ordinated and planned the rescue.

If you have ever wondered why it is important to cultivate personal relationships with people then you need no further evidence than this. Because we in the operations room had made a conscious effort to reach out the hand of friendship we suddenly had allies offering to help.

Consider the Americans. They were deployed in Afghanistan on a different mission than us and had no formal command relationship with us whatsoever. They had no need to help, no formal arrangement for doing so and no moral obligation. Yet because we had a personal relationship they were willing not only to help but to risk their lives doing so.

As soon as the situation was broadcast they were on the VOIP phone to offer anything they could - including an AC130 Spectre gunship if needed! This is no small thing. Time and time again, crisis situations prove that personal relationships trump 'the rules'. We as human beings can demonstrate incredible selflessness when we have a friend in trouble and amazing indifference if we don't.

It is common in the UK to bad mouth the American forces, possibly out of a sense of rivalry. I will hear none of it. When you have callsigns in trouble and someone comes to offer a hand as soon as humanly possible when they have no official requirement or obligation to do so it is not something that you can forget.

THE THINGS YOU OWN, OWN YOU

As much as what being resolved tells you what you should care about, it should also tell you what you shouldn't care about. The warrior can have no time for attachments to material goods. If we think about it sensibly we will realise that it is ridiculous to kill yourself earning money to buy a flash car. If everybody had an amazing car they would have no appeal. The desire for conspicuous consumption of goods is something you must avoid.

People will often misquote the Bible when they say 'money is the root of all evil' but the correct quote is 'the love of money is the root of all kinds of evil'. [16]

This is an important distinction. It may be that money comes as a consequence of your successful endeavours. It may be that you get a private pleasure from beautiful things. I am not talking about the aesthetic appreciation which has always been an important part of living life. But to do things purely from the love of money and the acquisition of more 'stuff' is corrupting. Our regard for the things we own overtakes our freedom.

This is a type of self-imposed slavery. If you are caught in this trap you need to do something about it now. The best thing you can do is quit your job before your life flashes by before you. This is a necessary first step for you in becoming Battle Ready.

Meditation on death is also the way in which we can free ourselves of the attachment to material possessions. The true awareness that all turns to dust in the end should free us from the desire to acquire possessions for the sake of acquiring possessions. Instead, all possessions become a means to an end - a fast car could be a way for you and your partner to have an enjoyable drive around the roads of North Wales. An unexpected sales bonus at work means you can take an evening class in a craft you have always wanted to learn and so on. Money and goods then give opportunities, rather than being things that hang around your neck.

All these attachments, be them to money, possessions, status or even how others think of you are competing interests that will divert you from your resolve. It is said that man cannot serve two masters. In actual fact the normal state of man is to serve a whole host of masters, never being in genuine control of himself. We can be enslaved by a whole manner of things such as others expectations of us or the expectations of society.

There is a temptation to give up things in order to try and regain control. We can give up drinking and all vices, give up our possessions, detach ourselves from others, move to a log cabin and so forth. This is not true control though. In actual fact we fall into another trap - that of being attached to our un-attachment. Think for a moment about what many vegans are like - insufferable bores that only talk about what they DON'T do.

Remember that we wish to be surfers on the waves of chaos and for that we need to know what it is to get wet. To try and wish all these other elements away is futile and does not aid the development of a robust and resolved character. There is a time to be teetotal and a time to get drunk. There is a time to be celibate and a time to enjoy physical love to its fullest. There is a time to heed advice and a time to ignore it. There is a time to be exceptionally polite and a time to be exceptionally rude. The resolve of the warrior dictates his behaviour.

HUMOUR

One aspect of his behaviour which acts as a window to the warriors resolve is his humour. The very term 'laconic' comes from that particular kind of humour associated with warriors in general and originating with the Spartans. There are historical examples recorded by Herodotus and Plutarch regarding the Spartans wars against the Persians. When it was claimed that the Persian's arrows were so numerous that they will blot out the sun, the Spartans replied, 'Then we will fight in the shade'.

When the Persians demanded that the Spartans lay down their arms, the Spartan King replied 'Molon labe' - 'come and take them'.[17]

The pithy and humorous retort is also displayed by Admiral Nelson when ordered via signal flags to call off an attack at the Battle of Copenhagen. He is said to have lifted his telescope to his blind eye and said 'I really do not see the signal' and continued his attack.[18]

There is a story I heard when working with the Royal Air Force from the Battle of Britain; an RAF plane had been involved in dogfight with a German Mescherschmitt. As the RAF plane was disabled and hurtling down to crash land to the certain death of the pilot and gunner, the pilot reportedly got onto the radio and uttered his last words 'cancel two late suppers'.

To be able to face danger and extraordinary odds and yet still keep our sense of humour is only made possible by RESOLVE. When we have selected our AIM we need resolve to maintain it. All kinds of distractions and obstacles will try and throw us off the path we have selected. It takes the resolve of a warrior to stay on course and not be deflected.

RESOLVE IN COMMON LIFE

This is all very well if you actually are a soldier involved in the profession of arms and of killing and being killed. But what of our everyday lives? To be resolved from the beginning in every task is to identify and accept the worst that can happen. This does not mean that you ALLOW it to happen but that you have already come to terms with it. What do you then have to lose?

Think about what keeps you up at night worrying or making you anxious. I guarantee it's thoughts of what MIGHT happen. It's the unknown. Fear feeds on mystery. We constantly extrapolate the consequences of our actions in all possible permutations. Usually we focus on negative outcomes.

Imagine for a second that you have one day to live and therefore your actions have little consequence. How would you approach things differently? Imagine you wanted to rob a bank. How powerful would it make you to act without any fear of consequence? What if those around you knew you had only a day to live. Would anyone pick a fight with you? You have nothing at all to lose. This makes you a most dangerous opponent.

But it is in our power ALL THE TIME to decide how much we feel we have to lose. It is simply a matter of perspective. A suicide bomber chooses to decide he has nothing to lose. We all potentially have this power. I am not suggesting we make the evil choice of the terrorist. But we need to recognise that we can choose a perspective other than perpetual fear of the possible outcomes of what we do.

Here is how to do this in a simple, practical way:

1. Ask yourself 'what is the worst thing that can happen?'. Write it down.
2. Assume this WILL happen for a moment and write down the consequences. Find a way to accept and live with these conse quences. For example, you may identify that will lose your house. This means you will need to find somewhere else to live.
3. Do everything in your power now to improve the situation from that worst case scenario.

Like all of the best advice, this is intellectually simple to grasp but you MUST NOT underestimate the power of this perspective. It is something that I did daily in combat operations and is 100% effective in keeping you out there, making decisions without curling up in despair. It is not exaggerating to say that doing this can change your life.

Only the decisions you make in this instant can change your situation, you cannot make those decisions in the past or the future. This does not mean that you do not plan. Not at all. But in planning you work out what to decide now and what to do.

Crucially, you develop your contingency plans - Plan B, C, D and however many you need. An often quoted military maxim is 'No plan survives contact with the enemy'. Mike Tyson paraphrased this when he said 'Everyone has a plan until they get punched in the mouth'. We plan because we need to be able to develop our strategy, but the tactics often change.

Let us look at a military example. Remember that 'Selection and Maintenance of the Aim' is the master principle of war.

Imagine you are the commander of an infantry company deployed on operations. You receive a mission:

'To destroy the enemy on Hill 362 in order to facilitate the movement of the brigade down Route Badger.'

When you get to Hill 362, your reconnaissance elements report that the enemy is twice as strong as was thought having re-enforced. This is not good. How will you now destroy the enemy and achieve your mission? Do you need to abandon the whole thing and admit defeat? This would mean that the brigade cannot move down Route Badger and time is ticking away. But you know not only what you have been told to do but also why you have been asked to do it, so a number of options are open.

We can time our attack to merely 'tie up' the enemy force, fighting a delaying battle until the brigade has passed. We can smoke off the whole area so that the enemy is blind as the brigade goes past. We can lie in wait until the enemy moves to attack the brigade on Route Badger and ambush them. We can request our own reinforcements in order to destroy the enemy as planned.

While all this is going through your head you receive a radio communication that the brigade plan has changed and they are now going to advance along Route Weasel as airborne forces have captured a bridge on that route making its use possible. Just as your lightning quick mind is beginning to plan the withdrawal already, you receive orders to make the enemy think that the brigade is still going to use Route Badger. Suddenly the contingency plan of screening the enemy location with smoke and fighting a limited, delaying battle is looking pretty good. You get onto the radio and relay the new orders to your subordinates.

At no stage was there any need to panic. Even though the enemy was twice the size planned for, your contingency plans were put to good use. This can happen only when you really understand what is trying to be achieved. If we had only been told that we had to destroy the enemy without the reason why, we would have begun a fruitless and pointless action that would have cost lives for no tactical benefit. It is a tragedy that this has happened many times over countless operations and in many different armies.

To be able to operate in this way, without panic and switching tactics when necessary we need certain personal qualities. Developing these personal qualities is what this book is about, after all! We simultaneously need agility and robustness in the Moving, Emotional and Intellectual Centres to make this work.

The military example demonstrates an extreme case, but this process applies to so many of the big events in life, from making investments, to moving house, to planning for an elderly relatives future or the education of children. It particularly applies also to running your own business or to running any project with a defined goal.

The reality of war - the reality of LIFE is that things go wrong often. This is because we live in a world where chaos exists. Indeed chaos MUST exist in order for life to exist. We must accept chaos as a part of the universe, neither good nor bad but ever present. We can mitigate its effects by selecting an AIM and by maintaining it with discipline and contingency plans. We do not cross our fingers and hope for the best. The best is unlikely and if it does happen, then great.

More often than not though, things go wrong, either a little or more than a little. We expect this. We certainly have no expectation that everything will go as planned. The universe couldn't care less about our plans.

There is a great scene in the film *The Outlaw Josey Wales* where Josey (played by Clint Eastwood) has made it over a river with his companion to escape a group of marauders hunting them down to kill them. The river was crossed on a 'pontoon' ferry by means of system whereby a ferryman, having loaded his mounted passengers on, pulls on a rope stretched across the river to move the pontoon from one side to the other.

As Josey gets off at the far side of the river, he can see the marauders reach the near side. It is possible for Josey and his companion to ride off at high speed as the ferry still has to go back over, pick them up and take them to the far side. Working out that they would still be caught before nightfall anyway, Josey dismounts, sits down by a tree and goes to sleep for a while!

As the group draws ever closer towards them on the river,

Josey's companion nervously reminds him that they are coming. Undaunted, Josey stands up, takes a rifle out of his saddle bags, waits until the men coming to kill him are in the centre of the river - and then shoots out the rope the pontoon is being pulled along on. As the current begins to sweep the pontoon down the river, the horses panic and fall into the water.

This is the essence of the Battle Ready warrior. *The Outlaw Josey Wales* is often referred to as Clint Eastwood's finest film. He has made a career out of playing archetypes - men who reflect the essence of certain type of human character. In this film he gets the Battle Ready man spot on. When Josey Wales rides in alone to make peace with the fearsome Native American Chief Ten Bears, Ten Bears recognises that Josey is RESOLVED to die, or resolved to live if that is what transpires. Either way, he sees a fellow warrior whose values are the same as his own.

This is the WILL of the warrior. He is RESOLVED to his AIM come what may. Nothing can stop him. Our AIM is to become Battle Ready by training the WILL.

PREPARATION

If you are reading this book, then you already have the desire to develop. But to get results we must ensure certain conditions exist and some preparation is done. For example, no progress can be made if we are addicted to drugs, alcohol or any activity that we are slave to such as gambling. Neither can we make progress with eating disorders or genuine mental illness. If this is you then you need to solve this bit first.

If you have a highly disruptive home life then this also needs sorting. This is because your time and emotional energy will be depleted to the extent that you will not have enough for work on yourself. Likewise you need to be in a position where you are not working the entire time. But neither can you be in a position of dependance upon the state. You must have enough freedom of time and resources to be able to commit to progress.

PERSPECTIVE

One of the problems of ever more urbanised living is that we can lose perspective and live in a bubble of man-made landscapes. This artifice can fool us into thinking that it is 'natural' if we become too familiar and accustomed to it. Our perspective on life focuses on the artificial and a thousand stupid and meaningless concerns worry us to death. All that is needed to clear these out is to change our perspective. We need to get out into nature and find the stars. The light pollution in our cities increases the illusion that we live in a bubble. We do not, we live in a universe of unimaginable size and complexity.

Mostly, we cannot see this during the day as our blue sky provides a canopy. But at night we should be able to view on a daily basis the reality of our position in the universe. In our cities however the blue (or grey) shield of the day merely gives way to a black one at night.

By getting out and finding the stars we can quickly and easily change our perspective. I mentioned the importance of getting back to nature by killing and eating an animal. Many people in our cities feel like this - that their existence lacks 'authenticity'. We have no connection to the reality of where even the food that keeps us alive comes from.

I have a student I train that works in a software company and earns a good living. He told me that every now and then, the other people in the office will comment that they 'should be out in the forest chopping wood or something', rather than stuck in an office.

It is no surprise that spiritual sensitivity wanes as the population becomes ever more divorced from natural surroundings.

How can we spend time reflecting on the eternal and that which is beyond ourselves if everything we see is created by man? Our religions instead become urban ones - 60,000 people crammed into a temple of football every weekend, singing hymns such as 'the referee's a wanker' and worshipping their deities on the pitch.

We live artificial lives in artificial environments with arbitrary rules that we make up. When we get back into nature we become aware again that there are natural laws that govern our existence. We may also find that, on reflexion we are not much of a big deal in the grand scheme of things and that's ok - in fact it's the ONLY place to start.

Get out into nature and wake your ESSENCE up. Go walking in the mountains, find the stars and come back with a fresh and rejuvenated perspective.

CHAPTER 5
TRAINING YOUR WILL

For the great Roman emperors and for generations of conquerors and famous rulers alike, there is one shining example of the human being as leader. The man that they most esteemed and sought to emulate was Alexander the Great.

Alexander became king at the age of twenty and over the course of the next 12 years created an empire the like of which had never been seen. The consequences of his conquest were so great that even now, our Western civilisation is largely based on Greek culture, politics and thought.

It is evident that what made this all possible was the leadership of Alexander himself. Alexander's life is shrouded by myth and speculation but one thing we know for certain is that his education and training came from his personal tutor, Aristotle.

Aristotle stands as a colossus of ancient thought and knowledge, his works ranging in scope from poetry and science to politics and leadership.

The reason for this breadth of study and investigation was that Aristotle's mission was to uncover and describe 'universal laws'; those things that constitute the very principles of all phenomena to which everything conforms. In a practical sense, our actions must be founded upon these principles if we wish to achieve a specified aim - such as conquering the world.

We find in every field of specialisation an inherent weakness created by its self-imposed lack of scope. This is no more evident in modern academic pursuits, particularly in the UK and USA where the growing tendency to become more and more specialised and limited in our studies creates less and less true understanding of underlying principles.

As one of my old philosophy lecturers used to say "we end up writing our PhD on something that only has interest to the other six people in the world that share our specialisation".

Imagine the man who has given himself the task of understanding a song and in his frustration begins to look so hard at the notes that he can no longer hear the music. Aristotle understood from his own tutor, Plato that nothing existed in isolation and all must be studied.

Aristotle and Alexander would study together in a cave and take walks around the countryside, with Aristotle educating and training the young prince amongst the flora and fauna of the natural world where the patterns of nature can be freely witnessed. Only a couple of years after this, Alexander would be a general in the Macedonian army aged eighteen and be king by twenty and begin his campaign of conquest.

It is said that Alexander had absorbed his attitude of rapacious curiosity directly from Aristotle and that this perhaps was the greatest part of his desire to constantly push further and further into foreign lands. Curiosity is not only the essential component of bettering ourselves but also that which compels us to find universal laws that reveal 'truth'.

It is the finding of 'truth' and how it relates to ourselves that enables us to learn. It is this curiosity and drive to find truth that was the greatest gift that Aristotle gave to Alexander and what made him one of the finest leaders the world has ever seen. We can call this drive WILL.

It is not our intention to suggest or in any way imply that the finding of truth is easy. In fact, its very difficulty produces a great conflict in us. The energy that conflict creates is vital in order to succeed. For those who are serious, the effort and hardship involved brings extraordinary rewards.

In order to develop this personal power, it is necessary to be aware of our own weaknesses. There can be no sentimentality or concern for causing offence about this. On many occasions you may feel a shock akin to being metaphorically slapped about the face on a cold day. For those who are serious the necessity for this is obvious and we are not looking for a gentle improvement in ability, rather we strive for excellence. For those who are merely 'playing at it', it is better not to bother because it will challenge many comfortable fantasies that you currently hold.

Training the will can be likened to the forging of a sword; It is only by deliberate and skilled hammering that we produce a sharp, resilient and effective weapon. If the steel we use is too inflexible, the sword will shatter under pressure. If the steel we use is too soft, the blades sharpness will be short-lived.

In the spirit of Aristotle and Alexander your training should be designed to prepare you for your coming campaigns, so that when the moment comes, you will be Battle Ready.

THE STATE WE ARE IN

You may have spent time wondering why people in general are not more capable. You will, I hope have wondered this about yourself too: Why am I so poor at getting things done? Why do I struggle to attain mediocrity? Why am I not as good at things as I dreamed I would be when I was young?

The answer lies within the question. That is, there is a LIE within the question. The lie is in the word 'I'. We use the word 'I' to refer to ourselves as if we are a single and integrated fully functioning unit. WE ARE NOT!

The simple truth is this: if we want to thrive in chaos we cannot ourselves be chaotic - but that is EXACTLY what we are!

We are a mess of contradictory little wills all with their own selfish agenda, pushing us and pulling us about all over the place. The idea that we even have freewill and choose what to do is a sick joke. In reality we just give in to whatever little will shouts the loudest at a given time. Do we choose to cheat on our loved one? Do we choose to eat the cake even though we know we are overweight? Do we choose to lie in when we should be active? Do we choose our profession or do we do it because we fell into it or it happened to us?

More often than not, we take the easy way out and then justify it with all kinds of nonsense. Then we have the arrogance to talk about 'I' in a pompous manner as if we are in total control of ourselves. Social media has done us a favour in the way it has held up a mirror to show us our monstrous vanity and self-concern.

Plato calls this situation the 'tyranny of individual passions'. In a memorable story in 'The Republic', Cephalus tells Socrates about how the aged poet Sophocles was asked if he was still capable of making love. Sophocles replied that he was pleased to be done with it and felt that he had escaped from a frantic and savage master.[19]

FEAR & PASSION

Slavery to our passions or indeed to fears is how we live our lives. There is a passage in Frank Herbert's masterwork Dune when the Bene Gesserit Reverend Mother tests the young Paul Atredis by placing his hand into a box that stimulates the nerves and produces agonising pain. The young Paul does not know that the burning sensation is not actually destroying his hand yet he must not pull his hand out but by an act of will keep his hand in the box. The Reverend Mother explains that the test is to see whether or not he is a 'human'. In other words whether his will is able to overcome his desires. His desire in this case being to stop the pain.[20]

Our fears create NO-GO AREAS that we avoid and which limit our potential. We are slaves to our ego which feeds a FALSE SELF-IMAGE. The false self-image is so greedy that it requires constant feeding in the form of praise and self-regard. How many 'decisions' do we make in life in order to feed this, from the car that we work hard to buy to the promotions that we take, the titles that we give ourselves, the company we keep, even the house we live in.

Our NO-GO areas are especially large in our modern world due to its relative ease and comfort. This is precisely why I recommend killing and eating an animal as a necessary preparation for serious development. This is one example of how to begin the process of becoming free.

Another example comes from my school days. My boarding school in Cumbria had a very long history and plenty of old buildings. Like a lot of young people with active imaginations I realised that I had an irrational fear of the dark and in particular, gothic buildings at night. This was greatly contributed to by my love of gothic horror stories!

The job of duty student included the task of making sure all the old buildings were locked for the night. The duty student would venture out in the pitch black in winter and often into very strong winds and pouring rain - this being the west coast of Cumbria. These conditions are perfect gothic horror story fare. One of these buildings was the school chapel, complete with dark wood carvings of eagles on the lecterns and all kinds of other gothic architectural standards.

I hatched a plan to cure my fear of the dark. On the first night of my duty I would spend a full minute alone inside the chapel in the darkness before allowing myself to leave, lock the door and go back to the warmth and light of my accommodation block. The second night I would spend five minutes and the third night an absurd ten minutes alone in the dark.

On this first night I ventured out into a howling gale, made my way inside the chapel and shut the heavy wooden door behind me. In my hand I held the enormous iron key for the ancient lock - the kind of key you imagine in Tolkeins stories opening the gates of Mordor. Inside the chapel was eerily quiet after the gale outside. It was pretty dark but I could see the cross on the altar silhouetted against the window behind.

I made my way up to the altar, rain dripping down my face from my wet hair. Turning around, I faced the wooden pews, now empty of the girls and boys that sat there in the light of each morning. I looked at my watch: a full minute I had promised myself.

But I was already creeped out. I daren't close my eyes for fear of some entity silently approaching me in the dark. No way I was going to last a full minute. I was ready to break into a sprint and get the hell out of there.

In my mind were all the demons of my imagination, the ghouls, the spectres, the phantoms, the wraiths, the banshees, the zombies, Dracula, the child catcher from *Chitty Chitty Bang Bang* - anything that had ever scared me.

Now at breaking point I was about to bolt. But I was suddenly frozen by fear. Literally frozen by fear to the spot. With my eyes now accustomed to the dark I could see the definite outline of a dark figure at the back of the chapel. The figure was roughly human shaped with broad shoulders and a small head. I felt fear expand right in the pit of my stomach and pulse outwards consuming my body. My heart was banging in my chest and my eyes were taking in more of the shape as the adrenalin sharpened my senses ready to fight or run. But run where? The door was at the back of the chapel, in the direction of the figure.

Even though I was frozen, after what seemed like an hour but was more like twenty seconds I knew I couldn't just stand there. The waiting and uncertainty was worse than anything else. Very slowly I took a step toward the figure and toward the door. For the first time, the figure moved towards me. I froze again. The figure slowly raised its arm up to challenge me with some object in its hand. Horrified I looked straight at the object. It was a key. I had a key too. What could this mean? I snatched a look down towards my hand - and realised my hands had at some time come up in a defensive posture. I was mirroring the figures movements! In order not to antagonise the figure I slowly lowered my hands and watched as the figure did exactly the same.

Emboldened I took a step forward and noticed the figure was in the glass fronted trophy cabinet at the back of the chapel that I saw everyday but had completely forgotten about in my fear. The knowledge flooded into my petrified mind that I was of course looking at my own reflection! I had been frozen by fear by my own reflection. The fear I had felt gave way to relief on the one hand and shame on the other.

Chastened by my own weakness and now laughing at myself I locked the heavy door stepping back into the gale. That key and indeed, any big old key now reminds me of the ridiculousness of my own fear, a symbol of how we can defeat ourselves in our imagination.

The second night I managed five minutes without difficulty and on the third spent far more than ten minutes exploring the chapel in the dark, defeating frightened imagination with knowledge.

There is no doubt fear hates laughter and is a powerful tool in conquering it. There is a great scene in an old Woody Woodpecker cartoon from the forties called *Pantry Panic* when the ghost of starvation does a demonic, classic ghostly laugh right into Woody's face - and Woody laughs right back at him.

Cartoons often depict the hero laughing at fear, think of how Jerry laughs at Tom trying to eat him or how Bugs Bunny uses humour to defeat Elmer Fudd who is trying to shoot him dead. Perhaps this is why cartoons appeal so much to children. The hero always seems to be overcoming enormous odds to survive, defeating fear with laughter.

MECHANICAL DOLLS

The other weapon we have to conquer fear is knowledge as we saw with worry - in my case darkness was the fear of the unknown yet again, conquered through experience which brought knowledge. The unknown became known.

In my experience, all of the demons on Earth, all of the ghosts and 'supernatural' phenomena are projections by us. As much as at times I have wanted there to be special beings they have turned out to be aspects of human consciousness.

My conclusion is that 'demons' are a negative manifestation of our individual passions - malignant mechanical dolls that take over. We need not look for the supernatural or alien, that which is within us is powerful and mysterious enough.

We should not forget that the human being has evolved over millions of years and is a supremely complicated and miraculous animal. It never fails to amuse me that despite huge funds and engineers of huge ability, no-one can yet make a robot that can genuinely walk like a human. Most humanoid robots walk like they have done something unpleasant in their pants.

The idea of the individual passions or fears as being like mechanical dolls comes from the work of George Gurdjieff, perhaps heavily influenced by Plato. What makes Gurdjieff's work stand out is that it contains practical methods of development. Within Platonism, Pythagorism, Stoicism and so forth we have a great deal of theory and some practical methods, but most of the things those schools did in detail is lost to us through the years.

In the case of Plato for example, we have his dialogues but not his lecture notes. For Aristotle, we have his lecture notes but not his other works. Many of the practical methods of training these schools used may even have been secret or not written down as they were constantly in the business of doing them and hence everybody knew them.

There is also the possibility that many of these techniques were only open to 'initiates' of one or other of the many 'mystery' religions at the time. Whatever the truth, it is fortunate that we have available to us knowledge of such powerful methods of personal development. In this chapter, those methods relevant to our aim - to be Battle Ready will be discussed and covered in detail.

Within many of us exists the desire to conquer fear and take on challenge. In our modern world this often involves doing a bungee jump or running through a muddy obstacle course and then putting all the pictures on social media to gather the approval and praise of others, many of whom we don't know very well.

The obstacle course promoters and organisers understand the psychology of this brilliantly. Firstly they give the event a suitably tough sounding name that gives an air of kudos for completing it. Then they provide items of clothing that you can wear to let everybody know what you have done. The participants then feel a sense of achievement which is reinforced by others who were there and by positive comments or 'likes'. But in reality you have just done an obstacle course which most people can do. Rather than 'taking the easy way out' why not join the army where you will get to do a lot of muddy obstacle courses and get paid for it?!

These events cater to a kind of aimless desire for one-off challenge that is not sufficiently taxing or rigorous to bring us any results. The same is true often of 'white-collar' boxing events in the main.

Often out of shape guys are taken and get trained to be a bit fitter with a few sessions over eight weeks or so. In many of these programs, the aim of the training is not to teach much boxing but merely to get the guys fit enough to last three two minute rounds. When the event is over, we go back to our normal lives. No permanent change has been made. Worse than that, we give ourselves credit and dine out on the story of what we achieved despite the fact that little lasting progress has been made.

A feeling of dissatisfaction with their sedentary, risk free and aimless lives made those guys sign up. This feeling is what we want to use to fuel progress but we must have a thorough, rigorous and worthwhile method that trains and challenges the individual physically, emotionally and mentally far, far beyond what they thought possible.

In my own training of men and women who have this desire, I teach and train every aspect of fighting which when practiced, creates a lasting and profound effect on the individual. The aim of this training is to develop WILL.

You remember that we likened the individual passions in human beings to mechanical dolls? We need to create a leader for those dolls to get them all working in the same direction toward a common aim. Imagine the mechanical dolls as soldiers in an army. The soldier that likes to drink, all he wants to do is drink. The soldier that likes to chase women, all he wants to do is chase women. The soldier who wants to go home, all he wants to do is go home. These soldiers get together with other like-minded soldiers and form themselves into loose squads or 'sections'. The sections form platoons and so on. The most powerful group in any moment decides what the army will do.

If the soldiers who like to drink are the most powerful, the army goes drinking. It is a matter of chance whether or not the army actually gets to do any fighting for its commander, subject to the small unit of soldiers that actually want to fight gaining temporary control of the others. No single WILL exists - all is chaos. What this army is in dire need of is a regimental sergeant major that will whip them into shape ready for the commander's orders.

All officer cadets at the The Royal Military Academy Sandhurst have a reading list to get through most of which they don't have time to read. One of those books suggested is Sun Tzu's *Art of War*. To be honest reading this book as a young officer cadet is a waste of time. It's a book for generals and the young officer cadet is far better off concentrating on the nuts and bolts of the job, the rest can wait. That said, I managed to get through the introduction which in my copy, translated by Lionel Giles, included an extract from a biography on Sun Tzu written by a man called Ssu-ma Chien, a Chinese historian from the Han Dynasty.

Ssu-ma Chien recounts the tale of the King of Wu who read Sun-Tzu's book and called him into the palace. To test Sun-Tzu he asked him if his techniques of drilling soldiers would work with women. When Sun-Tzu replied that it would, they gathered 180 woman from the palace and put them into two companies, each with its own 'commander'. The commanders appointed were the king's favourite concubines.

Sun-Tzu explained the words of command to them which they confirmed they understood. As soon as Sun-Tzu gave them a command they all fell about laughing. He explained the orders to them again, gave another word of command and - they all fell about laughing again. Sun-Tzu ordered the concubines leading each company to be executed by beheading.

The king immediately sent a message to Sun-Tzu saying that he was quite happy that Sun-Tzu had proved his point. Sun-Tzu replied that, having been appointed general there were some orders that he must ignore and went on and had the king's favourite concubines beheaded anyway. Then he had replacements installed as commanders for each company. He then gave another word of command which they obeyed immediately. He then continued to give all kinds of orders and march them up and down, all of which were done in silence and with perfect precision. When Sun-Tzu was satisfied he sent a message to the king saying that the troops were ready for inspection. The king declined to which Sun-Tzu, questioning his resolve said "The king is only fond of words and cannot translate them into deeds'. The king appointed him as his general.[21]

This is an example of how we must treat SOME of the mechanical dolls: the ones that have physical passions. However, not all of the dolls respond to this treatment. Some must be cajoled and some must be tricked but ALL must be made to work together as one. This is what we call WILL.

THE CENTRES

The differences in the dolls are due to the fact within each person exist 3 basic 'centres'. This is explained in Gurdjieff's system as the MOVING (physical) centre, the EMOTIONAL centre and the INTELLECTUAL centre. In addition to these centres, we have an INSTINCTIVE centre that runs are most basic functions like control of our organs. The SEX centre that contains our sexual energy is closely allied to the INSTINCTIVE and MOVING centres.

Although this concept has been further developed by Gurdjieff, the idea itself is ancient. We can find the 3 part (or Tripartite) psyche in Plato. In The Republic, the centres are designated as the 'Appetites' (Moving Centre), the 'Spirit' (Emotional Centre) and 'Reason' (Intellectual Centre)[22]. Socrates asserts that the health of an individual is due to having virtue in each part and being able to harmonise the different parts of the psyche.

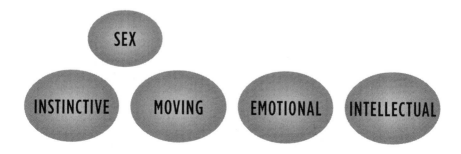

THE 5 CENTRES

I have found this to be the most useful to shape training and development. This concept of the 'centres' makes the essence of how humans are constructed understandable as a whole, rather than as poorly connected parts. For example, in typical scientific reductionist language we would talk about psychology, physiology, neurology and biology as separate elements in the human organism where in actual fact, no separation exists. The separation is a falsehood created by the desire to limit study in order to achieve detail.

This is not to say that this type of modern scientific approach is wrong, in fact many of the discoveries could not possibly have been made without it, but it limits our understanding of the how humans really operate. In particular, there is a real gap in our current scientific knowledge between what we call psychology and neurology. The question of how these are linked is a fascinating and ongoing scientific investigation. I have no doubt that over the coming decades there will be some major discoveries in this field that will create new technological and medical possibilities.

But the state of our modern appreciation of psychology is particularly poor. We still talk in clumsy terms about 'subconscious' minds and so forth, taken from the works of Freud who has been debunked by the scientific community and yet we continue to use his terminology as gospel.

This problem leads us to talking a lot of old vague nonsense. It does not help us that the 'scientific' experiments done in the name of psychology are often so badly designed. Time and time again you read a so-called 'famous' psychological experiment and find that the sample group were all university students or were such a small group that very little that is meaningful can be taken from it. The Stanford Prison Experiment is one such example that is often referred to as being significant.

The great advantage of the Gurdjieffian system is that it allows us to understand how human psychic equipment operates as a whole. Remember that this is a representation of how humans function. We do not need to get 'wrapped around the axle' debating the finer points of neurological or psychological niceties, these will obscure rather than clarify our task. Our understanding of our own processes may never be complete, but this system gives us the best 'working diagram' in order to improve ourselves.

When I train an individual to fight (a primarily Moving Centre task) I cannot ignore the Emotional and Intellectual Centres. They do not remove their minds and emotions and give me their body alone to train. I need to feed them physically to grow physically but I also need to give them sufficient emotional and intellectual training for them to gain real understanding. Real understanding or 'wisdom' is different than knowledge in that knowledge can be held in one centre only, but wisdom is knowledge across all the centres.

Think of all the people who can do something but not teach it or articulate HOW to do it. They may have knowledge in the Moving Centre but cannot articulate it as it is not also in the Intellectual Centre. This is knowledge held only in one centre. If I can explain something but not DO it, that means I have knowledge in the Intellectual Centre but not in the Moving Centre. I know plenty of people to whom this applies!

This also applies to something like bravery. Bravery is an expression of WILL. I have known many people who display physical bravery - Moving Centre bravery. These people can throw themselves out of planes and do all kinds of dare devil acts. Why then can some of them not summon up the courage to tell their girlfriends that they no longer want to see them? I have known one such individual that stayed in a relationship he was not happy with for years because he could not get the will together to end it. Yet the same individual could abseil down the highest buildings with no trouble at all. He was certainly not brave in the Emotional Centre however.

OUR SUBJECTIVE MIND - WE DO NOT SEE THINGS AS THEY ARE

On leaving the army, one of the tasks I set myself was to learn how to be a hypnotherapist. My theory was that this could be a very valuable training tool to help people learn skills better, particularly when it came to controlling the way they saw things and therefore how they reacted emotionally to things. What I was not prepared for was the revelation of just how subjectively we all see the world. It is worse in our modern culture because we see ourselves as being scientific and have the fantasy that we are cold and calculating. Nothing could be further from the truth.

Our individual perspective on everything we become aware of is almost hopelessly biased. Our behaviour and reactions are over-whelmingly controlled by a kind of machine-like mechanism which spews out our conditioned response to things. Most things we say or do come from this response without ever having gone through the Intellectual Centre for proper consideration. You know those dolls you get where you pull on a string and the doll speaks one of about six different phrases? This is us - someone pulls our string and like good little dolls we vomit our stock response. In the same way as the tape that stores the dolls responses, we have a memory bank that holds this information.

I found from doing the hypnotherapy course that sometimes we can develop a particularly strong response that we call a phobia. We can also develop a strong negative response to certain other stim-uli - particularly one of anger. We even commonly refer to this as 'pushing someone's buttons'. Some of us even take a perverse pride in having these responses, as if it proves we are fiery or 'human'. The reverse is true - it proves we are a machine that can be manipulated with a few words.

This feeling of being manipulated was what led me to sort out my own angry responses. One of the benefits of being in a group of blokes is that they will find a way of winding you up. This kind of interplay between men in particular is a very British way of social interaction. This gives you ample opportunity to find out where your 'buttons' are. We often say 'you are making me angry' or 'you are upsetting me'. But our own habitual responses are to blame for this. These are projections of our fear, feelings of inadequacy, hatred and ego. What are we worth if we cannot even control our reactions?

There is a story in one of the old 'Sinbad' myths where warrior after warrior enters the cave to claim the sacred jewel. Warrior after warrior fails as the cave has a unique defence mechanism. As the warrior enters, voices accuse the warrior of being a coward. As the warrior reacts with anger, the voice further accuses him of greed and every ignoble vice to which the warrior, driven by ego disintegrates into shame and rushes out of the cave and away from the truth.

Then the thief sneaks into the cave. The voices accuse him of cowardice to which he agrees saying that is why he is a thief and not a warrior. Then the voices accuse him of greed to which he again agrees saying that is why he is a thief. Then the voices change tack and say his mother was a whore who entertained half of Bagdad. The thief agrees but adds that she was also violent. Then the voices accuse the thief of being ugly. The thief says 'is it any surprise when I am the son of a thousand fathers?'. The voices stop as the thief reaches out and takes the jewel for his own.

The 'jewel' in this myth represents the key to mastery of the self. The thief knows that he is a shit and that's ok, so is everyone else. That knowledge is the beginning of self-mastery. The warriors cannot take that knowledge and reject it. They think that their achievements count for something.

In other mythologies a mirror stands at the gate to the cave of riches. Those proud warriors see themselves reflected in the mirror as they really are and can go no further from fright and disgust. The thief (or 'innocent' depending on the myth) already sees himself as he really is and so sees what he already sees.

One of the great problems in starting genuine self-development is that we may not survive having the scales taken from our eyes. We like to think of ourselves as 'good' 'honest' and 'noble' creatures constantly working from the best motives. But look around you. Is that what you see in other people? We can see their flaws but not our own. The answer to this is not to wallow in self-pity but to do something about it. This begins with getting in control of ourselves.

THE FORMATORY APPARATUS

In Gurdjeff's system this machine-like information store is called

The 'Formatory Apparatus'. It is essential for the smooth running of the human being that there is a way of connecting the centres together. This is the real job of the Formatory Apparatus. But because of our biased and skewed perspective, the Formatory Apparatus builds up a series of 'sub-routines' that run when a certain stimulus is received, short-cutting the involvement of the Intellectual Centre.

How many times have you been in a meeting and listened to an individuals contribution which is merely a repeat of a 'fashionable' viewpoint based on no evaluation from their intellect whatsoever. The Formatory Apparatus which holds all of our memories should be helping inform the Intellectual Centre in order to make good decisions. The propagation of 'fashionable ideas' is like never before with social media being a great forum of the Formatory Apparatus - a meeting place of human sub-routines. Barely an Intelligent or thoughtful contribution gets a look in.

We live in a time of great moral outrage, where the slightest thing that appears to go against the fashionable narrative is reacted to immediately. If you need proof about this, try and make an intelligent point about race. This is a current hot potato. Almost regardless of the point you are making, you will be on the receiving end of a collection of sub-routines directly from people's Formatory Apparatus. This is so strong that some will not even read through your comments fully before launching into it. Because it can act quickly, the Formatory Apparatus usurps the Intellectual Centre with its standard sub-routine responses. Our WILL is cut out completely.

BALANCING THE CENTRES

When we put the Formatory Apparatus back in its box and stop it controlling our reactions with its habitual responses we can start to go to work on involving the centres properly. We will look at how to do that later but first we need to understand why this is so necessary. To do that, we need to get into the mechanism of how the centres work. Stick with this and read it through a few times if necessary. Like anything new, it may seem unusual at first, but this is the missing piece in people's understanding of how to develop themselves.

The way I think of the centres is that they represent our 'Combat Power'. We all have resources. Some come with us when we are born, such as our instincts. We can call these part of our ESSENCE. Some of our resources we learn. We can call these part of our PERSON-ALITY. But with our ESSENCE comes a particular predisposition to certain things in life. A potential that represents our 'talent'. This is obviously true if we look just at the Moving Centre. Although I have a physical body and so does my mate David, my physical body is better disposed to playing rugby than it is to long distance running. My mate David however would snap in two playing rugby but is totally happy running up and down the fells in Cumbria.

This is true of 'artistic' or 'scholarly' dispositions too. All of us have them to a greater of lesser degree.

We all have aspects of each to varying degrees but most of us have a main 'centre of gravity' in one of the centres. A person who loves movement and ceremony has their gravity in the Moving Centre. A person who likes good things and is sentimental has their centre of gravity in the Emotional Centre. A person who loves intellectual argument has their gravity in the Intellectual Centre.

For example, I myself have a desire for the good things in life in some part and also enjoy intellectual debate to a degree. But when I look at the things I have done in my life - nine years as an infantry-man, then a salesman, then a teacher of self-defence and fighting, it becomes clear that my 'centre of gravity' is naturally in the Moving Centre.

There are a few - very few - who are balanced. Some are conditioned by heredity to be all rounders - but no one achieves proper balance without work on themselves. When we come to techniques, the first exercise will be to discover our own centre of gravity, to know what we are up against in the fight to gain a WILL OF OUR OWN.

The imbalance caused by our favouring one centre brings a lack of harmony. How can we make accurate decisions from a one-sided view? Bringing all our centres together means that we can finally see things as they are, in their totality rather than only in fragments, 'as if through a glass, darkly'.

The imbalances between the centres lead to many psychological problems and neurosis. Furthermore the wrong working of the centres i.e one centre doing the work that another should be doing leads to so much of the poor performance and contrary attitudes that we experience daily.

If there is a constant imbalance and argument in yourself, how will you be able to bring all of your Combat Power to bear? You cannot! You will never be able to reach your true potential. Being Battle Ready is having all of your Combat Power available and ready to deploy at a moment's notice.

ONE CENTRE DOING THE WORK OF ANOTHER

The most nerve-racking time for any colour-sergeant instructor at The Royal Military Academy Sandhurst is when the 'professionally qualified' new officers go to the range to learn how to pistol shoot. These new officers all have some professional qualification, be it legal, medical, dental or otherwise.

Rather than putting them through the rigours of the standard year-long officer's training course, they only have to complete a four week course, known informally to everyone as the 'Vicar's and Tart's Course', mainly due to the fact that the military chaplains also undergo this training (minus the pistol shooting).

The cause of the general nervousness amongst the instructors is the tendency amongst these more intellectual types to do something dangerous on the range. To be safe on the range when firing live ammunition, it is necessary to do exactly what you are instructed to do.

This is an act of imitation and is best done by the Moving Centre. The tendency with the professionally qualified officers is to think too much. Hence, when ready to fire, one of the firers would suddenly turn around to ask a pointless question - forgetting the fact that when you turn around with a short barrelled weapon in your hand, this small movement can point the weapon (loaded and ready to fire) directly at the instructor you are asking the question of. This is not ideal! The purpose of so much of military training is to drill actions so that they are carried out by the Moving Centre through imitation. This means that those actions can be carried out fast and done under extreme pressure. If the Intellectual Centre gets involved in these actions, the whole thing breaks down.

In the military context, the Intellectual Centre needs to be free of physical actions in order to make important decisions. The more tasks a military commander can perform without thinking, the more capacity they have to take in data on the situation and make appropriate and timely decisions. Good commanders can therefore stay ahead of the battle and begin to dictate the battle tempo, rather than merely reacting as best they can.

VISION

Taking again our 'master principle' of war - 'Selection and Maintenance of the AIM'. This is what we have to do to ensure that we can achieve mission success in any area of life from business, sporting or personal matters.

It is vision that allows us to select the correct aim and to continue to look for future opportunities.

Vision in this context means the ability of the individual to see what is happening in their environment and have the foresight to plan future events in order to create a successful outcome. Vision for the business leader means knowing how to develop a company based on the reality of the market. Vision for the military leader means having the battle awareness and experience to plan the mission. Vision for both means anticipating change.

One of the most impressive companies in recent years is the online retailer, Amazon. They are especially impressive in terms of vision. Let us say that we are a bookseller. What is our aim? Is it to sell books? Actually no. Our aim if we run a business is to make profit. Our current tactic to achieve our aim may be to sell books but if our vision is limited to this then we have a problem.

If the market changes we cannot be agile enough to move with it. Can you imagine Amazon having a board meeting and someone suggests selling more than just books? If they had seen their aim as selling books this could not have been suggested. Can you imagine someone objecting to that suggestion and saying 'no, we only sell books because we are booksellers!' They never would have become the huge company they became.

Not only that, but they had the vision to start hammering away at the perceived disadvantages of online buying. To make items easier to collect if you live in a flat, or easier to return if you are not happy, they put lockers in supermarkets and other places where you can do this. Again, this was a solution that needed vision.

What about the fact that if you go into a shop you can get your item immediately versus having to wait for the post from ordering online? If you have the vision you can come up with the idea of delivery to your house by drone! Clearly there are people at the top of this company who have vision.

A great military example we have already examined is Hannibal's army crossing the Alps - to even conceive of such a plan is remarkable. In a hierarchical organisation, the higher up the chain the leader is, the more vision they require, given that responsibility and the consequences of their actions increase with rank.

The unbalanced individual is limited in vision because their understanding is only in part rather than the whole. Modern life has us all furiously looking at details with every available distraction. But by being immersed in details, we cannot see the underlying patterns. If we pull back for a moment, we can see a broader view and our vision is raised. Those underlying patterns we call 'principles'.

LEVELS OF VISION

Let us start with the vision of a worm. It is only an Instinctive Centre creature. The worm has no vision, only signals arising from its simple brain.

Unlike the worm, the sheep has some vision because it has

some learned behaviour and some basic sense of fellowship with other sheep. A sheep receives signals from its brain and also from the secondary 'brain' formed by its complicated gut. The sheep has a Moving Centre and part of an Emotional Centre.

Even the lowest type of human is more sophisticated than this, having thinking power and enough integration to know of its own existence. We are all self-conscious to some degree.

The worm has no vision, the sheep has some vision and the human's vision depends on the centres and parts of centres in which he operates and at what strength.

MOVING Centre man has a vision that is primarily concerned with the gratification of the physical self. Everyone else he despises as 'ponces or geeks'.

EMOTIONAL Centre man has a vision bounded by what makes him feel good. Everyone else he despises as 'scruffs or philistines'.

INTELLECTUAL Centre man has a vision that is bounded by the rationality of his sharp intellect. Everyone else he despises as 'thugs or wasters'.

Most people are unlikely to be as stereotyped as this but every individual has a natural leaning to one of the three centres, leaving him lob-sided in his vision. An individual's vision represents their potential Combat Power, much like an army is composed of a blend of infantry, cavalry and artillery for example. The broader our vision the more potential Combat Power we have and the more flexible, adaptive and effective we can become.

By working on ourself, by training with a specific aim for example in learning to fight, we can acquire the VISION of the other centres and vastly increase our potential Combat Power and therefore our ability to EXECUTE our mission.

SKILL IN EXECUTION

If vision allows us to select the correct aim, execution allows us to carry it through to a successful conclusion. If I need the power of all the centres to have a high vision, I also need the power of all centres in execution. In fact my ability to execute the plan to achieve the aim is dependent on how much energy I have available across the centres - think of this as AMMUNITION.

In describing the qualities necessary to successfully execute our plans, two qualities can be described, those of agility and robustness. On the face of it, these qualities may seem mutually exclusive. Think of the old martial arts adage of 'be like water' made famous by Bruce Lee but covered in depth by Musashi. Water has both these qualities, it is agile enough to fill any container that it is put in but robust enough to level entire cities. There is much more to say about this and how we focus our energy.

But the first step in this is to stop losing the energy we have 'out the back' in the form of negative emotions.

NEGATIVE EMOTIONS

Negative emotions are the greatest immediate cause of energy loss in the centres. They deplete our Combat Power and deprive us of our ammunition.

The Moving, Emotional and Intellectual centres have a POSITIVE and a NEGATIVE half.

The first thing we need to do to regain control of ourselves and start acting like a free human being rather than a robotic slave is to express NO NEGATIVE EMOTIONS. In doing so, we begin to prevent the chief way in which our behaviour is trapped into negative spirals.

Each centre has a limited supply of daily energy - think of time when you have been physically, emotionally or intellectually exhausted and you will know what this means. Remember we suffer the delusion that our negative emotions are caused by outside events. In fact they are inside us.

The external influence is used to justify them and therefore no attempt is made to struggle. We hear this often when people say 'you're making me angry' or 'you've destroyed my confidence'. In reality, no one can push the emotion of anger into your body or remove genuine confidence.

The expression of negative emotion strips energy away from us that we need to use to improve and achieve. With work, you can exercise WILL to choose your emotional expression.

The more we express negative emotion however, the more it gains control and the more machine-like we become. Think of how an army's Combat Power is undermined and sapped by low morale amongst the troops. Only by resisting, only by 'not expressing ', can we build a first seal against energy loss.

Although we still have a way to go before the psychic apparatus is sufficiently explored for our purposes, we have reached the place where the creation of FREEWILL starts.

Let us take some examples - in Britain we have a great preoccupation with weather. You will know some people make a misery of their day because the weather is not to their liking. The same weather to other people working in the same place will be a matter of indifference or even of pleasure. These 'weather miseries' are indulging in the expression of negative emotions. One usually finds that they moan about their mother-in-law, the neighbours, the government and what they see as breaches of law and order as well as the weather.

Really bad cases involve energy from the sex centre and we are on the receiving end of a gale of complaint. Unfortunately there is something racy and rather stimulating about the energetic expression of negative emotions (we are, after all, pulling on the sex centre). We feel purged, released, excited. It so easily becomes a habit - part of our style. Go into any office building and you can find individuals who constantly express negative emotion and suck everyones energy up like a morale Hoover.

NEGATIVE EMOTIONS EN MASSE

Being deployed on the ground in Northern Ireland during parades was a great way to see the expression of negative emotions writ large. During these parades, the two opposing factions of Protestants and

Catholics face off, with the army and police in the middle. The normal pattern is for them to scream abuse at each other and then throw rocks, petrol bombs and in some cases, acid at the army and police.

The 'buzz' that develops in a crowd feeds off negative and often sexual energy. This buzz spreads and can become uncontrollable

On one memorable occasion, as the excitement was building before violence broke out, a lone woman rushed out from the body of the crowd and ran towards a soldier on our baseline. Judging the situation perfectly being an experienced soldier, he remained alert but made no move that could set the crowd off.

The lone woman, in her excitement tried everything to plant a kiss on the soldier's face, despite the fact that he was wearing a helmet and visor. The woman's husband rushed forward to drag her away, even managing a mumbled apology to the soldier in question.

Negative emotions in crowds typically lead to the kind of pointless and wanton destruction we see on our television screens during riots; on the face of it caused by an 'issue', but in reality an excuse to vent negative emotions *en masse*.

NEGATIVE EMOTIONS IN BUSINESS

In the business environment, certain chief executives express a most destructive form of negative emotion by seeming only to notice and comment upon what they consider to be lapses of performance. "You didn't do so and so ..." is typical. This is an easy trap to fall into because one of the manager's main tasks is to maintain performance levels. But a sub-standard action should not only be examined in relation to the difference between it and the target. It should be examined in relation to the total work load and an assessment made of that which was achieved.

No expert would ever make this error of isolating the segment of performance which was not achieved. If you were to point this out to the chief executive concerned you will discover a 'can of worms'. For this negative complaint is but a cover for a lazy way of managing that gives only the appearance of control but in fact avoids the hard work of managing properly and having the vision to appraise the total performance against the aim.

Take away the option of expressing the negative and we will not fall into this trap. I am sure that you can immediately think of people whom you know who when you ask them how they are go into a diatribe of negativity. There are some in particular who just love to moan, about health, about football, about their work, the boss, their wife or husband, how expensive everything is, the government, anything at all!

NO OPINIONS

The second thing we can do is to express NO OPINIONS. This may seem like you will condemn yourself to becoming a boring party guest and in the short-term, it probably will. But we must break the habit of merely switching on our sub-routines. Rather than express-ing opinions, we make decisions. In order to weigh up options, we present facts or information and acknowledge the source.

We can recount past events without making a conclusion which represents a biased and subjective opinion. By doing this, we will soon identify what we hold as fact is more often than not just our Formatory Apparatus sub-routines.

ACTING

In my experience, it really bothers people to let go of expressing opinions. The alternative way is to consciously present a viewpoint as being 'one way of looking at things'. There is no need to reveal your own personal opinion as it stands. This is a job of acting at the beginning but something you can soon get used to. Our society puts importance on the fact that everyone can express an opinion. But just because we have that freedom it does not mean our opinions are therefore worth a damn.

A good example of this is that people I have just met often feel a need to express an opinion about conflicts that I have been involved in as a soldier. Typically they state their opinion as a fact, taking the moral high ground one way or another but with no direct experience or any understanding of the complexities of the situation they are so certain about. How often have we ourselves offered such an opinion based on a similar lack of genuine knowledge?

THE GROWTH OF THE CENTRES

We come into the world with a complex of faculties that make up the ESSENCE, including the default balance of our centres. Our PERSONALITY is formed as we experience life.

The way in which the two interrelate is seen in a growing child. The child is born already with an Instinctive Centre.

During the first seven years of life each of the remaining three centres grow. The growth of the Moving Centre dominates the first two years. As this is only an addition to the Instinctive Centre almost no personality is created. The innocence and truthfulness of the Essence remains.

The years from two to five are dominated by the growth of the Emotional Centre, fuelled by a knowledge of language. Now the Essence begins to be covered by the fragments of experience we call 'Personality'.

The years from five to seven see the awakening of the Intellectual

Centre and many more adjustments to life - and therefore the creation of many more fragments of Personality. During this time, the Sex Centre exists but its reflection is in the essence. Attitudes to sex begin to be formed in Personality but they wait until the end of the second seven year period (fourteen) to be developed.

Three periods of seven year growth are determined by the interaction of the two systems. We will be examining the formation of WILL - but we need to note, under this examination of the inter-action of the two rivers of behaviour, that Essence is essentially truth whereas Personality is essentially false.

The river of Essence comes from outside our life. Can you see that a thing coming from outside our lives must be true? It has not yet had the opportunity to misunderstand, or create fantasy, or behave selfishly or be half asleep when the experience happened!

Personality, on the other hand can only be made up of experi-ence which starts after the age of two, when we can pour something into the empty vessels of the three centres.

Falseness of Personality comes from the lack of our ability to register events truthfully.

ESSENCE is PASSIVE. PERSONALITY is ACTIVE

ESSENCE is SINGLE. PERSONALITY is MULTIPLE.

Problems arise when Personality grows too strong for Essence. Ordinary people are ruled by the reactions of Personality. In some people Essence can actually be stifled to death.

Do you remember what we said about getting into nature? Well our man-made cities are false like Personality, whereas the natu-ral world is true like Essence. It is not practical for us all to give everything up and go and live in a forest. Neither is it necessarily desirable either because we need Personality to grow Essence.

But we do need to go and wake our Essence up first by chang-ing our tiny perspective and meditating on the true size and scope of our environment. Growing Essence is easier nearer to nature due to the truth of the natural world. It is also easier in situations of danger and risk, as the battle between 'yes and no' is more profound and frequent.

So when we consider the formation of WILL we remember that our aim is to grow from the truth of the Essence. But the corollary is that to have a strong will to accomplish this task, we need a strong 'character', which is largely a creature of Personality.

To make progress towards our avowed aim of achieving FREE-WILL we need to engage in a battle which allows a subtle weakening of the false personality, to allow good things to grow the truthful essence.

TO SUMMARISE: Our basic psychic equipment consists of five centres, badly connected.

1. Our behaviour is in two 'rivers'; truthful essence and false personality.
2. The three personality centres of moving, emotional and intellectual have two halves - positive and negative.
3. We can start our growth now by ceasing to express negative emotions and all opinions.

THE WORKING OF THE CENTRES

Here we come onto how we can train to begin to harmonise the centres and increase our Combat Power. In working through this, you will be developing your understanding of how to learn anything.

THE SEX CENTRE AND THE INSTINCTIVE CENTRE

The Instinctive Centre is our 'animal' centre, the interrelated control of every organ and system in the body. This facility is part of our Essence. All these controls take place without our having learned them. The Sex Centre is closely allied to the Instinctive Centre, but in a more sophisticated (learned) way. It is also tied to the Moving Centre.

The three centres of Moving, Instinctive and Sexual form a group which is the 'animal' in us. We can function as animals without feelings or intellect and you may have noticed that some individuals do little more than that.

THREE PART CENTRES

As a final part of our explanation of the centres, we can now locate specific actions. Before doing this is a further sophistication has to be added. The diagram below illustrates a further division of the Instinctive, Moving, Emotional and Intellectual Centres. They are in turn themselves split into Moving, Emotional, and Intellectual parts. The Instinctive centre does not have a positive and negative, but the other three centres are split into three, in both positive and negative halves.

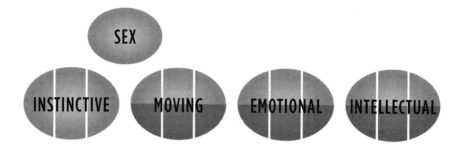

Here is a guide to what feelings and actions take place and where.

INSTINCTIVE CENTRE		
MOVING Habitual sensations	EMOTIONAL Animal love and hate	INTELLECTUAL Intuitions
MOVING CENTRE		
MOVING Reflexes, imitation	EMOTIONAL Acting, love of activity	INTELLECTUAL Inventiveness
EMOTIONAL CENTRE		
MOVING Like and dislike	EMOTIONAL Aesthetic and Religious	INTELLECTUAL Higher creation
INTELLECTUAL CENTRE		
MOVING Knowledge gathering	EMOTIONAL Desire for knowledge	INTELLECTUAL Creative thinking (or fantasy)

The wrong working of the centres continues within the three parts. In a person heavily biased towards the Moving Centre the bias will extend to the moving part of each of the other centres. From the table we would read as follows:

HABITUAL SENSATIONS	REFLEXES AND IMITATION	LIKE AND DISLIKE	KNOWLEDGE GATHERING

The moving part of each centre is the most primitive as we can see from the result above. A high percentage of people do not escape from this level.

The less primitive person works in the emotional parts in addition to the moving parts. From the guide on the table we add the following less basic feelings and actions:

ANIMAL LOVE AND HATE	ACTING & LOVE OF ACTIVITY	AESTHETIC AND RELIGIOUS	DESIRE FOR KNOWLEDGE

An extremely rare individual, operates in all parts of all four centres. From the table we add the following to the primitive actions and feelings of the other two parts:

INTUITIONS	INVENTIVENESS	HIGHER CREATION	CREATIVE THINKING

This individual's Combat Power is now maximised. He has all of his possible resources 'on-line' and available to use. His vision is in all parts of his centres. This discovery is vital and is light years beyond the typical understanding of our own psychic processes. Its significance is that practical techniques can now be followed to make us 'Battle Ready'.

WORK

How do we in practice do this? How do we grow our Combat Power and become Battle Ready? By doing WORK. It should not surprise you that there are no short cuts. But that does not mean that we cannot work smartly. For most people, that work should begin with the Moving Centre and develop outwards. When we look at systems of personal development throughout history and around the world we find this same solution. This might be in the Yoga of the Indian Yogi, or the T'ai Chi of the Chinese Taoist or the dancing of the Sufi Dervish - or the drill movements of all the best armies of the world throughout the ages.

In our modern world, it is precisely this aspect which is likely to be under-developed as we have seen through Chapter 1. The good news is that the physical body provides us with an instrument for growth where results can be easily measured and our progress clear.

You will remember that WILL is developed through the battle between 'yes and 'no'. That battle is simple and straightforwardly arranged when we take a Moving Centre skill as our vehicle.

Done correctly, learning this Moving Centre skill will increase power in the Moving Centre and activate the Moving parts of the Emotional and Intellectual Centres. This means, looking again at the table, that we gain control over 'like and dislike' and begin to use and exercise our powers of 'invention'.

I am not saying that by doing this, we achieve all we ever need to in life. If we look at the table we can see the areas in the Emotional and Intellectual Centres that we are not directly effecting by this method. However we are creating the necessary first bridge across all the centres in order to build a firm foundation for building a harmonious individual in control of their own life. The Warrior has this foundation in place. What the Warrior does from there is beyond the scope of this book - but the vast and increasing majority of people never get to the Warrior stage.

You should be at the point now where you understand why we need to learn to a physical skill to a good level and why the skill of fighting is ideal for this job. Joseph Campbell said that in life we should 'follow our bliss' as the best way to develop. Our sense of 'bliss' or enjoyment is a place of truth and most of us have experienced the sense of enjoyment of bliss from physical movement.

The words of Joseph Campbell were often misunderstood and

years later he said that he wished he had said we need to 'follow our blisters'. In other words, some people took his words as meaning you need to turn on and tune out rather than work hard at what you enjoy and take it to a high level, which is only possible through hard graft.

By talking about taking a physical skill to a high level we need to know what we mean by this and set our expectations to a sufficiently elevated level.

Put simply, our physical body is the most direct way we have to experience life and from that direct experience we can develop a sense of what is true and what is false. Only from this can we build our foundation on solid ground.

In English mythology, we have a great example of this in the story of Robin Hood. What does it mean when Robin Hood splits the arrow? He shows his mastery of the art of archery - his level of being has risen to the stage where he has learned objective truth. He can bring his divided wills under control towards a specified aim, metaphorically represented by literally aiming at a target! There is no bluffing or fantasy here, he either hits the bullseye or he does not. Such a measurable task shows us the level that we really have regardless of the lies we tell ourselves from our false ego.

TRAINING THE MOVING CENTRE

You remember the story of how my father got a knife through his hand? Well one of the characters who worked at the bacon smoking factory was a certain Benny Horovitz. He didn't just work at the factory though, he also sold newspapers. Benny would get up at some ungodly hour in all weathers, pick up the papers, sell them in the street then start work at the bacon smoking factory at seven. After a full day's work he would then pick up the evening papers and sell them on the street too. He did this six days a week.

Benny had had the kind of life that could only have come from that period of the twentieth century. He had grown up in the Warsaw Ghetto, an area established by the Nazis to contain mainly Polish Jews like Benny. In conditions that can only truthfully be described as unimaginable, Benny and his family had to survive.

Estimates of the death toll in the Warsaw Ghetto in the two and a half years of its administration are around the four hundred thousand mark. Many of these were from simple starvation. Benny was further challenged by the fact that, possibly as a result of this upbringing, he was a dwarf with a hunchback. This had not stopped him.

My father tells a story about him that is, in turns, both heart-breaking and inspiring. Rats were a constant scourge in the factory, brought by the plentiful supply of fat from the meat. Open warfare had been declared between rat and man, without hope of any final victory for man. Rather, the menace had to be contained somehow. When a rat broke cover and dashed across the warehouse floor, a great cry of 'BENNY!' would go up from the men.

Now alerted, Benny would grab a meat hook and get the rodent in his sights. With astonishing speed, he would hurl the meat hook towards the rat, skidding it across the stone floor until the animal was skewered like a kebab. My father said in all the years he had witnessed this, he never once saw Benny miss. The reason Benny had acquired this almost superhuman skill was down to the fact that, from childhood, he had had to kill rats in order to eat.

Can you imagine that? This was no child learning a sports skill to chase the dream of becoming a professional sportsman, but a child needing to learn a skill to avoid dying of starvation. A child learning to play tennis can have an off day, or a day where they don't 'feel like it' or a day when they throw a tantrum and refuse to prac-tice. Not for Benny. If he didn't hunt rats, he didn't eat. If he didn't eat, he would get weaker and die as so many of his countrymen did in their hundreds of thousands.

There is a profound lesson to be learnt about Moving Centre skills from this. Benny had to eat every day. So every day he prac-ticed his skill of hunting rats. Every day, little by little his skill built up. He could not do it for five minutes then complain that he wasn't naturally 'good at it' or he wasn't physically 'suited' to it. He was a hunchback dwarf. He had none of the physical advantages that you or I take for granted. But his motivation couldn't be stronger. He didn't have the option of coming up with an excuse for why he couldn't do it so he got on and did it anyway.

So many people come into my gym to learn and then after 10 minutes claim that they 'aren't any good at this'. This is because in our soft modern lives we forget that we can't just pick up a Moving Centre skill in the same way that we can quickly understand an intellectual concept. Remember the story of the professionally qualified officers pistol shooting? We often try and use the Intellectual Centre to learn the Moving Centre skill. This is never going to work. We cannot use our brain power to learn something physical. Our bodies must learn it for themselves.

Think of learning to drive. In order to drive a manual car, we need to perform many physical skills at once - under pressure. When we are at the early stages and have to think about what we are doing, it often goes wrong. Only when we cease having to involve our Intellectual Centre can we actually drive properly. Even when we can drive, if we come under intense pressure we can suddenly forget if we start to think about it too much. Imagine the task of being a 'getaway driver'. If that getaway driver starts to panic he can lose the relaxation needed to let his Moving Centre do the task of driving. He tries instead to do it with his Emotional Centre. This is why we sometimes stall the car under pressure. We can mitigate this by practising under rising levels of pressure - this is possible for the racing car driver but not so much for the getaway driver!

If we understand that learning a Moving Centre skill means repetition and letting the body learn by itself we can start to make good progress because after all, we have evolved to be able to learn skills as human beings.

One of the frustrations of teaching students in self-defence is when they constantly stop repeating an action because it is not perfect. This is not the way the body learns. Rather, it learns by trial and error and gets more and more refined in its actions the more an action is performed. To stop to think about it is totally counter-productive.

One way of appreciating this is to think of how an artist sketches the figure of a man. The artist does not sketch one part of the figure perfectly and then moves on to the next part. The artist makes a general rough outline and then goes over those lines again and again, making them more accurate each time until a firm and accurate outline is created. Then he goes over the lines again but only this time in more detail and with more technique. But he would never try and get the detail right from the outset. This would make his sketch lifeless and disjointed.

If we apply this approach to learning to drive we can see that the best and fastest way would be to have a student just practice gear change after gear change - without pressure before going out on the roads. It should be no surprise at all that learning to drive Formula 1 cars involves a similar process. Can you imagine if every school taught learning to drive in a simulator as part of the syllabus? There is no reason technologically that an actual car could not be used for this process with simulated scenarios and scenery.

The key element is that the student gets repetition after repetition of the basic coordination of hands and feet that is the core skill of driving. When they go out on the roads and then need to use judgement, in quiet areas at first under low pressure, the basic motor skills are already there. How many repetitions could we fit into a 2 hour period on a simulator? Hundreds.

We need to understand that learning all Moving Centre skills is essentially the same. The difference between the highly skilled and the unskilled is overwhelmingly a matter of application.

In teaching people the skill of fighting in self-defence or for sport, one of the key obstacles to overcome is the perception in many peoples head that they will be either good at it or bad at it - all down to the luck of genetics and/or God given talent. Think of Benny Horovitz. He had no physical advantages of any kind yet was able to take a physical skill to an almost supernatural level. And what we need to learn to fight is not even as difficult as that!

It IS true that some individuals will pick up a skill to a good level faster than others, either because they have previously done something similar or because they have a natural very strong centre of gravity in the Moving Centre. But this need not overly worry us. We can ALL get to a level of skill beyond our highest expectations by WORK.

Speed of learning by imitation (in the Moving part of the Moving Centre) is very strong in children who have not yet developed the Intellectual Centre enough for it to get in the way. I am sure you will have observed many times how amazing and sometimes uncanny a child's ability to imitate is. There is no doubt that this is a perfect time to learn a Moving Centre skill.

When we take away the molly-coddling culture that we have developed, we see what even very young children are actually capable of. There was a documentary filmed where the footballer, David Beckham went into the Amazon to meet the Yanomami tribe. Something particularly remarkable was children as young as 3 years old using knives with incredible skill and speed to prepare food. Clearly, being a Western father he was worried about their safety and asked what happens if they cut themselves. The reply was 'they learn'.

I am not suggesting that we adopt this model - but it shows what human beings are really capable of even at such a young age if we change our expectation and remove restrictions. You can see footage of a tiny Novak Djokovic smashing balls around a court for example. For sure, if we start that young we can become the best in the world at a certain skill, such as playing tennis. But our aim is to get control of ourselves by learning a skill that demands our centres work together, we need not try and be the best in the world!

DRILLING

What learning these skills have in common is DRILLING. The repetition of an action over and over again to cement it into the Moving Centre. ALL skills are best developed this way. The artist needs to sketch over and over. The sniper needs to spend time on the range. When we look at all individuals of great skill we find that they have drilled their skill. This holds true even for a creative genius like William Shakespeare.

Shakespeare as a poet and playwright was supremely skilled in the use of verse and meter. He had gone to a Grammar school, which had been newly created at the time. What the boys did at that school was drill Latin grammar, spoken aloud and in rhythm over and over.

One of our famous local comedians is Ken Dodd. His astonishing machine gun joke delivery was drilled over and over before his performances and before he became famous he drilled it under the pressure of a live audience on brutal touring schedules as part of variety shows. Not only did he have to make the audience laugh, but he had to finish his set exactly on time, to the second, or face the wrath of the producer who controlled whether or not he got paid. Also on these shows were jugglers from Italy and Ken Dodd watched them literally practice all day every day before the shows without fail.

Think of Benny Horovitz again. His skill may seem supernatural, almost impossible, but it is no more remarkable than many of the skills we see in the modern circus, such as the Cirque du Soleil.

On the internet, we can find video of 'the fastest workers in the world'. One that stands out is of Chinese piece-workers packing playing cards into boxes. The speed at which they move has to be seen to be believed. Their motivation for this speed is simple as they get paid by how many they do. Their skill is so deeply embedded into the Moving Centre that it looks instinctive rather than learned. But - it IS learnt. They can even look around and talk while there are doing it, no thought whatsoever is required to perform the action.

The workers are often from China or India where they get paid very little and so have to develop this skill to a high level. Our Western workers by comparison are painfully slow and lazy - because they can be but this makes them soft. Speed is the real hallmark of the action fully learnt and operating from the Moving Centre.

We may ask ourselves 'why don't we learn a skill like this then?'. But remember our task is to begin the work of harmonising the centres. We need a skill that involves parts of the Emotional and Intellectual Centres as well - and then allows us to go beyond.

We also need a skill that is directly relevant to thriving in chaos and coping with crisis. But these serve as examples of what our expectations should be - much, much higher than we think. Often people learning in my gym will say 'it's not fair, you make it look so easy!'. But here's the truth - it IS fair! Fair is exactly what it is. I make it look easy because I have done it so many times. If they also do it as many times as I they will make it look easy too. The human being will sometimes do anything to admit that the answer is to do WORK. Not talent, not genetic predisposition but WORK. Everyone can acquire a tremendous level of skill this way.

We must not fool ourselves though. On one occasion an individual told me they had been training for one year. When I watched them I wondered what they have been doing all that time as they demonstrated little skill. Then we get down to how much training they have actually done - 1 hour a week. For a whole year? He was on holiday for 2 of those weeks and sick for another 2 weeks. Then the kids were off school so chalk off 4 more weeks, all in all 1 hour for 44 weeks or 44 hours. Then we take into account a warm up of 10 minutes each time and we are talking about a lot less than 40 hours actual training.

You can train for much more time than that in one week. In fact, I had just come back from training in Spain at the time and we had trained for seven hours every day for seven days. A total of forty nine hours training and we had only warmed up twice a day, once in the morning and once after lunch. In real terms, he had been training for around a week!

If we think about classic military training we can see this work in progress. Take the Commissioning Course at The Royal Military Academy Sandhurst as an example. This is the course that all army officers attend. It is forty-four weeks in duration which doesn't seem a long time at all. The initial phase of training before you have a couple of days off is only five weeks. Five weeks! But after that time many officer cadets return to their families unrecognisable.

There is no trickery in this, it just shows what is possible with good training. The training syllabus for this period is seven days a week with Sundays consisting of attending chapel and orienteering competitions. That is the 'day off'! The rest of the time is solid training on basic soldiering skills.

The entire twelve week course of basic soldier training for army recruits is completed in five weeks for the officers, based on the fact that they have been selected for their ability to be trained amongst other things.

Generally the day starts at 5am or earlier to enable the cadet to get their room ready for inspection. Typically that cadet may have been awake until the small hours preparing kit for inspection for the next day. The rest of the day is drill (marching up and down to commands), endurance and fitness training, weapons training, signals training, field skills training, platoon drills and tactics training and so on. What I remember more than anything in this initial training period is drill, ironing and polishing. There is a whole lot of that.

In order to be allowed to have a couple of days off at home after that period, each training platoon must 'pass off the square'. This means completing a series of drill movements as a squad and also individually in order to meet an expected standard of reaction to commands and in terms of your turnout and standards of dress. This is not just a test of the individual or of the platoon, but of the instructor as well.

The British Army is unusual in that its officer cadets spend most of their training being taught by senior non-commissioned officers - typically recruited from the infantry but also other arms too. These instructors are of staff sergeant rank (known as colour sergeant in the infantry).

They are drawn from the top 5% of those of that rank in the army. These are the men and women who will go on to be the regimental sergeant majors of their units and from then on to commissioned rank and vital jobs such as the quartermaster of their battalion.

One of the great strengths of the British Army culture is its huge emphasis on the quality and responsibilities of the instructor. If a soldier does not know something or cannot perform a drill correctly, the responsibility lies ultimately with the instructor who trained him. Likewise the instructor will be given great credit if his charges do well. This means that as the member of the training platoon, you will get to the required standard whether you like it or not!

In reality though, every member of the British Army is a volunteer and, in particular, every officer cadet is rightly expected to be self-motivated and have a drive to exceed the standards required.

The colour sergeant instructors are on hand almost all the time during that initial phase. I remember clearly on day 2 of my training at Sandhurst being so frustrated with trying to iron a collar flat in just the way we had been shown that I almost launched my iron through the window. That would have needed some explaining. Fortunately I checked my anger before I did something I would later regret and marched off to see the colour sergeant for help.

This was at 11 o'clock at night. Explaining my problem to the colour sergeant, he leapt up from his chair and marched me to my room. With seemingly infinite patience he took my through the process on my own ironing board and with my own shirt and did one side for me. Checking that I had taken this all in, he then watched me do the other side correctly before going back to his office. The next time I saw him it was 6 o'clock the next morning when he, immaculately dressed, was inspecting our rooms.

One effect of going through this training yourself is that you know what's possible in only a short space of time. Most people would not believe the standard you can get to as they only think in terms of 9 - 5 with breaks for lunch and so forth. The potential of every human being is vastly beyond what they typically think.

TRAINING THE EMOTIONAL CENTRE

After 'passing off the square' I went to see a girlfriend that I had only recently started seeing. I was well over a stone lighter, I walked differently and talked differently and had the constant rhythm of the training in my head. I had been a civilian only five short weeks ago.

Suddenly I was a soldier. If you work it out, I had done over five hundred hours of training. My girlfriend was a little bit of a hippy. A lovely girl but she had been very concerned about my training to be an army officer anyway. When I came back suddenly indoctrinated in mind and body it was too much for her.

From being soft and woolly in body and mind, my movements were sharp and crisp and my reactions and decisions immediate.

In every training platoon at Sandhurst there is a ritual observed when the first 'Dear John' letter comes in. Over the hundreds of years that soldiers have been trained in the British Army, they have been receiving letters from girlfriends saying they no longer wanted to see them. Becoming a soldier means stepping out of normal civilian life in a not too dissimilar way that becoming a monk does (both love beer). It is true that the soldier does not live a holy, celibate life, but he does join an old established institution with its own rules, rituals and language.

Those that have understood the workings of the centres will observe that the way of the soldier is in the Moving Centre with its physical orientation, whereas the way of the monk is in the Emotional Centre with its religious orientation.

As fate would have it, I received the first 'Dear John' letter in my platoon. Nowadays it's probably just a text message. The ritual to be observed was that I was awarded a bottle of champagne and my letter was to be read out to the platoon as we were waiting to go out on parade.

The person nominated to read out the letter was a good friend who went on to join the Household Calvary. He was a perfect choice as he had a beautiful 'cut glass' Queen's English received pronunciation voice, dripping with the air of gentlemanliness and history.

He stood before us, all six foot four of him with his lantern jaw and matinee idol looks. He did me proud, putting plenty of pathos into every sentence. There were groans when he read out 'it's not you it's me' and jeers when he read out 'I hope we can still be friends'.

He even managed to put a little hint of timbre in his voice as if he were crying while imagining writing it out to me. By good luck, my ex-girlfriend had written a pretty standard corny break up letter that when read out was in turns funny, tragic and hammy all at once.

It may seem like a fairly brutal thing to do, to read out someone's very personal correspondence. But the effect it had, not just on me but on the whole platoon was important.

Everybody was going through the emotions of leaving family and loved ones behind as they followed this path. We were also taking on a new identity, leaving the old versions of us behind. Reading out the letter in this way was a kind of catharsis for all of us.

We British people don't like to spell out in words our love and support for each other, we prefer to do it with gestures and rituals. The gesture of the bottle of champagne and the ritual of reading out the letter felt like we were all in this as one. There was an obvious contrast in the banal and insincere words of comfort being read out from my letter and the sincere gesture of support that my comrades were showing me.

Generations of soldiers had had this bond tested to the limit. We didn't know it then, but we were to have that experience as well. Black humour is a powerful weapon against difficulties and after sharing a good laugh we got smartly on parade and the matter was dealt with.

ESPRIT DE CORPS

One of the most under-appreciated elements of military training is the emotional aspect. Think of an army barracks for example, and let us chose an infantry battalion of the British Army. It is designed and presented in a way that reflects the ethos of the unit. There are signs and symbols up that attest to the history and achievements of that unit. Often the kerb stones are painted in the colours of the regiment.

Then you walk into the officer's mess. The place is like a museum with old paintings up of campaigns of the distant and not so distant past. Regimental silver is on display, often looted from one country or another. In pride of place as you enter the building and staring you right in the face are the Regimental Colours. Colours are called the 'heart of the regiment' and each battalion of that regiment has its own.

'Colours' are flags - 'standards' if you will that were used historically to identify this or that unit on the battlefield. Originally, these would have been the coat of arms of the aristocratic officer commanding that unit - a practice that goes all the way back to the days of medieval knights. Colours came about as many of the captains in the infantry were 'low-born' meaning they had no coat of arms. Colours were used instead to signify their units.[23] As the infantry continued to grow and noble or ennobled commanders became in shorter and shorter supply, colours became the norm.

You can see old colours 'laid up' in the military chapels of cathedrals across the UK. Often they have holes in them from where musket balls have gone through the silk during battles. Emblazoned on the colours are the names of the battle honours that the regiment has won over the centuries. On the colours of my own regiment "Namur 1685' was the first.

The effect of the symbols and representations of history is what? It's an emotional effect. There is a constant reminder of the traditions of bravery, pride and excellence of that regiment designed to fuel the ethos and espirit de corp of the current body of men that make up its number.

It is possible to define exactly why this is needed if we once again reflect on the centres. Within the Moving part of the Emotional Centre is this basic emotional feelings of 'like and dislike'. Without ethos, without espirit de corp, without pride, to fight in a battle and risk your life is one big fat DISLIKE to the individual.

So much of the military apparatus that we see is to turn this big fat dislike into either indifference, or even better than that an actual LIKE of the benefit to the whole. The process of doing this, we call DISCIPLINE. We should not think of this as some sort of 'con' or swindle - LIKE and DISLIKE can be equally arbitrary.

But we must move the individual from a focus on the 'dislike' of the hardships of war to himself to the 'like' to the benefits of his service to the unit, the army and perhaps even to his country. Otherwise he is simply going to run away. We can also negatively motivate the individual too, by turning the idea of running away into an emotional 'dislike' by making it a taboo and a disgrace.

In reality, more often than not in my experience, the concept of 'Queen and Country' is too abstract for the individual when on operations but the feelings of responsibility to his immediate comrades is very, very strong.

This phenomenon of discipline is the battle between 'yes and 'no' or 'like and 'dislike' that we have mentioned earlier and it is the key to unlocking FREEWILL. This is NOT the will of our own but it is the necessary first step. Put in the most simple terms, to begin with, we must learn to obey before we can expect to lead ourselves or for that matter, others.

THE COLLECTIVE

There is a great fashionable zeitgeist to focus on the individual and paint the collective as sinister and evil. Learning to obey has become something to be railed against as 'conformity' or 'oppression'. The irony is that those individuals who are so vehemently attacking this are not even in control of themselves! It is a trick to think that you 'go your own way' and 'dance to your own tune'. The most popular song played at funerals is 'My Way' by Frank Sinatra. How pathetic. The people who claim self-mastery and who sneer at those who choose to learn to obey are simply lazy and cowardly.

This claim of individualism is really self-glorification, vanity and a way of just giving in to whatever the loudest mechanical dolls say to do. Then we praise ourselves for our 'rebelliousness' and in our heads we are a folk hero on a par with our fantasies about Che Guevara.

No one can achieve mastery of themselves without learning discipline first. This discipline if correctly applied can become self-discipline with WORK. We simply do not have it without. And that struggle is constant.

Think of the classic image of the drill sergeant shouting at the troops. What is the purpose of this? During our room inspections in training, if an item of clothing or piece of equipment wasn't up to the required standard it was often launched out of the window into the rain.

For the first five weeks of training we were marched everywhere at some ridiculous pace - for what? The reason for this is one
of ATTITUDE. The attitude we must acquire as a soldier is one of
emotional robustness and of a sense of urgency. This is a preparation for combat operations. If we can develop an attitude of being
able to ride out emotional, physical and intellectual challenges, we
will make ourselves useful in difficult circumstances.

Although the experience of being 'bawled out' by a figure in
authority may seem horrifying, it's just someone making noise.
Although the experience of watching your carefully pressed and
prepared shirts flying out of the window and into a muddy puddle
seems distressing, it just means you need to wash and iron them
again. And that's it.

The tactics and techniques of this training are designed to take
you beyond the immediate slavery of your likes and dislikes and into
a kind of indifference. It's true also of the hardships that soldiers face
in the field. Most civilians would be rendered useless through being
consumed with the emotion of dislike or disgust at having to live in
a wet hole in the ground. This state of indifference was highly sought
after by the Stoics and is recalled time and time again in Marcus
Aurelius' Meditations:

> *"Pain is neither intolerable nor continuing,*
> *provided you remember its limits and*
> *do not let your imagination add to it."*[24]

Our normal psychic state is one of mild trance, perfectly illustrated by the countless numbers of people who walk along engrossed
in mobile phones. Their level of awareness of their environment is
not far off being a state of hypnosis. The mind will drift off into
daydreaming if we do not grip it tight into the present.

The effect of military training is to ensure your mind is constantly alert and ready to go. Day dreaming when you should be looking
out for the enemy has predictably fatal consequences. The phrases
'get a grip' and 'switch on' (normally accompanied by expletives) are
standard training ground utterances and designed to keep the mind

alert and actions fast and timely.

The attitude of mental awareness, emotional robustness and urgency of action is precisely that cultivated by learning to fight. It is a thing that cannot be cultivated by learning from books or by talking about it.

The ancient Greeks in Plato's time had a word for the process of developing this: *agon*. *Agon*, from which we derive the word 'agony' means in this context the struggle between 'yes and no'. It means the way in which we develop discipline and gain control over ourselves. The physical body is the place to start, being the most simple and clearly observable way of making progress. Being so clearly observable, it is also the least subjective way to grow.

Sweat and pain are visceral things that we can be certain we have experienced! There is a great truth in facing an opponent in that we are aware of our own ability in reference to theirs. It is difficult to get too carried away with ourselves during tough training as we all encounter difficulty. Even if we claim to have found it easy later on out of braggadocio, deep down we know the reality!

FALSEHOOD

It is common now to 'talk up' our achievements and to pontificate and wiseacre on every subject under the sun as if we know something about it. We all feel like we have an equal right to comment upon all sorts of things without any knowledge or experience in them. By taking a tough, physical discipline as our training tool we can start to experience something genuine - honest sweat.

Think of all the people working away in offices basically bullshitting and dodging their way through their working life. This provides no firm ground on which to develop. There are other types of pursuits that involve *agon* and can bring results. Some of them have additional benefits over the physical route. I am referring to the learning of serious craft or artistic skills such as sculpture, painting, jewellery making, silversmithing and so on.

These are sound methods if we can find instructors who are

rigorous enough to teach them as a proper skill at a high level and if we have an artistic talent. But the rigour has gone out of many of these pursuits. The apprentice of these crafts used to spend an initial seven years learning the foundations. This is not the case now.

When we appreciate that modern man is less physical and more slovenly than ever, we can see why the *agon* of learning the physical craft of fighting should be our path.

For the ancient Greeks, *agon* was a religious observance. This is an indicator of what value they placed on it. What is religiousness if not a way of identifying what we value most?

At its best, this means that we put the correct value on those things that help elevate our level of consciousness and being - or to put it in the language we have been using, that elevate our Essence. This is why we call certain things 'sacred'. It should not be because we have developed a superstition or because we fear retribution in an imagined afterlife. Rather, it should be that which improves us in this life.

This is why the ancient Greeks marked it out as being a sacred task. Even if we feel a bit strange thinking of it in that way we nevertheless should place that value on it. Look at our modern world. What we value is upside down. You would not have failed to notice this. We value a pointless game of kicking a bag of wind from one area of grass to another more than we value matters of real importance. We pay the people who kick that bag of wind far more than the best scientists, inventors, physicians and so forth. But what we value is merely watching it, not even doing it! We have become voyeurs and mere spectators.

How much people are paid is only a reflection of how much they are valued. We should not seek to make any political points here, other than to say that what we should value most in our own lives are those things that improve us. That does not mean that we don't go and watch the football if that's what we enjoy doing for entertainment. But we save our feelings of what has the most value for things that matter.

THE AIM OF SPORTS

As that great civilisation of Greece was coming to an end, one of the indicators of their decline was the fact that they began to place too much value on sports and winning laurels. This was a key observation of the Roman civilisation that superseded them. The Romans knew that the Greeks had stopped being truly martial and healthy when their values started to degenerate. The winning of sports events became more valued than participation and personal improvement. They lost their military vitality and so they were no longer Battle Ready.

Here we see a clear difference in learning combat sports and learning for combat. In his book *Combat Sports in the Ancient World*, Michael B. Poliakoff highlights the Roman view of Greek obsession with games:

> *"The indirect military training that the palaestra could provide seemed idle diversion to the Romans: even Cicero, who was by no means hostile to the Greek civilisation, considered the ephebic exercises absurd training for the army. Roman poets mocked the Greek youths, " who are lazy from their devotion to the palaestra, who are hardly capable of carrying their weapons," youths who "have learned from their lazy pursuit of wrestling to endure (only) a soft, shaded contest, who delight in shining with oil."*[25]

It is clear that the Romans are chiefly attacking the value that the Greeks placed on combat sports contests rather than the physical exercises themselves. The difference is the attitude that the activities engender. The Spartans too, who made the cultivation of the Battle Ready man their primary activity also made the distinction:

"the bold athlete is not necessarily a bold warrior".[26]

This does not mean that the Spartans did not practice pankration (mixed martial arts) or hold combat sports events - but they were done specifically to develop the desired Spartan mentality, not for the vainglorious pursuit of personal victories:

> *"Unlike the citizens of our states, the Spartans cultivated combatative group contests. Each year, the two youth teams would gather on an island, fighting each other wildly, gouging, biting, and punching, until one team drove the other into the water. Spartans also had team sports that involved quite a lot of fighting over a ball."*[27]

The Greeks may have lost their way over time in fetishising sporting victory - as we do now, but the concept and original intention of the *agon*, as demonstrated by the focus on 'attitude' of the Spartans is a good example.

We should not be obsessed with winning medals but by developing ourselves. For a civilian seeking to obtain a Battle Ready attitude, we need not spend time learning how to be a soldier as such, this is not relevant to our lives. But to learn self-defence and how to fight for real without weapons or with improvised weapons is.

Part of this training, as for the Spartans, as for the Greeks and Romans may involve combat games such as sparring and grappling. The training benefit of those activities specifically will be discussed in a later chapter.

The *agon* we are fighting is not against others but against ourselves. The confusion comes in the fact that we may measure and test our progress against others. But who wins is meaningless if we are not developing. This is why we should be humble in victory if we happen to win a sporting contest - we seek a much higher prize. To give up all in the pursuit of beating other people is a corruption of personal development.

Sports people are unbelievably selfish and self-orientated in the main which is why they are so boring in conversation. Ultimately, sports prizes are meaningless. We even see sports stars celebrating a great victory when the best person in the world could not compete due to injury! Neither do they celebrate any less when an obvious error has been made by the referee, handing them the win.

We may be tempted to take from this then that the glory is not in winning but in 'taking part' as Baron de Coubertin the founder of the modern Olympic movement would have it. But this has become a mealy mouthed cop out and an idea that you should not try too hard. In our schools it is translated as 'everybody is a winner'. This is not so.

Poliakoff uses the example of the Nuba tribes in the Sudan as those who recognise that winning is not the point. In their wrestling matches, particularly when they wear heavy sharp bracelets, serious injury can occur. But the younger fighters are given praise if they challenge and fight the most powerful wrestlers, regardless of the outcome. This does not mean that they can just turn up and curl into a ball, but that they go out and give it everything whatever.[28]

This is the purpose of the contest and how they keep their fighting spirit alive. An obsession with winning for the sake of winning is not true fighting spirit as it lacks true aim. We become obsessed with the correct interpretation of the rules and whether the playing field or arena was of the right condition.

A particularly illuminating and disgraceful example of the corruption of winning for the sake of winning occurred between the world's two best footballers, Lionel Messi of Argentina and Cristiano Ronaldo of Portugal. Every year an award is given for the world's best player called the FIFA Ballon d'Or. Media representatives and national team coaches and captains get to vote for who should win it.

In one particular year it was obvious to everybody that these two players were the best in the world. Both Messi and Ronaldo got to vote as captains of their respective countries. Each voter has to nominate a top three and then all the votes are counted up, five points for a first place, three for a second place, one point for a third place.

Neither Messi nor Ronaldo had the other in their top three! These are men who are already wealthy and famous beyond anybody's wildest dreams behaving like selfish children at a birthday party! For all their skill in kicking a ball, little development of character at all has taken place.

The best way to develop the attitude we require then is to base our training around combat, rather than sport. We can use games and competitions to aid this aim, but the winning of prizes must not become an end in itself. If we happen to be soldiers in an army, then the type of combat training we must do is obvious. We need to prepare ourselves for modern warfare using all manner of weapons as this is what we must prepare to face.

For the civilian - for you and I - the combat training we must do to develop ourselves must be self-defence for the modern urban environment because this is our reality. We, who are prevented by law from carrying weapons must learn how to use our bodies as the weapons and improvise them where we can.

In some aspects, this is more difficult and challenging than training to be a soldier as it focusses more on the individual.

Only when we train to face life and death do we attract the kind of energy we need to make genuine FREEWILL.

TRAINING THE INTELLECTUAL CENTRE

If we look back to the table of the 'three-part' centres, we can see that 'knowledge gathering' is in the Moving part of the Intellectual Centre. Using our vehicle of learning to fight, we must focus on 'mastering' this activity in order to begin our aim of harmonising the centres and becoming Battle Ready.

When we talk of 'mastering' the activity we must not think that this means doing it to a point where there is no more to learn. This is not possible. There is always more for the Moving, Emotional and Intellectual Centres to learn, at least while the universe remains mysterious to us!

To claim to be a 'master' in that sense in anything is hilarious - for the most part, we do not even know why we are here on earth or if what we sense is truly real or not! This does not mean that we should tear ourselves apart worrying about these things but we need to have some humility at least!

Those that claim to be masters in the main do not even have the skill of a Benny Horovitz, not to mention a Caravaggio or a Shakespeare. The actual state of things is that we are all trying to get better, whatever level we are at currently.

For our purposes, the term 'mastering' means understanding ALL aspects of the subject physical, emotional and intellectual. Therefore we must gather all the knowledge we can.

This knowledge gathering should be to the aim of understanding the essence of the subject. It is the job of the Intellectual Centre to tie all this together.

You remember those people that are amazingly skilled in something but cannot teach it for toffee? If this is the case, it is because they do not truly understand its essence in the Intellectual Centre. It is then impossible for them to put it into words. The ability to teach is not the same as the ability to do, but the very best teachers have understanding across the centres.

Our intellectual processes work by comparison. That is, when we attempt to understand an intellectual concept, we do it by comparing it to something we already know. The best teachers understand this and use the language and metaphors that their students already know to push them into the understanding of something new. For example, I often have people come to me to learn self-defence who have combat sports backgrounds. I explain the concepts of self-defence by using a combat sport analogy to explain the differences.

If they have no background in physical activity I use experiences that people have daily to use as comparisons. Everybody has been in a crowded place surrounded by people for example. This is not rocket science for sure, but so many teachers and instructors cannot do this and the ones who can make it look deceptively easy.

To explain concepts to students in this way should give us a clue about how to study our subject of fighting. This passage is from *The Hagakure*:

> *"It is bad when one thing becomes two. One should not look for anything else in the Way of the Samurai. It is the same for anything else that is called a Way. Therefore, it is inconsistent to hear something of the Way of Confucius or the Way of*

the Buddha, and say that this is the Way of the Samurai. If one understands things in this manner, he should be able to hear about all Ways and be more and more in accord with his own."[29]

The Way I have been brought up in is not the Way of the samurai. I do not live in medieval Japan. Neither am I a Buddhist or Confucianist. It makes no sense for me to try and be a samurai or to convert to Buddhism. I have a 'language' and experience that I have grown up with and can use as a foundation to compare things to, to help my intellectual development.

Using the language of a different or alien Way does not help me, other than to *'be more and more in accord with my own'*. This is how I have used the above passage for example! The metaphors, myths and experiences I have grown up with are Christianity, Western philosophy, Western science and medicine.

I do not talk about chi or ki or yin yang to explain or teach because it is not a strong understanding for us in this part of the world. I can no more use these metaphors and language authentically than someone who is only a Mandarin speaker can truly understand all the nuances of Shakespeare by reading a translation.

Think of the words in Shakespeare - the English language is his tool and the musicality and meaning flows from it. If I read a Japanese *haiku* in an English translation can I get the meaning that a native Japanese gets from it? No way. Not even close. Even someone that speaks Japanese but then has to translate the words in their head cannot get all the meaning out of it. This is because a *haiku*, like Shakespeare's verse relies on the sounds of the words as much as the meaning.

If the culture those words are conceived in is very different than your own then much of the true meaning is lost.

You will be aware also that many words in a language simply have no accurate translation in another language, coming from a particular culture and environment that exists in that country. The Spanish word *duende* is associated with flamenco and Andalusian culture - best of luck trying to get its whole meaning in English! You generally need a few paragraphs!

This does not mean that we arrogantly assume that the metaphors and language we grew up with is 'the best' or somehow superior to all. But it is the most fruitful place to grow out of, rather than trying to adopt wholesale a Way of thinking that is not our own. I am not saying that this is impossible but the time that it would take to do it is better spent following a familiar path. If we are honest we will see that people like to adopt other Ways purely because they seem exotic and different.

Think of all the people who delight in having tattoos written in other languages - especially the very exotic like Mandarin, Japanese and Arabic. But it's also true that the Japanese think that the Western script is exotic and cool! How more interesting and edgy is it to say that we have become a Buddhist? It conjures up a world of colour, warmth and exotic temples in Phuket rather than the familiar settings of the local parish church on a cold, grey Sunday morning in Wigan.

We need not despair though as our own culture is rich enough to provide us with sufficient material. Our language and thought is a result of our history. Our history has developed from the Greeks, Romans, Britons, Anglo-Saxons, Normans and so on. All of these have left marks on our language and ways of thinking.

This means that Pythagoras, Plato, Aristotle, Jesus Christ, Plotinus, Marcus Aurelius, Seneca, Bede, Machiavelli, Shakespeare, Einstein, Jung, Tesla, Gurdjieff and so on are in our cultural and intellectual short hand. We may miss the full meaning from some of these due to translation, but the cultural environment that they came from is sufficiently close to our own way of thinking to remain relevant and fertile ground for our understanding.

Other influences are vitally important as a way of being 'more and more in accord' with our own way (I do this throughout this book in fact) but they are not a rabbit hole that we want to travel too far down, lest we lose our grip on firm ground.

The best way to understand the essence of fighting then is primarily via our own cultural heritage of science and investigation rather than trying to squint dimly through the lens of oriental philosophical systems. So I'm going to leave well alone ideas of chi and ki, yin yang, and all that stuff and instead talk about geometry, lever-age, balance and the laws of physics.

Understanding the essence of a thing at first is a bit like gath-ering intelligence upon enemy forces. What we need to have first is information. The difference between 'intelligence' and 'information' on the battlefield is one of analysis. Information might be that the enemy has two battlegroups moving towards Target A. Intelligence is that this means that the enemy intends to reinforce Target A and create a defensive position in order to block our advancement. In other words, this information is now put in context.

In the next chapters, we will be developing our knowledge and analysis of fighting. My aim in this will be to boil fighting down to its essential principles in context. Your work will be to go and DO it in order for it to be activated throughout your centres creating 'wisdom'.

DISCERNING TRUTH FROM FANTASY

The first step in understanding the essence of anything is to clear the decks and remove what is false in our current assumptions. We cannot learn anything if we think we already know it.

This is the purpose of the 'Socratic Method' we find in Plato's dialogues. I was somewhat annoyed to find when I began my master's degree in 'Philosophy as a Way of Life' at the age of thirty that Plato's dialogues were easy to read, funny, practical and good stories to boot. I felt rather that the academic world had been 'hogging' them and making them sound inaccessible except to those initiated and steeped in the Classics.

This is far from the case, I found that I was able to understand many of the themes in the dialogues to a deeper level than the dry academics, many of whom did not have a great variety of experience of life.

Plato's dialogues, ironically are not 'academic'. I say ironically as the term 'academic' comes from Plato's school - the Academy. I would have had the courage to dive into them far sooner had I known!

Take Plato's *Symposium* for example. It's the story of a group of men getting drunk and talking about the nature of love and sex. They banter, entertain each other with tragic and funny stories and challenge each other's ideas. There is a great warmth to the meeting and it's a very human story that is recognisable to us even thousands of years later. The figure of Socrates appears in the Platonic dialogues always as the questioner, the one who challenges what we think we know.

In our modern age, we have recently developed this idea, particularly amongst young people at university that any challenge to our ideas is 'offensive' or makes us feel uncomfortable when we should be in a 'safe space'. Socrates takes the view that we constantly need our ideas and beliefs challenged and tested if we are to get to any truth. The chances are that if you are an eighteen year old at university, you probably don't know everything. In fact, taking myself as an example, looking back it's safe to say I didn't know much about anything important! I needed my ideas challenged and continue to need them challenged to this day and every day.

I count myself very fortunate that my philosophy professor at the University of Liverpool was Stephen RL Clark, a man who exemplifies everything that is good about the academic world. I saw from Professor Clark that he was deeply curious about the world in general and had no snobbery of any sort where knowledge gathering and investigation were concerned.

He was an authority on science fiction literature and his advice for what to read put me onto countless delights that I continue to get great pleasure from. What in particular I learned from Professor Clark was the necessity for intellectual rigour. It was not enough to take things at face value, one had to get underneath them and separate the wheat from the chaff.

Often in a tutorial, a student would question the meaning of a sentence in Plato. The professor would say 'well, let's have a look at the Greek', pull a dusty tome off the shelf and read it in the original Greek. Often he would correct the English translation we had with a substitute that far better reflected the meaning of the phrase.

Translators often get it wrong and sometimes miss the whole

context of the passage of a work, resulting in poor understanding. This is never more true than in the New Testament of the Christian Bible. If you are interested at all in the Christian story, you must at least go back to the direct translation of the original Greek that the New Testament is written in. You will find a host of incredible surprises.

Consider the Christian idea of 'repentance'; if we go back to the Greek we find the word *metanoia*. Our basic concept of repentance is admitting guilt, saying sorry and making up for it. But this is not what *metanoia* means. Not even close. *Metanoia* means 'changing your perspective'. Many clergymen and biblical scholars from Martin Luther to John Albert Broadus and beyond have bemoaned this terrible translation.

Take the word for 'sin' - *harmartia*, which means 'missing the mark' and comes from throwing a spear at a target. If we view this in terms of spiritual development then, if we 'miss the mark' we need to 'change our perspective'.

This is expressed in terms which makes us have to do something about our lack of understanding, rather than simply feeling guilt and saying sorry for doing something forbidden. It puts the emphasis right onto us to do the work to try and understand our role in the universe. How this idea became corrupted into going into a box and spilling your guts to a celibate man behind a screen and then being ordered to say some prayers is the subject for another book entirely!

Professor Clark has written extensively on animal rights. I remember well that he wore 'vegetarian' shoes and owned nothing made of leather. I believe I am not doing him a disservice by saying he was no lover of the military either. In spite of this, or more accurately, because of it I learned a great deal from him and was inspired to learn more by his example. He would not let you get away with any assumptions and continually challenged the 'accepted view'.

My training partner and friend is a Brazilian jiu-jitsu black belt and also teaches mixed martial arts and boxing. He has a scientific approach to teaching and keeps himself right up with all the latest investigations and techniques evolving in the sporting world. Part of my desire to challenge my own understanding of fighting made me join his Brazilian jiu-jitsu class as a student.

Off the mats, we often discuss fighting and many other topics besides. Within this friendship is a continuous process of challenging each other in order to improve our thinking and behaviour. This makes the friendship productive as well as enjoyable on a personal level.

It is vitally important that we seek out people who can challenge our views with rigourous and informed debate. This prevents us from disappearing into a solipsistic fantasy. It is not 'losing' an argument if you find that the other person is right or that your thinking was based on an incorrect assumption. In fact, you have won as you have learned something!

DISAPPOINTMENT

Most people that get to the stage where they seriously start looking for improvement do so out of a feeling of disappointment. This is a disappointment with themselves for achieving no more than mediocre things and disappointment with other people for being less than they thought.

We need to be clear on one thing. Everybody is a shit. Far from being depressing, this realisation should free us from unrealistic expectations of others. Whenever you drill down into the motives of others you will find selfishness and self-concern. If this is true of them, then it is true of you and I also.

Many of us go to incredible feats to mask our own selfishness, particularly if it involves charity work. Occasionally, people will surprise you and do something for its own sake. These moments are to be treasured. But it should not raise our expectations of them.

For survival, any organism must evolve selfishness and the ability to primarily look after number one. None of us would be here if it was not for this. We should not think of this as evil or good but rather just the way things are. If you are able to have some objectivity for a moment to examine your own motives you will find that self-concern drives you more than anything. Even acts of kindness that you perform will be for recognition, self-esteem or because you expect something in return.

The most important thing is that we do not involve ourselves in the fantasy that we are 'good' people and that others therefore should be 'good' people.

The realisation that everyone is a shit allows you to have the correct attitude to everyone. If you think well of people you have expectations of them. Because you are continually disappointed when they do not meet your expectations you begin to dislike them and moan about them and make bad decisions regarding them. If you think everyone is a shit you have no expectations; and because they occasionally surprise you by acting better than a shit you like them, have true compassion for them and make first class decisions regarding them.

Now you can truly love them and involve them much more in your lives for mutual benefit. For yourself, know that you are a shit and resolve to try and be less of one!

To break down everything to what it is, without romanticising it or giving it virtues it does not merit, let us briefly examine again the Meditations of Marcus Aurelius. He is another example for us of the Battle Ready individual, strong and harmonised in the centres.

Pierre Hadot in his work *Philosophy as a Way of Life* chooses this passage as being illustrative of Marcus Aurelius' approach:

> "These foods and dishes.....are only dead fish, birds and pigs, this Falernian wine is a bit of grape juice; this purple-edged toga is some sheep's hairs dipped in the blood of shellfish; as for sex, it is the rubbing together of pieces of gut, followed by the spasmodic secretion of a little bit of slime."[30]

The purpose here is not to belittle things, merely to see them as they are without varnish. In the Stoic school of philosophy, this exercise was done in order to see things objectively. Hadot chooses the words of Epictetus to further illustrate this point:

So-and-so's son is dead.
What happened?
His son is dead.
Nothing else?
Not a thing.

So-and-so's ship sank.
What happened?
His ship sank.

So-and-so was carried off to prison.
What happened?
He was carried off to prison.
But if we now add to this "He has had bad luck," then each of us
is adding this observation on his own account.[31]

He expresses no negative emotions nor does he express an opinion, merely recount the facts as they are. This is the process of boiling things down to their essence by stripping away our own subjective views on them as much as possible.

We can become Battle Ready by learning to fight, by understanding the essence as a vehicle. Firstly, we need to be able to discern the truth from the fantasy of our subject. This process should serve as an example for what you must do to begin ANY investigation into any area of study. As our study is fighting, we must shed our assumptions and subjective views about it, the myth and mystery of fighting must give way to a cold assessment supported by the facts!

By training in this way, we can build the Warrior by developing the Moving Centre and the Moving parts of the Emotional and Intellectual Centres. This will make us Battle Ready and form a solid foundation for further development throughout the rest of our lives.

CHAPTER 6
MYTH AND MYSTERY

———

*"We are but warriors for the working day; our gayness
and our gilt are all besmirch'd with rainy marching in the painful field....But, by the mass, our hearts are in the trim".*

William Shakespeare, Henry V.

It took me less than ten seconds to realise that I was wasting my
time learning martial arts for self-defence. In those ten seconds I
had witnessed a fight between a monster of a man in a Leeds United
shirt and my friend Tommy.

Tommy was minding his own business in the pub when this
guy had taken exception to Tommy's Manchester accent. When this
monster went for him, I knew Tommy would get the hiding of his
life. Instead, Tommy shoved his cigarette up the guy's nose, picked up
a bar stool, smashed him across the head with it and walked briskly
out of the premises, right passed the monsters' stunned mates.

I could see Tommy through the window, pausing to light another cigarette before disappearing into the night. What I had seen was
brutal, unbelievably quick and massively effective. It may even have
saved Tommy's life. At that point I went home to rethink a few basic
assumptions.

Tommy had never trained in martial arts in his life. He was,
however an excellent rugby league player, agile, fast and blessed
with superb vision and decision making. I was lucky to play on the
same team as him. He was also used to being the smallest man on

the pitch, being 5' 5" and barely ten stone. With no training other than life itself, Tommy had developed a mindset - a way of thinking that had nothing to do with technique but everything to do with survival. This mindset had saved him from hospital or worse.

For me, it was a bombshell. I had been training in martial arts three times a week for years, collecting techniques and thinking I was pretty handy. After that, I stopped going. If that guy had come at me, I would have been half-way through deciding which of my 101 techniques to destroy him with when he would have taken me apart.

A few years later, I was reminded of the 'Tommy incident' from an unlikely source. A legendary veteran World War 2 platoon commander was giving a lecture to the young infantry officers on the platoon commander's battle course. Someone asked him a complicated tactical question and ended it with 'What's the best thing to do in this situation?'. He replied, "I don't know but do anything quickly enough and aggressively enough and it will probably be right". A stunned silence followed.

All young infantry officer's aspire to being tactical geniuses and spend plenty of time arguing about tactics. I know I did. In fact, I had made the same mistake twice in thinking that greater complexity is what is needed.

Our WW2 veteran had developed his mindset through blood sweat and tears on the battlefield. Tommy had developed his as a weedy kid on the streets of Salford. Both were born of survival. Experience had refined their approach into a simple, brutal and effective reaction under pressure. They had an ATTITUDE that was ready to go at any time.

Such is the human desire to complicate and intellectualise things however, this lesson must be learnt over and over again. It's not about how complicated you can make it, anyone can do this. It's about how simple you can make it, then how good you can get at doing the simple thing well under pressure. To get to the essence of what the simple thing is regarding self-defence, we need to first challenge our basic assumptions.

THE SHADOW OF BRUCE LEE

The popularity of martial arts in the modern era stems largely from Bruce Lee movies. Bruce Lee movies are not documentaries about street fighting. Fights in Hong Kong Kung Fu movies are a way of telling a story without dialogue. The 'style' of fighting each character employs reflects their personality and says something about them. The hero needs to fight heroically and the villain needs to fight villainously. A comic character needs to fight comically. These fight scenes are for our entertainment and need above all to be dramatic and work as a piece of cinema. We also need to see what the hell is going on. The cinema makes fighting look exciting and cool - everybody wants to be Bruce Lee, he is the coolest fighter of them all.

Bruce Lee is an interesting case because in the popular culture, he has become mythologised into being a super-human; the ultimate fighter capable of beating anyone. This is based largely on the the four and a half movies he had the starring role in. Bruce Lee is more than this however. He is more responsible than anyone of his generation for reconnecting people with the study of fighting.

If we read his words and understand what he was trying to do with his fighting system of Jeet Kune Do, we can see how outside of the movies, he was looking to break down outdated and formal ways of thinking and create solid principles based on fighting reality. When you look at videos of his training and demonstrations, you will see that compared to modern sports fighters, he was not technically as proficient.

This will seem like heresy to some so it is important to go and find the footage on the internet and compare it yourself with the best sports guys. Often there will be arguments about how Bruce Lee would have performed in a modern sports competition like mixed martial arts. Go and compare his training videos with those of modern fighters at his weight and make up your own mind. We will discuss more about this in the next chapter.

If everybody wants to be Bruce Lee, then everybody wants to be James Bond too, but James Bond films are not documentaries either. Spies for real are data analysts and agent handlers, they are not in the business of getting into fist fights in exotic locations. Without exception, all of the members of the Security Services that I came into contact with were geeks, super intelligent for sure but nothing like James Bond. Perhaps that kind of thing existed once in a less exaggerated form but now, it's only for the movies.

Movie magic has a way of getting into our consciousness and making us believe it is real. After all, the very essence of moving pictures is illusion! A large part of us wants to believe that what we are seeing on screen is real or at least could be real. We want the world to be more cool, sexier, more exciting than it really is. Especially if our own lives are a bit mundane. This is a nice fantasy.

Fighting for real is not like the fantasy version. It's shocking, grubby, unfair and never cool or sexy. Even the tamed and more civilised type of fighting in combat sports is too real for most. Many times I have seen young guys come into the gym to start to learn a bit of mixed martial arts or boxing, take a shot to face, taste their own blood in the back of their mouth and never come back. Too much reality, thank you very much. No doubt they go home, get on the internet, claim to be a fighter and then argue with some dude about who would win in a fight between Freddie Kruger and the Candyman.

I once said something similar to this when I was taking a seminar and I heard the guys laugh and nod their heads. Then a voice piped up...."yeah but seriously, the Candyman wouldn't stand a chance as Freddie would take him into the dreamworld". Before I could interrupt another voice replied 'yeah but Freddie would need to get the Candyman to sleep first so that's bollocks mate". How men love to argue about nonsense! I say men as I have never yet heard any women arguing like this.

The more subjective and pointless the subject, the more men seem to enjoy it, and there is nothing more subjective and pointless than arguing about who would win in a fight between two entirely fictional supernatural movie villains.

Much of the martial arts is like this; full grown men arguing about who would win in real fights between this system or that system, between a karate guy or a taekwondo guy or a jiu-jitsu guy or a boxer. Although comparing systems as training methods may be relevant, the only answer to the question of who would win in a real fight between such and such is "who knows?". Systems and styles don't fight each other, people fight each other and if we are talking about fighting for real, we need to forget about fair fights with rules, one against one and so forth.

What if I have never trained in my life but wait for a Brazilian jiu-jitsu black belt to leave the gym whilst I hide around the corner. When he goes past me, I hit him over the head with an iron bar and he is knocked out cold. Do I then assume that Brazilian jiu-jitsu as a form of self-defence is a lot of old cobblers?

I once heard an exchange between two soldiers, one an army boxer and the other a fairly humble character. The army boxer told him, "If we had a fight I would smash your face in, I'm too quick and strong for you." The humble character replied "Yeah maybe, but just remember this, when I pick up a bedside table it can move far quicker than a sleeping soldier!" Fair point. I imagine our boxer kept one eye open that night.

Everybody is vulnerable, regardless of how much training you have done. People in movies can take all sorts of punishment. Look how many massive punches Rocky can take and look at the injuries John McClean in the *Die Hard* movies simply shrugs off, from pulling broken glass out of his feet to pulling shards of cable out of his shoulder.

Anyone who has children in the family knows how painful it is to step on Lego with bare feet for heaven's sake. Imagine having pieces of broken glass sticking out of them!

We need to accept that we have no guarantees where fighting is concerned and no magic either. It seems so obvious to say that we need to recognise that movie fighting is not real, but time after time, we see martial arts training that is based on movie style fighting with one person attacking at a time. Movies are best as a way of inspiring us, of getting us excited about learning fighting. But we should never assume they reflect reality.

A great deal of the 'magic and mystery' of the martial arts is based on a false appraisal of the past. For example, we assume, because a martial art is old that it is therefore tested and has therefore stood the test of time.

To be able to decide which martial arts or self-defence methods to pursue, we need to ask ourselves if the training reflects the kind of situations we may be in for real.

If we look at threat in terms of self-defence we can see it in terms of an ambush. This is quite different to the threat posed by a sport martial art, where the time of the fight is fixed as well as the environment in which you fight. No-one in sports fighting is surprised when their opponent attacks them. For self-defence however, the attack is a surprise and is not on ground of our choosing. If we can begin to understand the reality of the threat we face, we can design training appropriately to counter that threat. No more and nothing less.

It's the 'warriors for the working day' approach to self-defence; no fancy outfits, no grand sounding titles and no high sounding morality or ideals. You will not learn how to give someone a heart attack in three month's time by pressing on their meridian points. Neither will you learn how to knock people out without touching them, or learn the skills of a ninja in medieval Japan. You won't learn these things because they are either spurious or irrelevant to learning how to fight to protect yourself in our modern world.

You will not learn therefore how to wield a bo-staff or how to use nunchukas or little chain things with spikes on the end. I have been to seminars where they teach these things and the kind of people who regularly train with these seem to be the same kind of people that go to Star Trek or Star Wars conventions. There is nothing wrong with this at all - but people go to indulge their fantasies.

I can understand the motivation behind wanting the fantasy, it's bound to be more enjoyable, less difficult, more ego boosting, safer and generally more agreeable.

The reality of something is less glamorous, more difficult and contains no glory. But it's real. To take an analogy, we can get our kicks by looking a pictures of perfect, naked, passive, airbrushed human beings on the internet or we can enjoy the imperfect, occasionally awkward but active experience of having a physical relationship for real.

It is worth saying here that we may not think that this is too big a deal and that indulging in fantasy is harmless fun. But I'm going to make this very clear. Indulging in fantasy is going to be one of the major challenges of our generation. We have never faced this problem in this way before. Certainly mankind has faced the problem of people losing themselves in the oblivion of drug addiction for a very long time. We continue to face that problem.

But we now add to that the numerous ways in which technology has evolved to give us an alternative illusion of reality to get lost in. Of particular and immediate concern is the effect of internet pornography on the sexual function of our young people and young men in particular.

I say young men in particular as these are a generation that has reached sexual maturity with this technology available. In my youth, pornography was found discarded in hedgerows by the side of the road, now it's available in every home at any time. I am not interested here in the morality of pornography, That is an irrelevant issue to our aim of becoming Battle Ready. Nor am I talking about occasional use – it's the habitual use that's the issue here.

What is relevant is the way in which, through classical Pavlovian conditioning, young men are becoming sexually orientated towards the fantasy of pornography at the expense of being able to perform it for real.

The statistics back this up - more and more young people are presenting with the kind of sexual dysfunction associated with old age. The reason is simple. These young men have been conditioning themselves to be sexually aroused by pixels on a screen which they then masturbate to. They condition themselves to be voyeurs rather than participants.

It becomes difficult for them to then be aroused by contact with a real sexual partner as their habitual sexual experience is sitting in a chair watching a screen. It is typical for these men to no longer be able to achieve an erection standing up for example! Many men experience the problem of not being able to orgasm via real sexual intercourse. In simple terms, their brain has been rewired.[32]

The problem is compounded in that internet pornography

seems to provide endless novelty of stimulation and the human male is evolutionarily predisposed to find novelty of sexual partners arousing. But this is just the illusion of novelty rather than the reality.

So what's the result of this? A generation of people with serious sexual dysfunction. Increased anxiety, increased depression, increased relationship problems. Are these people Battle Ready? Their potency has been dissolved in fantasy. This is a recipe for disaster.

Beating any addiction is tough, though the solution is simple. Total abstinence from artificial sexual stimulation is the cure. The brain will eventually rewire and full sexual power will be reached. You cannot overestimate how grave this problem is. We are heading in a very bad direction and good sexual function is vitally important to our society and to the relationships of love that bind it together. We are turning away from reality and into fantasy.

Once we appreciate the essence of this problem we can do something about it. Can you see how this problem of fantasy extends to everything we do? The fantasy is easily accessible and takes little effort, it allows us to be kings in our own minds. Sexually we can have any partner we want and we are all powerful. Physically we defeat any and all opponents. In computer games we are assassins and special forces snipers. Everyone is Bruce Lee, Batman and James Bond rolled into one.

To understand the essence of real things is essential in becoming Battle Ready. A big part of that is being critical and questioning what you have been told. I absolutely expect and encourage you to be critical about what you are about to read and only take it on board when you have tested it and found it to be true for yourself. This goes for anybody, regardless of their qualifications or what they have done in the past. Listen to what they have to say, file it under 'pending' and take the effort to do it yourself and see what happens.

It has never failed to amaze me how supposedly well-qualified and well-regarded people can produce work of such little quality. On the other side, it's just as likely that someone you have never heard of gives you the golden nugget of truth that helps you understand a thing for yourself.

You must be genuinely critical of everything that is taught.

This does not mean that you are negatively inclined from the outset, rather that you view it neutrally before coming to any conclusion.

In the age we live in, where we can comment on things instantly, it's a real trap to get into the habit of making snap judgements of good or bad. Social media does black and white very well but it does shades of grey very badly. We even click 'like' on content, there's no button for 'having a little think about it, will test it then reply with something sensible'. It tends to be all or nothing. This does not help the honest desire to learn one bit. The sheer amount of information out there is staggering so we need to exercise some discernment in what we pay attention too.

Often a little research goes a long way. This is never more true when examining the incredible claims made in the name of some oriental martial arts. We are led to believe that kettles can be boiled with Chi energy and that many 'magic' techniques exist if only we go on live on Wu-Dong mountain or some other such place to learn them from 200 year old Taoist monks and sages.

Skin can supposedly be made impervious to blades and even withstand boiling oil. That these things are possible is a 'fact' reinforced by movies and popular culture. We like to believe that someone, somewhere has secret techniques that can give unlimited power. The popular conception of ninjas is that they could magically disappear and were capable of astounding feats. The association of ninjas with incredible and magical abilities is deep and leads some to believe that real secret abilities are to be found there.

According to Leung Ting, the origin of these supposedly magical abilities in oriental martial arts comes from groups known as 'The Vagabonds'. The Vagabonds were street performers who would tour China and whose shows combined martial arts, acrobatics and illusions. They were a kind of forerunner of the circus and of illusionists.[33]

Heavily imbued in Chinese culture and mythology is the idea of magical spirits and demons and The Vagabonds used this rich source material as a narrative to create amazing performances that would shock and delight audiences who would then give money in appreciation.

Superstition, religion and science were all woven together to create these spectacles. Often tricks were used that would cheat an unsuspecting mark out of their hard earned money. You can still see such tricks used around the world in side shows with things like 'Find The Lady' or the game where you try to keep your eye on a ball placed under one of three cups. In some ways, these events were a kind of travelling carnival or circus.

The performance aspect of the Chinese Vagabonds is important in understanding much of the myth and mystery associated with martial arts. It continues to this day with West End shows featuring the Shaolin monks.

The tales of the Shaolin monks are as legendary as the ninja but their performances are similar to the tradition of The Vagabonds, featuring a mixture of martial arts, acrobatics and amazing feats that people pay to go and see. But circus people can do the same things without claiming mystical powers.

The point is, they are designed for entertainment, rather than learning how to fight. Where the making of money is concerned, this has to be the overriding consideration.

The modern Shaolin temple was re-established as a tourist attraction, having been dissolved by Mao Tse-Tung and left empty for many years. There is no doubt that the Shaolin temple had a role to play in the development of martial arts, particularly the martial arts in Okinawa, Japan and from there across the world. But it is important to separate the reality from the legend if we are to find a real understanding. This is especially true if we are to try and understand something that comes from a culture that is not our own.

Too often, we lose the historical context that underpins the subject and tells us what it was originally intended for. If this is true for the performance art tricks and acrobatics of Chinese Vagabonds, it's also true for deepening our understanding of ninjas and samurai in Japan.

The reason we must uncover the reality of what are considered authorities on martial arts and therefore fighting generally, is that so often, people base training methods and techniques from historical sources that they do not fully understand. Then this becomes a kind of unchallengeable gospel truth that leads us down the wrong path.

LEGENDARY WARRIORS

A great deal of mystique and romanticism surrounds the samurai and ninjas but a little reading uncovers a much more prosaic reality. Firstly, our modern view of honour was not the same as theirs. samurai were professional warriors that collected enemy heads on the battlefield to prove their kills.

Not only did the collecting of heads serve this function of identification but there were people employed to divine the future based on the eye direction of the decapitated head. The heads were proudly displayed on spikes for the 'Head Inspector' to come and verify the kills. The higher ranking the enemy was, the more reward the samurai got. More like headhunting bounty killers than the modern perception.

Also, we tend to view the samurai sword as being the soul of the warrior, but during the main fighting period of their history, the sword was just another tool in the warriors armoury. The sword was not treated with any special reverence and was not even the main fighting weapon of the samurai, with spears and bows being much more important.

Antony Cummins, in his book *Samurai and Ninja* explains how archaeological research has shown that the vast majority of samurai were killed by projectile weapons such as arrows and musket balls, rather than by swords. This makes sense when compared to modern warfare as well, with far more soldiers being killed by weapons that function at distance rather than close up.[34]

He further explains how our typical view of samurai and ninja as being separate, antagonistic groups is also false. The ninja (Shinobi) were specially trained troops used by samurai armies for reconnaissance and covert operations.

As part of the field army, they had roles akin to a modern Brigade Reconnaissance Force or to classic commando type units. As well as gathering intelligence on enemy positions and strengths, they would also conduct night raids into enemy territory with planned withdrawals (a typical modern commando task). Their role in marking out positions for friendly forces to take up prior to attack and in guiding units in darkness is a task familiar to modern reconnaissance platoons.

A great many of their techniques and knowledge surround the making and carrying of fire and fire-making materials in order to operate at night. We take the creation of light for granted, having battery powered light sources with us constantly, but the Shinobi needed to be quite the chemist in order to have sources of reliable light when it was needed.

Shinobi were also used as spies, both within their own armies and in enemy forces. The composition of the Shinobi reflected the conventional samurai fighting forces; some were of samurai class and some were of the peasant class.

The legend of them being all anti-samurai freedom fighters may have come from the fact that they developed tactics and techniques specifically to defeat conventionally trained samurai and enemy forces. This is much more of a tactical necessity than a political statement. It should be borne in mind that an important part of a Shinobi's task was to cancel out the activities of the enemies Shinobi.

The romanticism of the samurai during the periods of constant warfare was done by later samurai, looking back at this 'golden age' during times of peace. Hence we have a process of greater and greater embellishment of a time in history when pragmatism and harsh realities were the order of the day.

Always we seem to lose track of the fact that people need to make money to survive and those that have money generally want more money or power or influence. It may upset our idealist views of this warrior cult but ultimately it should free our minds to focus on the present, without wishing to be in an age that never existed in the way we thought it did.

As the fantasists we are, we imagine that we are modern samurai, learning mystical fighting arts. But most of us come from a social class more analogous to peasants or merchants than to nobleman. The good news is that there is much to learn from the real history as opposed to the legends.

It is interesting the importance that is often placed on 'lineage' in the modern expression of 'traditional martial arts'. Perhaps though, we can view an 'old' martial art as being more likely to have been corrupted and misunderstood over the years. This is in addition to the fact that, even if the training is 'authentic', the circumstances that the training was designed to prepare you for no longer exist.

We often regard respect for tradition and lineage as being a very typical trait of oriental martial arts and there is a great deal of truth in that. It is ironic then that the most celebrated Japanese swordsman of all, Miyamoto Musashi had no time for lineage.

We equally need to understand that their idea of honour was not the same as we imagine. After all, the Japanese have a word 'tsuji-giri' that translates to 'trying out a sword on a chance passer-by'.[35]

To begin to unravel some of these threads however, we can see how legend and folklore combine with our delight in the mysterious and secret to create falsehood. When we uncover the truth of a thing, it's important to ask ourselves whether it is relevant to our purpose. We could, for example, completely dispense with all 'traditional martial arts' and start from scratch. This is what Musashi claimed to have done. But maybe this is throwing the baby out with the bathwater.

Ultimately, it's possible to get to truths about fighting purely from your own experience, but this suggests that your experience is so wide ranging that you know everything. When this is not the case, in order to enhance our learning, we would need to learn from the experiences of others. When we do this, we need to ask ourselves how relevant that experience is.

This holds true not just for street fighting and combat sports, but also for military combat. When I was going through my military training, a couple of my instructors had been in the Falklands War seventeen years earlier. All of the instructors had experience of Northern Ireland and The Troubles. Some had experience of conflict in the Balkans and some had experience of the Gulf War.

Generally speaking, there was enough genuine experience to convey the principles of warfighting in basic terms. But far too much time was spent on complicating tactics and on making platoon attacks seem more cerebral than they really are. As we have seen from the history of the samurai in and out of peacetime, this is common during even short periods of peace.

Very quickly, during the campaign against the Taliban in Afghanistan, soldiers added their experience to their training to adapt to the reality. In some cases, training on certain aspects of warfighting was found to be insufficient and the reality they were facing was not quite the reality they had trained for in the beginning of the campaign.

This did not mean a wholesale rejection of their training however, rather an adaption or modification, with the general principles holding true, but the emphasis altered. As one company commander in Afghanistan remarked to me "once again the British Army has to re-learn the importance of over-whelming firepower".

Sometimes in peacetime we can develop an approach of tactical 'cleverness' or 'trickiness', when the truth lies in simple things done very well. Generally speaking however, our training (which is basically learning from others peoples experience) was a good foundation on which to build. All this means is that the recent traditions and experience of the British Army was relevant enough to the next conflict to give us a strong foundation.

Following Afghanistan the standard of instruction went through the roof. More or less every instructor had direct experience and many of them had extensive experience. Training became simplified and more direct. Attacks and tactical decision making was trained as a drill rather than a game of chess. The learner can always add elements later if the foundation is secure.

I have occasionally come across the opinion from some sport martial artists that is not even possible to train for street self-defence as there are no 'solutions'. This is an interesting point. It's interesting because in some ways it's correct. There are no 'solutions', if solutions means guaranteed ways of dealing with certain situations. In any case, each situation is different. But this is true of military conflict as well. Again, there are no guarantees.

We even say 'no plan survives contact with the enemy'. So does that mean we don't train? Of course not! But our training must reflect the fact that nothing is guaranteed and flexibility and adaptability must be our emotional attitude.

When you compare a trained soldier with a random civilian off the street, it's obvious that the trained soldier is a great deal better prepared to fight the Taliban than your average Joe!

Whilst we are on the subject of the military, it is necessary to deal with the myth of how military personnel are 'magically' equipped to deal with the kind of unarmed street violence that is dealt with in this book. People often ask me if I know about street self-defence from being an infantryman. The answer is no! The type of fighting that this involves is with a rifle, at an enemy also with a rifle with other parts of the armed forces in support from artillery to aviation, fast jets, bombers and so on.

Even acting on its own, a modern infantry battalion boasts mortars, anti-tank weapons, heavy machine guns, automatic grenade launchers and so on. The troops do not lay down their arms and fist fight the enemy. Neither does the enemy put down its arms either. When you see this in films, it's pure Hollywood. When it comes to running out of ammunition, you use a bayonet. If your bayonet breaks you use an entrenching tool. If you have no entrenching tool you use a knife, if no knife you better start sharpening a spoon!

If I am engaged in empty handed fighting with an enemy that also means that he has run out of ammunition and all those other items too. Not only that but all the other soldiers in our respective units would have had to have lost all their weapons too! Hence the military should not be automatically regarded as experts in street self-defence because it is not something that is a battlefield reality. Only in movies do people throw down their weapons and decide to do things the 'old way'!

That is not to say that fighting at very close quarters does not happen but it would be wrong to think of this in the same terms as street self-defence. When I joined the army, there were still serving veterans of the Falklands War. I think it is fair to say that we held them in a kind of awe, knowing some of what they had done.

Our Academy Sergeant-Major at Sandhurst was one such man and I can still picture him telling us about the effect that the bagpipes had on the morale of the Scots Guards before they went into the attack at Mount Tumbledown. We had either been told about or had read about the bayonet charges that the Scots Guards had done that day. This is incredible stuff and some of the reported engagements in our time in Afghanistan were super close too but fist fights they were not.

One aspect that does serve us well from the military is the approach to training and the attitude that it engenders as we discussed in the last chapter.

Looking into the traditions of the martial arts then, we need to be sure that their experience is relevant enough to our next conflict to be worth something. We should have no truck whatsoever with those that religiously claim one system or another as being 'the best', nor should we concern ourselves with a respect for tradition and antiquity by itself. All we need to do is see what's relevant. Often it helps to look at the history of a martial art or fighting system and see what it was designed for.

For example, the great educator and founder of judo, Jigoro Kano updated the battlefield art of the samurai; Ju-Jitsu. Ju-Jitsu itself was designed to train samurai to fight against opponents wearing armour and the emphasis on joint manipulations reflects this. They found that the punch was less effective against an armoured opponent. Their training included this kind of empty hand fighting in case they found themselves disarmed. Many of their techniques involve how to enter into the close distance of an armed opponent and nullify their advantage.

The reality of the samurai's experience drove the technical aspects of their training and not the other way around.

We should therefore see training for fighting in an entirely pragmatic way and not seek to complicate or try and 'elevate' it above the purely practical.

It is a real curse when instructors and practitioners attempt to attach mystical and arcane philosophy to their training, in the mistaken belief that it needs this to be profound.

Like any craft, the value is contained within its simple truth, not its complex fantasy.

FORGETTING HISTORY

In many cases, things are forgotten and have to be rediscovered. This is perhaps true in the case of the importance of grappling on the ground in mixed martial arts. If we look back at the depictions of the ancient Greeks in pankration, we can see the heavy emphasis placed on grappling. When mixed martial arts (modern pankration) was introduced, that lesson was learnt all over again.

I once read a piece from a very well respected and excellent MMA and BJJ coach on how lucky young people were today because those early MMA pioneers had shown how important ground fighting was. They had shown that styles of fighting that don't include them are super vulnerable. Basically he was saying that MMA found the truth and prevented people from wasting time on phoney martial arts nonsense. There is a massive big fat chunk of truth in this.

But he failed to mention that it was largely his generation that caused all the misconceptions about martial arts and fighting. It was his generation that grew up on Kung Fu films and had created the worldwide marital arts scene in the 70s and 80s and so on. The ancient Greeks knew the truth!

The combat sports events of boxing, wrestling and pankration in ancient Greece were known as the 'big events' because the people who competed in them were physically big people. This is because there were no weight categories. It may seem obvious, but if you have no weight categories, does this mean all the champions are big? Well, actually yes it does.

We have a twisted view of this as we are so used to our sports competitions being in weight categories - boxing, MMA, judo, wrestling and so on. Even light contact combat sports like new style Olympic Taekwondo are in weight categories! This is how important size is.

If we had no weight categories today, would we have ever heard of Floyd Mayweather, Manny Pacquio, Oscar de la Hoya, Conor McGregor, Robbie Lawler and so on? Probably not. If every combat sport was without weight categories, boxers would all be like the modern heavyweights, 6' 6" and taller. The MMA fighters would be big too, not necessarily all tall but all heavy, solid guys.

Size is so important in combat sports that fighters will regularly drop weight by 'cutting water' prior to a weigh-in. So, if my fight is on Saturday and my weigh-in on Friday, I will spend the week before the weigh-in driving water out of my body by 'water loading', drinking excessive amounts of water to get my body to flush it through. I then stop drinking water and my body continues to drive the water out.

If I also lose water through saunas (which allow me to sweat without losing energy) I can drop as much as 10 kgs (22lb) or more before the fight! Of course this is very dangerous but the top fighters get used to this routine. They then have a day to get fluids and salts back into their bodies.

When you meet these smaller fighters in person you get a shock at how big they are compared to what they weigh-in at.

Of course, this creates a weight cutting 'arms race' to see how big you can be for the weight division you fight at. I have cut weight for competition and it's a miserable experience. The feeling of thirst on the last day is horrible. Fighters go through this though as pride, money and fame are the rewards for winning.

Size is an advantage not simply down to strength. The bigger man also may have more range to his strikes so can engage an opponent at a distance where he can strike but not be struck back. In a competition over many rounds, this advantage can be a very big one by itself.

The bigger man may also be able to generate more force in his strikes. If we accept that both parties in these fights have equally trained strikes then in general the bigger man can deliver more force. This is a case of him being able to recruit muscles of bigger size and strength and to utilise the momentum of a bigger frame.

There are fighters who are a bit shorter than their opponents in the same weight class, but they are still in the same weight class. Often the shorter fighter may be more muscular so will need to mitigate the opponents range advantage with movement.

Even in Brazilian jiu-jitsu which was designed for the smaller man to defeat the bigger man, there are weight classes in competitions.

You may ask why this is - surely the point is to be able to beat bigger guys? But Brazilian jiu-jitsu was developed to defeat bigger guys that had no ground training. Once the bigger guy knows jui-jitsu or grappling of another kind, he has the advantage unless the other man is very much more skilled.

I have watched my friend grapple with men 30kgs heavier and tie them in knots. But he is a BJJ black belt with 17 years of training and these huge men were beginners by comparison. Also, with no striking allowed, skill in grappling is of course, paramount.

On the ground, if you are of comparable skill level but the other guy is significantly bigger, you are in big trouble as a general rule.

We know that so many of the martial arts have traditions that do not necessarily reflect the reality of being attacked in normal everyday life. If this is so, we need to go back to our purpose and if our purpose is to protect ourselves for real we need to look at how we might be attacked and go from there.

If we begin with this as our starting point, we may well find that much in traditional martial arts that is useful. If we find things that are not useful, we can discard them. As Bruce Lee said "Absorb what is useful, discard what is useless and add what is specifically your own". This is an often repeated quote, not just because it is a good one, but because it is very easy to say and to understand.

The difficult bit and the bit that is poorly understood is how to do this. For that, we need to understand PRINCIPLES - and how to train them.

CHAPTER 7
THE ESSENCE OF FIGHTING

"Yet there will be people in the world who think that even if you learn martial arts, this will not prove useful when a real need arises. Regarding that concern, the true science of martial arts means practising them in such a way that they will be useful at any time, and to teach them in such a way that they will be useful in all things."

Miyamoto Musashi, *The Book of Five Rings.*

"Doctrine is a guide to anyone who wants to learn about war from books: it will light their way, ease their progress, train their judgement and help them avoid pitfalls. Doctrine is meant to educate the minds of future commanders...not to accompany them to the battlefields."

Von Clausewitz, *On War*

The aim of this chapter is not to be a comprehensive technical manual of all the possible techniques of fighting to defend yourself. You must learn that in the Moving Centre by attending physical training lessons. What can be done in a book though is to educate the Moving part of the Intellectual Centre on the essence and principles of our subject. Then you will be able to separate the wheat from the chaff and know what your physical training should be geared towards. You will know then if it is relevant to the particular problems, challenges and opportunities that exist in a fight to defend yourself.

This chapter should serve as an example of how we 'distil the essence' of an area of study. I have chosen self-defence as the vehicle in which to do this as the lessons we can learn from it are largely lacking in our modern society. When we know how to distil the essence of a subject, we can do it with any area of study.

Remember we start with the physical body because our body is the most direct way to experience things. We can know then that what we learn is 'real' and genuine, not just flouncy, untested theory. When you are pouring with sweat sparring with an opponent, you feel the TRUTH of it. This is the foundation on which to build. You are building your house upon a rock.

What's the aim of fighting in self-defence? Well, going back a step we can safely state that the aim of sports fighting is to WIN. But what about self-defence, where no belts or medals are available? You might say that the aim of self-defence training is to survive - and this is, of course, essential. But we should be reaching higher than that and aim to RESOLVE THE SITUATION.

Keeping this aim as our focus should mean that our training remains relevant. By 'resolving the situation' what do we mean? I can survive a street attack yet have physical and mental scars that last a lifetime. Whilst I cannot guarantee that this will not happen, it's not a price I want to pay. So my aim is to leave the situation pretty much as I was before it occurred. This is what I call 'resolving the situation'.

Maybe the best way to achieve my aim in a given situation is to run away. Can you see why fighting is not just a case of learning techniques? If I am victim to the FALSE EGO, I will not take the opportunity to leave a situation if I can and still feel good about it.

I spoke at length to a friend of mine who was very badly beaten up by a gang of five men. He had to take six weeks off work and still has numbness in his face where a key went through his cheek and broke off one of his teeth. The key had been sticking out of the fist of one of his assailants.

This friend of mine was a keen boxer who loved to come down to the gym to train and spar. He was a strong and well-built young man who trained hard. He had been waiting on his own for his girl-friend to pick him up after a night out in a part of Manchester. As misfortune would have it, a gang of men arrived looking to do injury to a man they believed to be in a pub near where my friend was waiting. Finding the pub shut but amped up on adrenaline, these charming characters looked around for someone to pick on.

Seeing my friend waiting by the side of the road they went over and began to ask him seemingly casual questions about where he was from and how many people he knew around here. My friend said he knew something was wrong when one of them started to walk around him.

Rather than take the opportunity to move though, he stood his ground. He was able to fire off some good punches back when the man at his side hit him, but after that he was attacked on all sides and ended up on the ground receiving blow after blow from his standing opponents. He was very lucky that an ambulance happened to be going past as he lay there bleeding and got him to hospital. I asked him why he hadn't moved when he realised something was wrong. He said "I have never run away from a fight in my life".

This is a fundamental error in thinking, made worse by the fact that he revealed to me that he had been a schoolboy champion sprinter! In battle, an army sometimes has to do a 'tactical withdrawal'. If you like you can call it running away. On occasion, a good tactical withdrawal lays the foundation for future success. Dunkirk instantly comes to mind as one such example.

A tactical withdrawal occurs when a commander sees that he cannot win or that the cost of trying to defeat the enemy would be too high. Rather than waste combat power, the commander withdraws his force so that they can fight another day. If a commander cannot do this out of personal pride (false ego) he risks losing not only the battle but also the war. If an enemy commander can see such a weakness in his opponent he may even try and provoke him to attack in an unwise situation when he is outnumbered and outgunned.

If you are facing five men and you are on your own, you are definitely outnumbered and most probably outgunned. The only way you would seek to fight this number is if you have no other way of trying to resolve the situation. Unless you are an absolute beast and the five guys are the world's worst fighters, you are in serious trouble.

To be able to run away and live with yourself is possible if you realise the truth of this and do not rely on 'being tough' and 'facing up to anyone' to feed your ego. It is simple mathematics to realise the odds are not in your favour. Talking of 'being honourable' and so forth is romantic nonsense - you do not need to 'act honourably' to those who show you no honour. The codes of honourable men only apply to other men of honour. This is why in the days of duelling, a gentleman was not expected to accept a challenge from a man who was not also a gentleman.

If you are worried about proving your courage, there will be plenty of occasions to do that without paying such a heavy price when it is not necessary. To engage in circumstances like this without having to only proves that you cannot appraise a situation correctly.

It is rare among soldiers that have been and fought in places like Afghanistan to find one who boasts about how brave he is. In fact, I cannot think of a single one of my comrades who I have ever heard 'bigging up' their bravery. I can think of many who bravely admit being scared however. This type of fear is sensible and helps us to make good decisions.

Think of the difference between this fight and a combat sport like mixed martial arts. Even in a sport like MMA, which allows punches, kicks, elbows, knees, grappling and so on there is still a couple of very important rules. You know that the fight is one on one guaranteed. You know the opponent will not produce a weapon or pick up an improvised weapon like a bar stool or bottle. You know the time that the fight will take place and you know where the fight will take place.

You know what, you know when and you know where. None of these things are known in a fight for real. There is a general difference here between a consensual fight between two parties and a fight where we have an aggressor or aggressors on an un-expectant opponent.

The key difference is one of VULNERABILITY. In simple terms if we wish to state the difference between sports fighting and self-defence it is that in self-defence we are far more vulnerable. We often will not know anything about our attackers, nor will we know if other parties will join in, either on our side or on the other side.

We are vulnerable not only to our opponents but to damage from the environment as well. Because we do not know where the fight will take place there may be kerbstones, gravel, street furniture, actual furniture, walls, stairways, vehicles and so forth. We must have the same agility and robustness in the Moving Centre as we need in the Emotional and Intellectual Centres.

That vulnerability and danger is obvious when I think of the consequences of being knocked unconscious. In an MMA fight if my opponent renders me unconscious either by a choke or by striking the referee will stop the fight. If I am taking big damage, the referee will even step in and put himself between my opponent and myself to stop the fight. If this happens in a real fight, there is no referee and medics on standby to ensure my safety. Getting incapacitated could cost me my life. This is no game.

MMA is undoubtably one of the toughest sports there is. No-one should doubt that the fighters are incredibly tough and brave men and women that face serious injury every time they step into the arena. But that risk is mitigated by rules and safety precautions. As dangerous as MMA is, it does not carry the same uncertainty as the 'ambush' of a real fight.

I am not claiming that people who train in self-defence are somehow intrinsically tougher than those who train MMA. It is simply not about that. After all, MMA fighters are not training with the understanding that they will try and avoid a fight if possible! They train, knowing the risks and yet still choose to fight! In training self-defence we prepare to fight but do so only if this is the best or only way to resolve the situation. The great benefit of training in both sports and self-defence will covered later in this chapter.

The aspect of 'preparation' is an important one. The referee asks the fighters before a bout if they are ready. In a real fight, no-one asks if you are ready. You will get some warning or you won't but in any event you did not enter that place at that time to fight.

Perhaps you just went out for a drink, or for a walk with your wife or husband. Maybe you went to watch a sports event with your family. Sports fighters go to a specific location at a specific time with the precise intention of fighting. Their adrenaline and endorphin levels are up, they have their mouthguards in and gloves on. Their senses are on red alert ready to go. They bounce up and down and stretch ready for action and stripped to the waist. They may have been preparing for this fight for a number of months, studying their opponent. They know what's coming. When the fight starts they are not surprised when the other guy comes out and tries to do them harm!

If we accept this, then at the least we can say that the unexpected nature of the non-consensual fight creates a different emotional and intellectual dynamic. We are not emotionally prepared, nor is our mind ready to go, visualising possibilities and going over and over our game plan. So we at the least need to train with this in mind - but what about the physical differences? Isn't it just the same as MMA, even if we bear in mind that the element of surprise and lack of preparation is a factor? Well, no actually.

Here an analogy may be helpful. Think back to the duellers who fought with rapiers. The rapier was invented as a weapon for duelling. It gives us good length in a forward direction and is thin and sharply pointed in order to thrust. Often it was teamed with a very small round shield known as a 'buckler' or at the height of the art, with a dagger to form a two bladed style.

In a duel, I know that I will be facing a similarly armed opponent, in fact the rules demand it. This will be a one on one fight guaranteed. All my problems, and all my potential problems will come from the single reference point of my opponent. I can see my opponent at all times and he can see me. We are face to face. Neither of us is wearing armour.

How would that change if I knew for a moment that I might be facing more than one opponent? Well, a clever answer would be that if I knew I might be facing more than one opponent I would have the chance to either not show up or to bring some of my own friends! This is perfectly true, but for the purposes of the analogy let us imagine that I have no choice but to turn up.

I would definitely want to be wearing some form of armour now as the attacks may come from more than one direction simultaneously and I cannot possibly cover them all. Even if this is just a helmet my chances will improve.

I may also wish to consider having a larger shield to protect me as well as the attacks may come from different distances depending on the weapons of my opponents. Given that a rapier is very good in one direction but not as a slashing weapon, would I also want to consider changing my sword for something that can strike in more than one direction? How will this change my strategy?

Back to the present time, how can I possibly train for the potential of facing more than one opponent given that I have no guarantee that my attacker will be alone? Even if I am attacked by a person who seems to be alone, how will I know that he does not have a friend behind me? How will I know that if I hit the ground, someone else might try and attack me when I am in a particularly vulnerable position?

Those of you that have watched street fights or have been involved in them may have seen a particular phenomenon, especially amongst groups of lads out drinking. Sometimes a fight breaks out between two people but as soon as one of the fighters hits the floor, others come over to attack - some of whom were not even involved at all in the first place in any capacity!

This is a sickening, cowardly but not unusual occurrence. It happens because the individual perceives that they are in no danger from an opponent who is floored so they suddenly get the urge if they are of a violent disposition, exacerbated by drink to do some damage without risk. Doubtless these characters then go and boast about how they beat someone up afterwards (leaving out a few details of course).

It is also the case that someone joining a fight will seek to get either behind you or in a position where you cannot effectively attack them. This is not necessarily a deliberate tactic, it's a result of person instinctively not wishing to expose themselves to your potential strikes. The safest place to do this is from behind, where they perceive that they can hit you, but you cannot hit them. This risk is always present if you find yourself in a situation where you need to defend yourself.

We cannot imagine it away or pretend that it doesn't exist and train only to fight a single opponent. If we train like this we can get in a habit of putting everything in our favour - we start to train without shoes on nice soft mats, we train with one opponent only and without much pressure or chaos. We train as if we are already expecting the attack, we train in a nice clear space in good light and so on. We end up training in such sterilised circumstances that it begins to bear little relation to the type of conditions we may actually find ourselves in.

A basic principle of any training is that we want to train in circumstances as close to the ones we will be facing as possible. This is as true for sports training as it is for military training as it is for self-defence training.

There will be certain limits. For example, in training for operations in the army, we cannot have actual live rounds fired at the troops. What we can do is have live rounds fired overhead from behind, live rounds fired off to the side, explosions in the form of 'battle simulations' going off and the troops firing live rounds on a designated range area. We can have indirect fire in the form of mortars or artillery being fired, we can have troops dropped off by helicopters and so on.

It may never be exactly the same as actual combat conditions but its close enough that relevant and appropriate training can take place. We know it works as troops often say that the training 'kicked in' after the initial shock of combat for real.

Because of the material we have covered in previous chapters, we can identify the fact that when training is described as 'kicking in', it means we have drilled those actions into the Moving Centre. This is absolutely vital as it means that we can free up capacity in the Intellectual Centre in order to assess the situation - which you will remember happens by comparison.

We also need to ensure that our Emotional Centre is sufficiently trained that it does not try to overwhelm us and try and do the jobs of the Moving and Intellectual Centres. That would be an utter disaster! You can spot when an individual is doing physical tasks fuelled by the Emotional Centre - the movements are frantic, erratic and inefficient. You can tell also when the Emotional Centre is trying to do the job of the Intellectual Centre as the decisions lack logic and common sense. In times of stress, without training, the individual will default to trying to do everything through his natural 'centre of gravity'.

The very best training for the individual will take this into account and work more on balancing out that tendency. For example, as I often train businessmen and women working in finance, software and the scientific industries I find many of the clients are strong in the Intellectual Centre. Their natural inclination is to try and do everything with the combat power they have in that Centre.

This means that they do an action then stop and try and review it, rather than just keep going until their body finds the rhythm of the movement of its own accord. To remedy this, I have a host of training exercises that force the individual to react quickly and without analysis. These are best when very simple and dynamic.

The army equivalent of these is obeying drill commands. You can see how if you try and react to drill commands such as 'left turn!' with the Intellectual Centre you will miss the timing beat needed to do it with everybody else.

The result of the wrong centre being used in a fight could be fatal - we fail to act fast enough to protect ourselves or we freeze which is equally bad! We need to let the Moving Centre do this job. Our thinking processes are too slow and just get in the way. If we try and do it with the Emotional Centre our movements will be uncontrolled and all over the place.

This is the secret of learning Moving Centre action and reaction. You will remember that 'imitation' is in the Moving part of the Moving Centre. Imitation is the first step in building these skills in the Moving Centre. There is no substitute for this but most people never get past this stage as they simply don't put the time and effort in necessary to sufficiently develop the skill. But there is nothing complicated about it. The difficulty is that in our modern world of short attention spans and a thousand distractions is that we do not do it.

Recalling the example I used of 'starting the diet tomorrow' we have a group of mechanical dolls that would very much like to have the physical skills we are seeking. But we have many other groups of mechanical dolls that would like to take the kids to the park, sit on the sofa and watch TV and so forth. If these seem the easier and more attractive option at the time, our training will lose out. This is most definitely not FREEWILL. This is our usual, divided, rather mediocre self.

We can never get beyond this phase unless we put the time in but it need not be torture. Having a training partner helps. But even alone, if we make the experience as pleasant as possible we are more likely to do it. I put on my favourite music for example if I am drilling movements. I take video footage of my training to review later. Most of all though, I use a timer.

Often when we train we do so at very little intensity. This means we spend an hour training but only really get ten minutes of actual training in. Far better to identify say, a twenty minute period of training maybe split into five minute blocks with two minutes rest in between. This is then more of less a half hour training session. It doesn't seem much but if we use a timer and train at high intensity we will find we get good very quickly. But we must work out exactly what we are training beforehand.

We will come back to training plans later but if you trained for half an hour every day you would be amazed by the level of your progress in a relatively short period of time. We must have the training frequency for our Moving Centre to develop the necessary skills. If we do a long duration but infrequently we will not get the same results. Every day, even if we can only fit five minutes in is better.

Everybody has five minutes available every day. Nearly all of us will have half an hour. We need not go to the gym, we can train anywhere we have some space. Most people have absolutely no idea of the high standard they can get too, simply by doing a small intense amount of training with high frequency. It is difficult at the beginning to believe this which is why so few of us actually ever get really good at anything. This is a tragic waste of your potential. Although the process is not easy, it IS simple.

RESOLVING THE SITUATION

By far, one of the most difficult moments in circumstances where a fight may occur is knowing when to run and when to fight. If we are attacked out of the blue the situation is clear - we need to fight to protect ourselves right now. Maybe the opportunity to escape will come later but in the instant, we need to react.

But sometimes these situations start with a glance or with a few words before escalating to a physical confrontation. If I keep in mind my aim of RESOLVING THE SITUATION it may not come down to that. Ideally we never come to blows as train hard as I may, there is always the chance that I come off worse. This means the risk of serious injury or death.

We need to understand why it is that people look to start fights. I have been around physical, aggressive men my whole life and observed their behaviour at work and at play. I have also observed my own behaviour over the years and seen many changes.

If we take for example, young men with a habit of drinking too much and of naturally aggressive tendencies. I now regard these men as being at an earlier stage of emotional evolution than myself. The young man's ego can be a delicate thing. Perhaps he feels that he has not yet 'proved' himself. Perhaps he believes that self-esteem is to be had by dominating others.

Either way, particularly when mixed with alcohol this is not good. I am using as an example young men - but this is not to say that they are the only people that start fights, not at all. We need only look at examples of 'road rage' to see that young men do not own aggression nor do they own foul language! But this group will give us a good working model for potential fight starters.

Rory Miller uses the term 'monkey dance' to explain the kind of ritual of looking to start a fight for reasons of ego. I like the term as it reflects the animalistic nature of seeking dominance in a situation.[36] Men doing the 'monkey dance' say things like 'have you got a problem?' and 'what are you looking at?'. When I was stationed near Newcastle, the joke was that the men in the town had developed this into an art form and that it had become 'are you looking at my mate's pint?'! These questions might be ridiculous but they are seeking dominance, either by the person they are directed at doing a gesture of submission or by fighting them into submission.

Sometimes then, the easiest way to resolve the situation is by giving them what they want. "Have you got a problem? "no mate, not at all.' 'Are you looking at my mate's pint?' 'No I'm not'. I remember an occasion when a total enormous thug of a bloke saw me staring at his girlfriend on a night out. I was staring at her with good reason. Not only was she movie star beautiful, she was dressed up to the nines and was wearing very little. It was impossible not to stare. In fact her whole look was designed to be attention grabbing. Perhaps this was the point. The thug had deliberately gone out on the town with a 'look at me' girlfriend to catch people staring at her who he could then intimidate.

Such a person is highly dangerous. It is likely his ego is pretty fragile and needs little encouragement. There is also a kind of girl that enjoys seeing men fight over her. Perhaps that is why she was with such a no-neck animal. This thug said to me 'Are you staring at my girlfriend?' This was a difficult question to answer because I was. In fact he had made eye contact with me as soon as I took my eyes off her ample and well displayed cleavage (which were like two perfect round blancmanges presented on a tray just for me). I said 'yeah, is she on Hollyoaks? (Hollyoaks being a local soap opera which has a cast of attractive women). He said 'No' and maintained his ice cold stare. I repeated 'No?' and looked away with a shrug.

Catching him out of corner of my eye I could see him not entirely convinced but in enough doubt not to take it further. His ego had been sufficiently boosted by me suggesting his girlfriend was attractive enough to be a TV star and pretending I was trying to work out if she was famous was just about good enough to excuse my stare. He was also expecting me to say 'no' and therefore contradict him.

Perhaps his next gambit would have been 'yes you are' followed by 'are you calling me a liar?' and so on.

Regardless, what I didn't say was 'yes I am looking at your girl-friend. I'm looking right at her wonderful boobies and I am wondering why she is with such an ugly fat gay bastard like you'. It is fairly certain that this would have made him swing for me! In that one sentence I would have pushed all his buttons of insecurity. Why else was he spending all that time in the gym to get inflated muscles that he did not need to use? Why else was he wearing a skin tight white t-shirt with a bottle tan but to show them off - to other men!

This situation was resolved on that occasion by my looking away at the end. Sometimes this gesture of submission is all it needs when these type of people try and stare you down. If they want to think they are dominant - let them. It should be no skin off your nose to do this if you do not have a fragile ego yourself. It never fails to amaze me how many people simply cannot bring themselves to do this.

Think of when someone gives you a shoulder bump walking down the street. This is a tactic some guys will use as a way of starting the confrontation in which they want to show dominance. A quick 'sorry mate' even if it's not your fault may be all it takes to resolve the situation.

There is another possibility here. Sometimes you may feel like the character of the aggressor is such that he will only be encouraged by a gesture of submission and takes things further. A friend of mine has a way of sighing when he is challenged and saying 'come on mate' as if he is slightly bored of the situation and its pointlessness. He also does this when beggars aggressively ask him for money.

For him it works well and I have used it myself a few times when you feel the aggressor is more of an opportunist who will cause trouble if he sees weakness but not bother if he sees you are not taking part in the game.

The word 'feel' is important here as it is down to your ability to read the aggressors emotional state. This emotional acuity comes from developing a sensitivity to read another persons feelings. I will explain how to train this later.

This also helps when we feel that a show of aggression from us will resolve the situation better. Years ago I was with a friend in Scarborough out on the town when a young lad started to provoke my friend by commenting on his premature baldness. My friend laughed him off. This young lad then took a step towards him and without warning my friend shot out his hand and gripped him hard by the throat. He very briefly suggested to him that he find his kicks elsewhere. The young lad disappeared quickly.

All of the above examples are to do with dominance. Firstly we have the problem of how to read the situation correctly and then we have the problem of what to do about it. We will never be sure that what we are doing is right until after we have done it. So how do we do this? What many conflict resolution books and instructors miss out or don't appreciate is that we need to be aware of the effect that we as individuals have on potential attackers.

For example, I once went to a session with a former nightclub bouncer who was talking about these kind of confrontations. He was talking about all kinds of tactics of how to question them to distract them and all sorts. It was all based on his vast experience of working the doors. But that is the problem. The dynamic he had experience of was as a huge, aggressive looking sober man facing drunk young blokes. He was backed up by others and was in a position of obvious responsibility as a doorman. This did not mean he did not get attacked ever, far from it. Some of my own students who are doormen and women can tell you incredible stories of their experiences. But for this particular guy, his size and look alone creates a different emotional state in his attacker than, for example I do.

I stand at 5' 8" and am around twelve stone. I look like I do physical activity but am not super muscular. Befitting a former British Army officer, I wear shirts with folded up sleeves and brown brogues as casual wear. In addition, I am tattoo free and have a sensible side parting haircut. I physically intimidate no one. Neither can I rely on others being cautious to start a fight with me.

If you have tattoos and a shaven head, stand well over six foot with a large build and have a face that looks like you have been hit with a bag of spanners you will find that people feel differently about you. I know this well as I used to hang around with guys like this when I played rugby league.

A couple of those standing next to me meant that I never had any trouble on our nights out. It was more of a problem not being allowed into venues as the bouncers would be looking at them thinking what a pain it would be to try and get them to leave if they kicked off.

The point about this is that if you recognise the effect you have on others, you will be better able to resolve a situation. It is not the same for everyone. My clientele is very largely businessmen and women - white collar workers who are your average family man or woman, not guys that look like they are heavyweight boxers.

Generally the dynamic is different between a man and a woman as well. It is absolutely a part of training to observe others reactions to you. Very often people ask me in the street for directions. Strangers will often talk to me and I am a magnet for the mad people you get on public transport. This tells me that I have a friendly face and people feel safe with me.

As a salesman, I was often praised for my affable style that made clients pleased to see me. If I am aware of this then I am aware of how I might need to conduct myself in situations of potential conflict. Certainly it is easier for me than others to gain the element of surprise by attacking first for example.

We have said how your training must be personal to you in order to take into account your natural strengths in the 'centres'. Your training furthermore must take into account your personal attributes, including how others are emotionally affected by you.

RECOGNISE YOURSELF

The entire process of training can be thought of as 'recognising yourself' 'Recognise' is the perfect word as it literally means 'know again'. We must lay aside the familiarity we have with ourselves and instead view ourselves as if looking at a strange foreign creature.

What are that creatures properties? How does it look? What

is it feeling at this moment? What is it thinking? Look at it now - losing its temper. Look at it now - frustrated trying to get in work on time. Look at it now - feeling pleased with itself after being praised.

One of the appalling problems of being human is our forgetfulness. I am not talking about the fact that we keep losing our car keys. The problem is much graver than that.

The basic human condition is that we forget our aims, forget what we should be doing, forget our responsibilities to others and more than anything forget ourselves. We cease to be fully attentive in a given moment and instead are absorbed into whatever daydream of the past or future we are involved in at that time. When we drive in a car our minds take a holiday and go into a state of hypnosis.

When we do a repetitive task our minds similarly clock off. When we are at work we dream of being somewhere else. When we are somewhere else we worry about work. Our mind does anything but be fully awake in the present moment.

SELF-OBSERVATION

Perhaps you have experienced an occasion when you thought your life was in danger. I will bet that the memory of it is clear and sharp. At times like these we actually live in the moment, thoughts about the future and past do not exist. These are times to cherish as we are fully conscious for once! If we are fully awake all the time we would remember everything as it was and be able to learn at a truly astonishing rate. Our memories that we hold dear are very often nothing like what actually happened.

It is always revealing to meet up with old friends to reminisce on old experiences. Time and time again our friends remind us of things we had forgotten and have very different versions of events we think we remember accurately. How often have you heard someone recount a tale of an experience that you were a part of and think 'that's not what happened AT ALL!'.

Sometimes people will remember themselves as the victim in a story when in fact they were the villain. Rarely are our memories actual objective records of the truth. One of the training preparations for Northern Ireland is going through a scenario simulator. This is like a video game in that it has a large screen that you stand in front of holding a rifle that has a gas system to give a realistic recoil. They play a scenario film in front of you with balaclava-wearing terrorists firing at you and you having to do what you think is right in the circumstances.

What was so fascinating about this is that when they debriefed you after, they ask simple questions about how many terrorists they were, what colour the cars were and so on. Every person that goes through the same scenario has different answers. When they let you watch it back you can't believe that you are seeing the same film!

If we are to properly recognise ourselves and be aware of our own natures, we will need to create a passive observer to remember them for us. This passive observer is like our very own CCTV camera that will record our every waking moment.

We can do this by imagining that we are duplicated and have a clone of ourselves. That clone takes up a position above us, floating in space but watching us at all times. Because this is our clone, we can see through its eyes and it can see through ours too. In this way, in our imagination, we can watch ourselves going about our daily business, our brains simultaneously receiving the input from our own eyes and from the clones watching us. We created our passive observer. At the moment, our observer simply records our actions. The observer does not analyse or comment.

It is nowhere near as hard to do this as it sounds. Do it now and you will see what I mean. The hard part is to remember to do it, which is, of course, the problem that we are trying to overcome. It makes sense to start by making sure this observer is switched on and recording whenever we train to begin with. By making this part of our routine, we can have the observer watch us doing physical training. He will have a lot to see as he watches us sweat and toil.

Training in any physical activity is very much the art of recognising yourself. We recognise ourself visually, we recognise our bodies spatially. We recognise our emotional state. Are we getting frustrated? Are we starting to feel angry in sparring as we cannot

SELF-OBSERVATION

land a strike on our opponent? Is our ego bruised by a good training partner that we perceive as being 'better' than us? The observer sees all of this.

As we train, we learn to recognise our bodies and where each limb is at a given time. We recognise our posture through trial and error. Our bodies begin to develop balance as the nerves feedback information which the brain becomes more sensitive to. Little by little, our body becomes better known to us. We cease to feel like we are numb and moving through treacle and instead feel sharp and poised. This happens by using the body in new ways, challenging our bodies to balance and move. The body responds to the challenge by learning.

Ultimately, if we can recognise our bodies spatially, we can control our bodies. If we can recognise our emotional state, we can control our emotions. If we recognise the environment we are in, we can control our environment. When I use the word 'control' I am not suggesting that that control is total.

To have total control over our emotions is a rare and advanced level! But we can have enough of a control to be able to achieve our aim of resolving the situation. The process is then continued with our opponent. If we can recognise our opponent's body spatially we can control our opponent's body with our own. If we can recognise our opponents emotional state we can control it.

This process starts with self-observation. We will also need an instructor. We need an instructor because we, as humans, are unable to see our own habits and our habitual behaviour. This is why, whatever level we are at, we need someone external to help us. We must not make the mistake of thinking we can do it all on our own. Simply put, an instructor's job is to make you more aware of yourself, not to do the job of learning for you. The instructor will of course give you technical information, but you could get this from a book. What you cannot get from a book is the continual process of becoming aware of yourself.

I once had a student come up to train with me who had only trained in self-defence previously from videos. He had spent many hours training at home from these videos and his technical knowledge was good. He suggested that he was now at an advanced level. He moved like a robot malfunctioning. What was happening in his head was not what his body was actually doing. Imagine his disappointment (disbelief at first) when I told him his actual level. I knew this would be hard to take so I filmed him training so he could watch it back for himself compared to what he thought he was doing.

Fair play to him, he then knuckled down and started to train with a renewed vigour - precisely the right attitude to have! I film training a great deal, it's a great way for a student to see themselves and know themselves better.

Fortunately with modern technology it's never been easier, you can do it on your phone and even use apps that can help you see it in slow motion and draw on the screen to show angles and so forth. My students can go home after a session with a visual record of their training and also of me demonstrating certain technical aspects they may be struggling with so they can review them later.

The process of the body learning awareness of itself is not easy to explain but imagine how people who have lost use of their hands can learn to use their feet to write, draw and paint with.

The first step in this is for their minds to recognise their feet and the individual muscles and bones of the feet in a way that it has never done before. This ability is latent in us all, yet we only develop it if we are forced to do so. Imagine the dexterity that a copper-plate engraver has with their hands. This is why the basic apprenticeship was seven years for these crafts - it takes that long to build the sensitivity and awareness to the skill level required.

Our work is more of a gross motor movement than this and so the basic skills do not take as many hours to develop. But like engraving, there is no limit to how skilled we can become.

Even though we use our limbs and body daily we only do so in a very small range of movement, especially if we work in an office. The body forgets how to move in different ways and we need to reawaken it. If you look at the movement of a child playing in a cardboard box you will see what I mean.

As children we all move up and down off the ground and seem to have no limit on our movement save for our imagination. When we become adults we stiffen up and only move as much as our weekly routine dictates. The vast majority of us have no idea of what our body is capable of anymore.

This is true of our emotions as well. If we get into a routine of familiar, limited situations and events we can lose the intensity and variety of emotions we experienced as children - joy, wonder, fear, delight, terror and so on. We even think of these emotions as being 'childish' but if that's the case then we are not sufficiently challenging ourselves.

One of the great satisfactions of training people is to see them experience emotions that they had not felt for a long time. They describe these emotions as feeling suddenly 'alive' again and this is a powerful feeling that we need to experience more in order to stay in contact with the full potential of the Emotional Centre.

RECOGNISING EMOTIONS

For me to be able to make a good judgement when a potential conflict is occurring, the best way I can prepare myself is by learning to recognise my own emotions and the emotions of others. This study will help me more than any intellectual appreciation of various conflict resolution strategies. I can learn them from a book. The ability to sense my opponent's emotional state I cannot.

When I train with others, if I have my observer in place I can record emotional reactions. If I have my observer in place when I am in crowds, watching sports events, concerts and so forth I will begin to focus my attention and really study myself and other people properly for the first time. By having a part of my attention passively observing without being caught up in habitual reaction, I can objectively see these emotions at work. By observing I can build a sensitivity to read the situation better.

I remember being in a bar with a group of friends. I could see one of our group talking to a big man whom I didn't know. My friend looked terrified. I went over to see what was going on, but stood near my friend without making eye contact with the big guy.

The big guy stepped in towards me, puffed his chest out and shoulder bumped me. I felt an icy ball of alarm right in my guts. Trusting my 'gut reaction' (literally) I grabbed the big guy's chest and punched him in the face.

He was knocked out cold and lay twitching on the floor. I marched quickly out of the bar. The bouncer on the door, not certain what had happened grabbed my arm. I said 'I'm leaving' and he instinctively let me go. I certainly did not want to rely on the bouncers having read the situation right. For all I know he might have been a friend of theirs. I didn't want to wait to find out.

Down the road I asked my friend (who had exited the bar close behind me) what the big guy had said to him. My friend's stony white face told the story 'he said he had just got out of prison and was going to hurt me to get back in'. No wonder he had looked terrified. What my gut had told me was that something was all wrong. The way the big guy had reacted was beyond the simple 'monkey dance'.

When I thought about it later I could piece together other clues that I may have subconsciously picked up on. He was out by himself. He didn't have a drink. He was a lot older than most of the people in there, he looked out of place. But mainly there was something in his demeanour that seemed serious. He was still and didn't seem agitated in the slightest. God only knows what he had been in prison for. He was serious enough that my gut felt fear and let me know in no uncertain terms.

I mentioned before about being aware of the effect you have on people. Maybe if I had been a big bruiser the guy would have attacked me first. Maybe he wouldn't have bothered at all. But by shoulder bumping a small guy not making eye contact he advertised his intention to do harm. He gave me a warning, thank you very much. Who knows how many other people he may have done that to, in prison or on the outside? Looking at me, he had no way of knowing the hours and hours of training I had put in on that single punch. The emotional content produced by the situation combined with the muscle memory of the practiced punch produced a strike of real power. In his head, after the shoulder bump, I imagine he envisaged a little bit more provocation for his amusement before he would be the one doing the violence. That is not how it panned out.

Of course, you are not always so sure. I remember walking home with friends late one night when we realised we were being followed by a lanky dude in a tracksuit. Eventually he was walking right behind my friend who turned around and asked him what he wanted. He was either very drunk or on drugs. What he said made no sense but he was fronting up like he was looking to fight and still coming forward. I put my hands out in a stop gesture and noticed the kerb behind him was raised. The ground after the kerb was a sharp descent down a grass verge. I didn't really feel it with this guy. He was being kind of aggressive but slurring his words.

The whole thing was unpredictable - he could just as easily have pulled a needle out or a knife. Or he might have suddenly have asked which bus stop to go to for the number 36. As he continued to come forward I cut the distance between us and shot both hands out in an explosive push.

Sure enough he shot backwards, tripped over the kerb and disappeared down the grass verge rolling like he had been unfurled from a carpet. He lay in a heap at the bottom, dragged himself to his feet and sloped off.

Some people are of the 'if there is any doubt, strike' school of thought but whenever you strike you have to understand that potentially you can kill that person.

This exact thing happened to an off duty policeman not long ago in Liverpool and there are many other examples. This is no game and judgement is necessary. It is not a thing to take lightly. If you strike someone and kill them or do them serious and lasting damage you need to live with the consequences of your actions. This does not mean you fail to act when necessary, but you do it with judgement.

Sometimes simple foreknowledge is all it takes. As a young man I was out and about in Leeds with some of the rugby league boys. I was chatting to one of our props when I could see a shifty looking guy hanging around and trying to get noticed. He came over and when my friend the prop caught his eye he managed to get 'what the fuck are you loo-' out of his mouth before my friend hit him clean with two straight punches. He scrambled out pretty quickly after picking himself up. I looked in surprise at my friend. He said 'that was the lunatic who broke John's nose last weekend in the Skyrack'. My friend had recognised him and acted appropriately.

THE OODA LOOP

If there is a single principle at work here despite the various tactics employed, it concerns the OODA loop. The OODA loop is also known as the Decision - Action cycle and it is used to describe the process that leads to an individual taking action.

It was created by John Boyd, an American fighter pilot who used it to explain and train the process needed to successfully engage an opponent in a dog fight in the air. It has also been used to focus strategic level military operations.

The OODA loop is one of those 'Holy Grails' of principles in that it is so clearly expressed that it can be applied to big actions, small actions and everything in between It's also perfect for describing the process we need to train for self-defence.

The OODA loop works like this Observation - Orientation - Decision - Action. It is a cycle because as soon as an action is taken the process begins again until the next action and so on. If I can do this process faster than my opponent, I am dictating the outcome. To do this process as fast as possible is what I am aiming for.

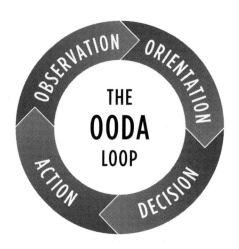

What this means for us is that our Observation needs to be trained within an inch of its life. By 'Observation' in this context we mean our ability to sense an input - visual, auditory, kinaesthetic. So we SEE an opponent coming in to strike. We HEAR him saying he is going to knock our block off. We FEEL him grab us or strike us. Collectively we can call our ability to sense these inputs as AWARE-NESS.

To prove that this principle of needing Observation first can be applied to all scales of action consider these words from Machiavelli:

> *The prince that does not detect evils the moment they appear is lacking in true wisdom; but few rulers have the ability to do so.*[37]

The key skill Machiavelli is taking about is Observation - our awareness of events. You can see now why rulers put so much effort into spies and surveillance!

Then we need to know what these inputs mean - this is Orientation. I see a person coming towards me and I assess he is looking to attack. I hear a person talking to me and can understand that it means he wants to fight. I feel a person grab me and know it's to hurt me.

In other words, I correctly interpret these inputs as being a precursor to an attack and recognise that person as an opponent. If I receive an attack out of the blue I have received an input - I need to have enough wits left to be able to understand what has happened! Clearly, if this attack leaves me unconscious or dis-orientated I cannot go any further in the cycle until my wits return.

My decision is then a response to what I have observed and what I have interpreted it as meaning. A person out of the blue launches a punch at my head. I see the punch coming and understand what it means - my head is about to be taken off. I 'decide' what to do - in this case get the hell out of the way as there is no time for anything else. This leads to my ACTION. I slip the punch to the left. The cycle then starts again. I see that he has over committed to the punch and is off balance with his head exposed. I know what this means as I have drilled this a thousand times so my ORIENTATION recognises the situation.

My decision is based on where my body is at that moment. I feel balanced and know that my own punch to his head is possible. My DECISION is made. My ACTION is punching his head. He falls to the ground. The cycle starts again. Observing that he is in no state to launch another attack I become aware that any extra action would be beyond the legal boundaries of the law of the land - I am orientated to the situation. My decision is to walk away which my legs obey and the ACTION is taken.

My opponent got through a whole cycle but his action was not fast enough to prevent me observing it and starting my own cycle. My success was down to my speed in the cycle. We can describe this as 'getting inside my opponent's OODA loop'. When we look at the nature of fighting an opponent, we should appreciate that at times, my decision is not made by the Intellectual Centre. Sometimes the decision is made - such as to slip the punch, by the Moving Centre and I only realise I have done it afterwards. The benefit of that is that my Moving Centre goes much faster than my Intellectual Centre can which you will remember works by comparison.

The driving analogy is useful here again. If a child runs out into the road in front of us the key is to observe the kid as soon as possible - this means we need to be paying attention and therefore have awareness. If we are not daydreaming we can orientate fast - what does the fact that we have seen a child run out in front of us mean? It means we are going to hit a child with our car. A decision is made by the Moving Centre and before we can even think about it, we have hit the brakes.

If we have observed the child fast enough, orientated fast enough, decided fast enough and our brakes are good we have a chance of not hitting the child. If we weren't paying attention to the road, or see the child but don't interpret what's happening quick enough we cannot make the decision fast enough to save the child. If we observe, orientate, decide and act fast but our brakes are poor the child dies too.

It will not surprise you to know that the answer to how to get better at this is training! I need to recognise my body and emotions and those of my opponent right? Because then I can observe and orientate fast. I can train to build fast decisions to the point where they are lightning fast REACTIONS. I can train my individual actions to the point where they are super effective. Like having the best brakes. This is the difference between having worn out drum brakes and the latest ceramic, vented disc brakes with enormous callipers.

It's essential to have the best brakes possible, but even they are no use unless I decide fast enough to use them! Now we can understand in detail why technique is NOT the most important thing when learning to fight.

The quality of our action is important but an 80% solution fast is better than a 100% solution too late. Emotionally I want to be able to operate without being overwhelmed and 'freezing'. Similarly, I need to have enough emotional control that I do not try and do a Moving Centre task with the Emotional Centre. Instead, my Emotional Centre should be utilised to understand the situation better and interpret what is actually going on.

My Intellectual Centre is utilised in this way too, comparing the potential for a conflict to previous experiences. I have in the past, walked into bars and then walked straight back out again, my Intellectual Centre having compared the current environment with previous unhappy occasions.

It is important to realise why we need to be balanced and active in all centres. What would be the use of having a strong and active Intellectual Centre that can recognise danger if my false ego, held in the Emotional Centre, is too strong to allow me to leave? This is not freewill. This is a group of evil mechanical dolls we call the ego, overpowering my common sense. I make no real decision, I am their slave.

My Intellectual Centre is also important in analysing a situation after my initial reactions. No conflict or fight takes place in isolation. In the aftermath for example, do I need to call the police? If my opponent is seriously injured do I need to call an ambulance? I am not talking about 'moral' considerations here, only pragmatic ones. If I don't call an ambulance or report the incident might this come back to me if the incident is investigated by police? A cool, calm and logical head is going to be very important in these moments. This is not something our sports fighter has to worry about or develop! We will examine the factors we should consider in these cases later.

TRAINING THE OODA LOOP

If I know the process I must go through before, during and after the fight I know what I must train for. Now we need to get really into the mechanics of learning to fight to defend yourself. My intention in this part of the book is not to exhaustively go through all the potential techniques that we can employ. This is much better learnt physically.

Rather it is necessary to use examples of techniques that demonstrate principles of fighting, along with suggestions for how we can train our processes. Our ability to use a technique comes from how deeply we hold it in our Moving Centre, not by how many techniques our Intellectual Centre 'knows'.

AWARENESS

A very simple and effective training drill that I first encountered when training with Justo Dieguez, the founder of the self-defence fighting method known as 'Keysi' is the 'black hand'. In the black hand, a group of people are contained within a small space. The small space can occur naturally from your choice of training venue, or you can mark out a small space with cones and have a penalty for stepping outside.

The black hand is a game where every man is for themselves. The aim of the game is to touch the other players on the back without them seeing you doing it whilst avoiding the same happening to you. The penalty for being touched on the back without seeing your opponent do it is to dive down and do two press-ups, then get back up and continue the game.

Many options exist for increasing the pressure in this game. We can change the rules so that ANY touch, whether seen or unseen results in the penalty. We can turn the lights down low and play in semi-darkness to increase the difficulty. We can have flashing lights and loud music playing and so forth. I have played the black hand with others in actual nightclubs borrowed for training sessions. The way that loud music and flashing lights change the dynamic is profound.

These training elements increase the activity of the Emotional Centre and can add confusion as well as sharpening the senses. Also, we can have every student 'shadow fight' at the same time rather than focus purely on touching the others backs. We can have everybody move around solely in the kneeling, sitting or lying positions or have some kneeling, some standing with those in the kneeling trying to touch the standing peoples' legs rather than back.

Many variations are possible with this game but it develops our ability to observe and orientate. It generates a kind of healthy 'paranoia' that becomes a habit.

Our great problem is that unless we have developed a habit under pressure we will 'forget' to do it for real - the behaviour simply won't be there to kick in unless it is habitual. Under pressure, the brain will 'go to what it knows'. The brain hates being confused so will latch on to anything to get out of that confusion. This includes freezing the body if unsure! What we want is to create a 'rugged highway' that the brain can follow when under pressure. It is a familiar highway as we have been on it a thousand times that we can even do it in the pitch black.

Training the 'black hand' reminds me of the situational awareness that we are forced to develop in army training. The constant cry of the instructors whilst training infantry attacks is 'get on your shagging belt buckles!'. This simply means that everyone needs to be either behind cover or making themselves as small as possible at all times during the attack, lying with your belt buckle pressed to the ground. You will never know if you are being targeted by a sniper until the round kills you.

Likewise in the chaos of the battle, shrapnel, bullets and all sorts are winging through the air. The human body is vulnerable, being soft and squidgy. So unless you are in an armoured vehicle you need to be aware of your personal vulnerability at all times. Failure to do this might be fatal. You may of course be able to stand up and walk about and by luck never get hit but why would you take this risk?! No one can tell what is going to happen but we can predict what MAY happen, based on experience. Any vulnerability is likely to be exploited.

Snipers are actively looking for just such an opportunity, the same way that there are 'street snipers' in a fight that will look to hurt you without danger to themselves. This does not mean that we need to lay on the ground during a street fight!! But we need to be able to mitigate the risk from potential threats just the same.

To train our awareness in every position; standing, kneeling, sitting and lying is a crucial part of our approach. I once got into a conversation with a martial arts 'master', who had seen me training in the gym, working my body movement up and down through the standing, kneeling, sitting and lying levels. He came up to me afterwards and said 'why do you spend so much time training at other levels than the standing position, surely you don't think you can be as good at these levels as in the standing position?'

'No,' I said. 'I can punch and kick best from the standing position but I train the other levels in case I end up there from being knocked down, tripping and whatever".

He said, 'In my system, we spend hours training our balance so we would never end up in that position'. I replied 'Have you ever watched gymnastics? Those guys spend ALL their time training their balance but even they fall off - and they don't have people trying to punch them at the same time! If your balance is so good that you can guarantee that you can stay on your feet regardless of your attackers, environment and all that, then all I can say is that you are a lot better than I am!'.

Rather than see my point, he walked off looking very pleased with himself. I think all he really heard was me saying 'you are a lot better than I am!'. The reality is that under pressure from an attacker we can end up in any position before we know it. This means that we will need to learn to fight to defend ourselves in all these positions. Perhaps more so even as we become more vulnerable to attack when we are off our feet.

To think that we become invulnerable just because we train is not only ridiculous but highly dangerous. Long is the list of black belts in one martial art or another who have been humbled in the street not through lack of skill or strength but from a failure to understand their vulnerability.

I have even heard certain martial artists talk about developing an aura through training that somehow dissuades others from attacking you. I have met many of the most highly regarded fighters, both in self-defence martial arts and in sports martial arts. I have never felt that they had an aura like this. The only aura is in people's minds who already know who they are and project magical properties onto them.

But this happens when you meet someone really famous too. Your previous knowledge of them creates an aura when you know who they are. But when you actually spend some time with them this quickly disappears! It IS true that you can pick up on a general feeling of calmness and competence in some people. It is also true that as a potential conflict develops you can sometimes feel like your potential opponent is not very scared. In no circumstances however can you RELY on an opponent not attacking you because of this.

People who have been in many, many fights in the street may well look not very scared. I know men like this. Their outward appearance seems to remain impassive and unreadable. This is no guarantee however that the opponent will respond to this by not being aggressive.

Being aware of our vulnerability is at the heart of our training. This feeling of vulnerability made me want to learn in the first place. I had come back from Afghanistan on leave and had a flat in Liverpool next to a park notorious for muggings. It was in a student area and the muggers would lie in wait to relieve the students of their electronic devices and any money and cards they happened to have on them. I was walking past the entrance to this park one night when a Chinese student came stumbling out in a very bad state. He was covered in blood and practically fell into my arms. High on adrenaline but badly beaten he told me he had been robbed of everything.

I phoned an ambulance and went to work on his cuts. His nose was very badly broken and blood was coming from a gash on his head. I had my gym bag with me from playing squash so wrapped him up in a towel to keep him warm, kept pressure on the wound on his head and kept him talking to calm him down and get his breathing under control. I also wanted him to stop moving about as his arm was hanging in an awkward fashion.

He told me there had been two of them and he had given them what they wanted but they still attacked him, dragging him onto the floor and kicking his head repeatedly. That explained the gash and the broken nose. The ambulance came and the paramedics took over and he was taken to the hospital.

What I felt was a sense of my own vulnerability. I seemed to be living in a different kind of conflict environment with different dangers. Crucially, I had no rifle to protect me, nor the presence of my comrades. It felt ridiculous to have survived riots in Northern Ireland, patrols in Iraq and deployment to Afghanistan and yet feel naked and vulnerable to danger at home! I had trained in martial arts as a young man, but the incident with Tommy made me realise its futility.

When I came across some footage of some guys training in Keysi on the internet, what impressed me immediately was the fact that they were constantly protecting themselves as they fought with their movements. This reminded me of the awareness we have to train for the battlefield. This can never 'guarantee' that you will be OK, but it sure as hell improves your chances!

After my first weekend of training with the Keysi guys, an enormous man who had been teaching us, said 'just remember, I could leave this gym today and a fifteen year old lad could sneak up behind me and put a knife in my back and I would bleed to death and not be able to do anything about it. So don't leave here thinking you are Tommy Ten Men just because you have done some training'.

I almost cheered when he said this as all I had previously encountered with a lot of martial arts training was a lot of macho posturing nonsense and blokes trying to act hard. Here instead was a big strong guy with tremendous skill and power making a point of his vulnerability rather than how strong and tough he was.

It also made me think of the time in my early twenties when I was blindsided with a punch outside of a nightclub. The punch hit me straight on the ear and when I looked up, my assailant was being dragged off by his friends. What if that punch had landed flush on my jaw? Make no bones about it, if we get hit cleanly we are in trouble training or no training. There are no magic tricks or shields of invulnerability. Every violent situation we are in is a potential disaster.

MOVEMENT

How we physically move and fight is going to be a reflection of the understanding of our vulnerability. Bear in mind that unlike sport fighting, I do not have to engage AT ALL necessarily. If my opponent backs away from me, I can keep backing away from him too - all the way home! Throughout this chapter I am going to use the comparison between sport fighting and fighting in self-defence. This is because all of us have seen sport fighting and this is useful to use as a kind of common ground. Indeed, many people labour under the impression that sport fighting and fighting to defend yourself are the same thing, but this is not the case.

In sport fighting I can fight with certain guarantees. The first and most important one as previously mentioned is that the fight is one on one. I need not develop a situational awareness that includes surprise attacks from any angle. If I am standing facing my opponent all of my problems are in front of me. I will, of course need to develop an awareness of the size of the ring or cage - known as 'ring sense'. I will need this to aid my tactics, 'cutting' the ring and so forth. I may wish to make my opponent fight in a smaller space, or I may wish to dominate the centre of the ring and so on.

I will need to know where I am but the ring is a codified size and shape and if I spend time in it I will get familiar with it. Compare that with the uncertainties in the street. The environment is not of our choosing, the time of the fight is not of our choosing, neither is our opponent or opponents. Because I do not know my environment or the number of my opponents my awareness must be of a different degree. I cannot take the same things for granted that I can do in sport. So much of sport competition is in the detailed preparation, the weight cut, the routine on the day, planning your meals and planning your warm up, staying relaxed and so forth.

When I started to compete in Brazilian jiu-jitsu I started to find a routine that worked best for me. I knew when to start to warm up based on the published time of my first bout. I could work out when to get changed, when to tape my fingers and so on. I could go and make myself familiar with what mat I would be fighting on. I could even go and look at my opponent in the knowledge that he will weigh the same as me. All this so I could be best prepared when the time came.

In the street the fundamental nature of the beast is that we are unprepared. We may be in clothes that you would never chose to fight in. We may have just eaten an enormous meal with a bottle of wine (or much more!). We are not warmed up. We are not stretched. We are anything but ready to go. Can you imagine going into a sports competition like this? Nothing is perfect, everything is sub-optimal. How can I prepare for this?

ATTITUDE

I need only ever train these two elements: ATTITUDE and BODY MECHANICS. Remember the words of the WW2 platoon commander - 'do anything fast enough and aggressively enough and it will probably be right'. We know now that this works because it gets inside our opponents OODA loop.

In the infantry, the expression used for this is to 'bounce' it. You suddenly come under fire from a location you did not expect only a short distance away. You can withdraw or you can 'bounce' it; amassing your available assets together as fast as you can and over-whelming this new target with speed, aggression and firepower.

To overwhelm with speed and firepower in a given moment in time is the principle of self-defence. We do not have to achieve this over a number of rounds or in a fair fight. Neither do we have to be tougher, stronger or faster than our opponent in general terms. We just have to be better than them in a single moment in time.

I imagine my worst case scenario of an opponent. Huge, strong and mean as hell. To fight him at all is not ideal. To fight him over a series of rounds with rules is crazy. He has all the advantages. To beat him I need to consistently be better, unless I throw it all into the first moments. But in a ring and with agreed rules there is little I can surprise him with. If my gamble fails, I am completely gassed out and facing the prospect of having to try and survive a long fight, outgunned and overmatched.

Think again of Tommy's solution. No way he could of fought a one-on-one fair fight with that guy. But why would he need to? Why conform to arbitrary 'rules' that you haven't signed up to? Everybody big and strong moans about 'fairness' and 'honour'. Why should I engage someone in a 'fair' fight who nature has seen fit to make 6' 6" and super strong! That's not fair! By making a fair fight, the stronger person eliminates all the chaos and surprise that could see him lose.

That is why competitions are designed to be fair, so that you can really tell who the better guy is. But we have no interest in this. Potentially, our life is at stake. We can save ideals of fairness for when we are playing games. For now, we need to be RUTHLESS.

The emotional attitude that gives us the potential to overwhelm our opponent in a single moment is ruthless, aggressive and desperate. I first came across the use of the word 'desperate' in a positive sense from listening to the country's top rugby league coaches. They often used the word to praise their players in the way that they had defended.

The attitude of 'desperateness' summed up the very best defenders when the opposing side was attacking their tryline. It's the all or nothing, all in attitude that lets go of consequence and focusses only on the single task. This is 100%, maximal performance with nothing left in the tank.

Aesop (of Aesop's fables fame) said "The rabbit runs faster than the fox, because the rabbit is running for his life while the fox is only running for his dinner." In this example, the rabbit is more desperate than the fox. This is oft quoted. But if the fox and its cubs are so hungry that they are in danger of starving to death, the rabbit better watch out! The attitude we need to develop is one where, if we engage in the fight, we fight in this spirit of desperation. How else really can I overwhelm my opponents? How else can the nine stone lady defeat the burly man trying to rape her?

I was once teaching a self-defence workshop to a women's group and was discussing this very point. One of the women asked if everybody had the potential to fight like this. I replied that everyone has it in them as a result of the evolution of our species. For many of us so called 'cultured' and 'civilised' individuals, it is buried quite deep but it is there waiting to emerge.

She told me that this was nonsense as she was a Buddhist and committed pacifist who could never bring herself to hurt anyone. I had noticed when she arrived at the workshop that she had been dropped off by a man (who I assumed to be a partner) carrying a cute little baby of about a year old. I said to her "what about if I tried to take your baby away from you to hurt it?". She looked shocked then confused and after a few seconds of mental gymnastics said finally spat out "yeah, I would kill you". The group dissolved into laughter.

She had illustrated a good point. Although we have the potential for this attitude, we generally do not go around 'wearing' it. For the purposes of living in an ordered society we have evolved manners and a way of dealing with each other. We could of course go around saying exactly what we think and feel all of the time. Perhaps you even know someone like this. I guarantee most people think of this person as a 'bit of an arsehole'. Living in a civilised society means considering others, appeasing them where necessary and generally trying to get on with the job of peaceful co-existence. People who are very good at this we call 'affable', 'charming', 'charismatic' even. A display of raw emotion is frowned on, especially in Britain.

The stereotypical 'English gentleman' is a master of subtlety, understatement, charm and composure. If we think of him being attacked by 'ruffians' we think of him calmly dispatching them with his umbrella, his heart rate never even rising. He pauses after the fight only to ensure that his tie remains perfectly straight. This is another nice fantasy. To accomplish this he would need an unbelievable, almost superhuman level of skill. And you don't get that just by being English!

In reality, we need to activate our raw emotion and unlock our full force and energy in doing so. For some, to bring this emotion out under control in a training environment is not too difficult. If we find it hard to bring this to the surface we will need to ACT THE

PART. Acting the part is the first step in developing the behaviour we are seeking. There is nothing 'false' in this. Think of the parts you play already in your daily life. They may be the part of the husband, wife, employee, friend, workmate. The difference between the roles can often be felt when they overlap - when for example your partner turns up at your workplace.

Because I both teach self-defence and yet am also a student of other martial arts, I play the role of teacher in a class and then immediately after play the role of student in another. The playing of roles is appropriate to what your aim is in each situation. If our aim is to 'rehearse' and develop the necessary attitude we need to overwhelm the opponent then the role we need to play is that of The Warrior.

The Warrior is you, but you with your fighting spirit activated and on full throttle. The clue to how to do this comes from acting. What do actors do but play roles professionally? An actor starts with the motivation for his role. The motivation you chose for this role may be to survive. More specifically, it may be to survive to see your family again. The Buddhist woman in my self-defence class might focus on the motivation of protecting her baby. Any powerful motivation that you can identify will do this job. Just like those actors who are trained in 'the method' of Stanislavsky, as the Warrior you must use these emotions to drive your physical actions.

Training at the beginning is a little like going on stage. But the role you are playing is a version of you so you have no need to worry about forgetting your lines. The Warrior is a supercharged, super aware human specimen, Battle Ready in every sense and straining at the leash. The Warrior remains contained but unleashes his power when needed in an explosive release of energy. Speaking from my own experience, I have a visualisation that greatly helps generate the attitude required.

When I was a very small boy I used to watch superhero cartoons. In the *Incredible Hulk* cartoons, the authorities were always trying to contain him by wrapping him up in ever stronger chains. Round and round they would wind these metal chains, with the Hulk getting madder and madder.

The whole story of the cartoon seemed to be leading up to the point where the Hulk would get so mad that he would triumphantly shatter these chains and they would fly off him in all directions in little pieces.

The Hulk may be an American comic book creation but he is an archetypal mythical figure, as I found out years later reading the Irish mythical epic *Tain Bo Culainge*. The hero of this tale is Cuchulain who, like The Hulk, turns into a fierce monster when he is made angry. This is known as Cuchulain's 'warp spasm'.

The first time Cuchulain experiences this 'warp spasm' is when he is five years old and he joins in a game of hurling without asking permission. The older boys decide to attack him, striking him with their hurling sticks.

The boy has his 'warp spasm' and transforms (with an eye popping out of his socket and onto his cheek). In a rage he kills fifty of the boys before he can be calmed down. The character of Cuchulain also has echoes of Hercules and many other mythical warriors.

There is a lesson for us here in the building of characters. Certain mythical archetypes occur again and again because they reflect an 'essence characteristic' in humans. These can provide powerful sources of inspiration for our roles. The closer the myth is to our cultural environment, the more powerful it will be.

Remember that this is simply a way of getting into the emotional state that we need. With practice, we will be able to summon up that emotional state at will. But to begin with we may need a little help and start adopting the characteristics we need in the mind through this method.

When I visualise breaking free, it's not the Hulk or Cuchulain but it's me, exploding into my attackers with the same abandonment and desperation of those mythical figures. The more exaggerated this is in my mind, the more of the emotion and ATTITUDE I will be able to translate. The central feeling is always the attackers trying to restrain and hurt me, followed by my explosive reaction.

This visualisation is rehearsed and made more powerful every time I train. In my visualisation it matters little what my attackers are doing when I go at them - they will all receive regardless. A nailbomb detonating is not picky about its victims, everyone gets a piece.

I had a demonstration of that attitude when I was posted to Northern Ireland. Ulster is the land of Cuchulain after all! My company commander was away on leave and as usual the company second-in-command (me) had taken command of the company. Our company was deployed onto the streets of Belfast around a place called 'Carlisle Circus'. We were deployed as part of the general public order provisions for a march that was taking place called the 'Tour of the North'.

We were not expecting much trouble on this march as year on year, it tended to go off peacefully enough. The route that the marchers took was not too contentious so there was generally less chance of riots between the various factions in the community.

Our company was about eighty men strong and we were tucked down a side street keeping a lowish profile with our vehicles and riot gear ready just in case. All of us were carrying rifles and kitted up as usual. Standing next to me on the street corner was our dog handler. The dog was deployed in order to search for explosives and the dog checked the area we were in to ensure no hidden devices had been planted as we were likely to be fixed in that position for some time.

The dog handler was a Royal Irish soldier from one of the part-time battalions. He was a Belfast man himself and had worked these streets for twenty years or so. Just before the march started, two small schoolboys were making their way up the street towards us, coming home from having been at primary school. I guessed that there were about seven or eight years old. One of the boys stood out.

He had the palest skin imaginable and a great shock of almost carrot-like ginger hair. On his back was a large rucksack, covering most of the rear of his body. The entire bag was in the form of the head of Darth Maul from *Star Wars: The Phantom Menace*.

It was a soft bag but had little horns sticking out from it, replicating the horns of the man himself. The expression on the face of Darth Maul was a furious grimace, showing his teeth. In contrast, the sight of this tiny boy and his companion put a smile on all our faces. He was a comical boy with a comical bag.

This little boy stopped when he saw the dog, a blond Labrador. He looked straight at the handler and said in an uber-thick Belfast accent "What's the dog for?". For whatever reason, the handler decided not to tell him and instead said 'Nothing, I'm just taking him out for a walk'. The boy furrowed his brow and said "No you're NOT! What's the dog for?' The handler again replied 'I'm just taking him for a walk'. At this the boy started to lose his temper to everybody's amusement.

Enraged further thinking that everyone was laughing at him, this little boy took off his Darth Maul bag and screamed 'No you're NOT! No you're NOT! I'll hit you with my bag!!'. He then began furiously whirling this bag around and around in a circle, like a hammer thrower, scattering the troops as he went. The fact that it was impossible to stop laughing fuelled the boy's rage and he went faster and faster like a miniature tornado, the face of Darth Maul becoming a blur.

Eventually his energy was spent and he stood glaring at the handler, his eyes blazing. His companion grabbed his arm and ushered him off and away before he could start up again.

At that moment an armoured staff car arrived and the brigade commander himself got out, flanked by his close protection team. He saw me and the boys still with huge smiles on our faces and I could hardly relate the story to him for laughing. That little boy was furious at being condescended to and you could see his point. In that moment he couldn't care less that he was in front of eighty armed men, he would take them all on with his soft bag. The attitude he displayed was like Cuchulain at the hurling game, no thought for himself just the urge to attack. Although the sight was comical, we all admired the boy's attitude and aggression. Like Cuchulain, the boy's warrior was awakened.

By training our physical movements and drills with this attitude we make them come alive. In fact, the training of the ATTITUDE is more important than the training of techniques. Remember the WW2 veteran saying 'do anything fast enough and aggressively enough and it will probably be right'? It's the ATTITUDE that gives you this. By playing roles and experimenting with our emotions we will learn to recognise them more, both in ourselves and in our opponents. Just as we need to flex and move our bodies to become more agile, we need to use our emotions in this way too. If this seems a bit like rehearsal for a stage play then this is good. Our training should be exactly that - a rehearsal for an event.

During the incident with the recently released prisoner, I felt a ball of energy in the middle of my chest, expanding to fill my whole chest and then travelling down my arm and into my opponent. This is not meant to identify any mystical or magical attributes I have, I am just honestly recounting what I felt. I have also felt physical sensations in other situations - like fear in the stomach, which I know from talking to others is common. The phrase 'bursting with pride' relates to a real physical sensation felt in the chest as well.

In moments of high emotion, I would go as far as saying that accompanying physical sensations are common. One that instantly springs to mind is the physical sensations felt when you are bereaved. At the other end of the scale, I felt the incredible feeling of floating once during a relay sprint race at school.

I was on the second leg and we needed to win this race in order to win the overall event prize. As the boy running the first leg ran towards me to hand over the baton, he slipped and fell down, barely able to hold up the baton whilst lying prostrate on the floor. I had already started running so had to turn around, go back and retrieve the baton from his upturned hand. Knowing how far behind we would be I ran without any thought of myself and the process of running. I was no longer concerned with my technique or even mindful of the passing of time.

The experience I had was one of floating, being pushed from behind by a great gust of wind. I had no sensation of my legs actually moving in my memory of the event. The boy I was handing over the baton to just seemed to get closer and closer like I was being simultaneously pushed and pulled towards him. When I handed over the baton, I had made up all the ground we had lost and we won that race.

Many people congratulated me and said it was the fastest they had ever seen me run and it was incredible that I had made up all that lost ground. I didn't feel like I had done anything at all. There was no feeling of endeavour. I had just been part of something that was happening to me. It was like I simply removed the thing normally preventing the circuit from being completed.

Once the circuit is completed, the electricity flows. Again, the feeling punching the convict was the same - a circuit being completed. These moments are rare but represent a small part of the true energy we have in the Emotional part of the Moving Centre. This energy can drive us into doing extraordinary things. The human body is a very mean machine and will only pull out all the stops when it can be convinced that it really needs to. This can be demonstrated in the way that certain drugs and chemicals effect the body.

The naturally occurring chemicals in the body provide the mechanism by which our emotional reaction effects our physical body. Following the emotion of stress and of fear, chemicals such as adrenaline, nor-adrenaline, dopamine, serotonin, endorphins and cortisol are released into the body in a 'hormonal cascade'. It is important to recognise here that these chemicals are one aspect of the mechanism by which emotions effect the human body directly.

If we don't feel the emotion, the chemicals are not released. If you are trained to a level where a situation becomes familiar, your emotional response of fear or stress is lessened hence the chemical reaction is less severe. Note the word here is 'lessened'. This is a key outcome of training for battle for example. We may not be able to replicate exactly the conditions of battle in training, but we can do enough so that the situation of battle for real does not overwhelm us emotionally. There are no guarantees here but the fact that trained soldiers can function in battle conditions at all is testament to this training approach.

This is true for fighting in self-defence as well. If my training is relevant and mimics the pressure of fighting for real, albeit imperfectly, I have a chance that my Emotional Centre will not overwhelm me. The human being has evolved this mechanism to aid survival after all. Adrenaline helps my heart beat faster to get oxygen to my muscles. Nor-adrenaline, dopamine and serotonin will keep me alert and ready for action. Endorphins block pain signals to keep me fighting through injury.

BODY MECHANICS

To the ATTITUDE we have just described, we need to add BODY MECHANICS. The training of our body mechanics (how to move my body in the fight to deliver or receive force or evade) needs to take into account the reality of a real fight in self-defence. Due to the hormonal cascade, muscle tension is increased. This is beneficial on the one hand as it will give us more strength and power. On the other hand however, it may inhibit our range of motion and control. We often say that 80% of our ability in training is lost in the real situation.

Whatever the correct figure, it is safe to say that a very large amount of the ability we demonstrate in the gym when training is lost in a real fight. This is unlike sport where we can train for a known situation. We know the limits of our environment and what our opponent can and cannot do. Even then, if we are a novice we will stiffen up, but in sport we can learn to relax as the process becomes more familiar.

I remember my first Brazilian jiu-jitsu competition - I was thirty-eight years old and had been training only a few months. We were in a nice warm building with friendly people and a great atmosphere. The worst that could happen was that I would have to 'tap out' - to submit to my opponent by literally tapping my hand. The pace of the match was faster than I had experienced in training.

Both of us were tense and strong, rather than relaxed and dynamic. My opponent had been training for around two years and it showed as he was able to take my back and apply a choke. The choke should have been around my neck but as I had dipped my chin, it went across my jaw. There was no immediate danger here as I was not being strangled. However the pressure was unpleasant to say the least as it was cranking my neck.

This is illegal at this level of jiu-jitsu but I didn't think for a moment my opponent was doing it intentionally. I heard three vertebrae in my neck click, decided discretion was the better part of valour and tapped out. I wanted to win the match, but not at the risk of an injury to my neck. I didn't then start complaining that it was an illegal move as it was clear that my opponent had better jiu-jitsu. Sport fighting is civilised in that we can submit and go into it knowing that we can do it. In the competitions to come, I was able to relax more and bring more control to the situation.

One of the interesting elements of being under the influence of adrenaline and other chemicals is that we can suddenly find ourselves in situations wondering how we got there. This happened in my first competition too - I suddenly found myself in my opponents 'closed guard', him underneath me with his arms and legs wrapped around me like a spider with a fly. I had no recollection of how we had got there. As I trained more I was able to recognise what was happening far clearer and this phenomenon disappeared.

This happens in street fights too but at a much more profound level. We have none of the familiar and friendly elements we find in sports competitions. We know we cannot 'tap out' if we are in trouble. Everything is emotionally supercharged.

When I was in my early twenties I was involved in a fight at a taxi rank which had been started by a friend I was with. Being outnumbered, I was swinging pretty wildly and was aware of my head being pushed down in the melee. I threw an uppercut out of instinct and felt it connect. The next thing I knew my back hit a tiled wall. This was strange as we had been outside at the taxi rank. As my back hit the wall my head came up and I was looking straight at the word 'POLICE' written across the chest of the person holding me.

I was suddenly aware that I was in a kebab shop. The policeman (who looked about the same age as me) said 'Do you REALLY want to hit a policeman?' he then repeated it over and over. He wasn't very happy. I said 'No, of course not' and I must have looked completely confused as he calmed down a little then.

To be fair to the policeman, he must have then realised what had happened and that when I had swung that uppercut I had no idea that it was him pushing my head down. As I was escorted out of the kebab shop, I could see my friend with a policeman holding onto him. My friend was mysteriously grinning from ear to ear. There must have been about ten policeman there at the taxi rank. Where the hell had they come from? After pleading with the policemen, they let us go without any further action on account of the fact that we had been seriously outnumbered.

As we walked away I asked my friend why he was grinning. He could hardly talk for laughing as he recounted how, when the fight had started the police very quickly descended. It turned out that the police used the taxi rank as a training ground for their young recruits as fights often occurred there.

Almost straight away my friend had been separated from the guy he was starting to trade blows with, without any damage being done. He then had a ringside seat to watch the rest of the fight - basically me swinging at four blokes. He knew exactly what would happen as the policeman tried to control me as I was punching without looking.

My friend had tears of laughter in his eyes as he said he saw my uppercut connect with the young policeman in almost slow motion. Three policeman had then pretty much picked me up and driven into the kebab shop, my progress only being halted by the rear tiled wall.

In sport we can get comfortable and familiar with the situations we are in to a large extent. The dangers become known and controlled to the extent that they can be. In a fight for real, everything is uncertain and the dangers much, much higher. Add to this the unexpected nature of the fight and we have a very different beast. We must understand that in self-defence we will always have a serious hormonal cascade that will stiffen us up and affect us physically to a large extent, far more than sport.

The solution to this problem is to habitually train with an exaggerated body mechanic. We deliberately train our movements beyond the normal range of motion with full awareness of the tightness we will experience in the fight. This approach is one where we are conscious of our own vulnerability, rather than accepting the fantasy of ourselves as cold-blooded assassin warriors! To train with a full knowledge of a weakness seems to be self-defeating. Nothing could be further from the truth.

Training for battle is precisely based on this awareness of weakness. We know we are physically vulnerable so we learn to take cover rather than walking around the battlefield like we own the place. We have everything written down in handy cue cards because pressure makes our brain forget.

The aide-memoires used in the British Army are a work of genius. Every process can be broken down and written out onto little laminated cards, waterproofed and ready to be whipped out of a combat jacket pocket at a moment's notice. Most of the time, memory will suffice but in times of great stress being able to refer to a written reminder is invaluable.

Imagine that I am receiving fire from an enemy location. What I really need to do is call in a fire mission and get the artillery boys to destroy the position. The section commander has been taken out of the battle. I need to step up and call in the fire mission myself. But my mind is blank on how to do it, even though I have trained it many times. The noise of battle is wringing in my ears and I can't think straight. I whip out my little card and get on the radio and call it in.

To me, one of the great elements of British Army training is this understanding of the reality of human frailties. Of course we train to be as robust as possible but we do everything we can to help. We understand that the human being will fall back onto habits in times of crisis and those habits sometimes need a little push even then. The phrase used is 'train hard, fight easy'. The fight is seldom easy in actual fact but the meaning of the phrase is that if we can train to an exaggerated level of difficulty, we have the best chance of success for real.

When we train this for self-defence then, we need to adopt this same approach. So we effectively 'overtrain' the way we move in the knowledge that we will stiffen up for real. We train for the worst likely scenario and we train individual moments in the fight to breaking point. More on this when we discuss movement with multiple opponents.

STANCE/BASE

Now we get to the technical details of the principles of fighting in self-defence. Remember that a book can only give you knowledge in the Intellectual Centre. It is up to you to build on this in the Moving Centre by actually doing it. When you do it, you will find a level of understanding far beyond what can be transmitted by theory.

The way that we stand in the fight (or kneel, or sit or lay, depending on the situation) needs to be a position from which we can deliver or receive force. This may sound obvious but in actual fact it takes serious training time to be able to move and change position whilst maintaining 'base'.

'Base' means that we have a physical position that allows us to transfer or absorb force from one part of our body to another. You will remember from high school physics classes that an object with a wide base and a low elevation is more stable as its centre of gravity is lower, making it harder to topple over. We will need to move our bodies however so it is not a simple case of forming a posture with a super low stance and then staying there. We need to be able to maintain a stable base from one position to another.

In any fight (such as a sports fight) where I have one opponent, my stance or base will always be in reference to them. Figure 1 shows this. I can move myself around my opponent, maintaining a single stance that gives me a platform to fight from. I may choose to switch that stance in order for example to confuse my opponent but I have no requirement to do so. Sport guarantees the single opponent. In self-defence, I cannot guarantee a single opponent and if I cannot guarantee this, I must train for multiple opponents.

I cannot guarantee either that the fight will be limited to standing either (like in boxing). It may be that the first thing that happens in the fight is that I trip over the kerb and suddenly have to fight for an instant in the laying, sitting or kneeling positions. I cannot ignore this fact merely because it is inconvenient, anymore than I can ignore the threat of snipers in my military training. True, it's a massive pain in the arse. But it's a massive pain in the arse that I must train for if my training is to be relevant.

When I have multiple opponents, my stance is then in relation to multiple reference points. I may be in a good position to deliver and receive force from one opponent but not from another. This means that I am required to train in every position that can give me

FIGURE 1

MOVEMENT WITH A SINGLE OPPONENT

WITH A SINGLE REFERENCE POINT, OUR FIGHTER CAN MAINTAIN A
COMMON STANCE IF HE WISHES TO, SWITCHING HIS STANCE FOR
TACTICAL REASONS BY HIS OWN CHOICE.

a base - from neutral, left stance and right stance in the standing to the same in the kneeling, sitting and lying positions. See Figure 2.

These positions give me the ability to move force from one part of my body to another with a degree of efficiency thus giving power. For example, in the standing position in a good stance, I am able to transfer the power from my whole body into my hand to produce a powerful punch. I cannot do this when I am off balance as I have no means of controlling my actions and transferring the energy.

When I have reference points that are continually moving, every position I am in, every stance or base has to be able to transition into any other. So I need to be able to transition from left stance into right stance whilst turning around 180 degrees for example. I need to be able to transition from a neutral base in the kneeling position to a left stance in the standing position and so on.

Furthermore in self-defence, an attack is often unexpected meaning that we must learn to receive force in a less than perfect stance and then transition to a better one. By training the neutral as well as the left and right stance we cover these bases.

This is a sharp contrast to sport fighting where we expect the attack. Because of this, we begin in our optimum stance. Because people often find it difficult to understand different stances, it is useful to explain it in terms of combat sports that we have all seen or can all easily look up on the internet. In boxing where I can only punch and only punch above the waist, the standard way of teaching is to have a very side on stance in relation to one opponent.

This gives me the advantage of showing less of my body to my opponent and it also means that my lead hand has more reach. If I change the rules to allow kicking above and below the waist my stance will need to square up to allow me to 'check' or block kicks against my legs. The squarer stance allows me to shift my weight more easily from side to side. If I then change the rules again and allow wrestling and the fighters to shoot in and grab each other legs, my stance will need to be able to square up further and drop down to receive and deliver force from there.

If I forget all about rules and introduce the possibility of more than one opponent my stance will need to be able to transition

FIGURE 2

MOVEMENT WITH MULTIPLE OPPONENTS

HERE OUR FIGHTER MAY BE REQUIRED TO FIGHT FROM A RANGE
OF STANCES AND POSITIONS, NOT BY HIS CHOICE BUT BY THE
REQUIREMENTS OF THE SITUATION HE FINDS HIMSELF IN. THIS IS FAR
MORE CHAOTIC AND SERIOUS TRAINING TIME IS NEEDED TO BE ABLE TO
FIND A BASE FROM ANY POSITION.

between all these elements. My only principle now is that I am able to receive or deliver force in that moment, whatever level I am at, on my feet or off my feet and in whatever direction I am facing.

BODY MECHANICS AND BASE

If the ability to maintain my base whilst moving is what I am aiming for, I need to develop the balance, strength and skill to move my weight through my centre of gravity. This is what allows me to 'move like a fighter', always in a position to receive or deliver force.

In order to train this, we can isolate certain movements that are the basis for all of these developments. There is nothing new in this - core movements have been trained by fighters for hundreds of years, not to mention by dancers as well. If you were to pop your head into any ballet school you will see the dancers practising these core movement drills.

The drills we train are driven by our need to be able to move in all directions and at all levels. Our approach is therefore 360 degrees. All these movements give rise to techniques of attack and defence. If you like, we can say that 'techniques' such as strikes or traps and so on are 'possibilities' within the body mechanics. Although I may use my hand to punch for example, in fact my whole body is involved in this strike (or it should be!). The kick is the same - my whole body should be involved. When I smash into my opponent to drive him back - again my whole body should be acting as one. At the beginning it can seem like my arms and legs have a mind of their own and my body does not want to act as one.

This is the process of recognising the body I mentioned earlier. Little by little the body starts to do what you want it to when you want it to do it. It does not come without practice however. This would be the equivalent of a gymnast jumping up onto the beam without ever training on it and expecting to have perfect balance. Don't forget that you are not even born being able to walk and have to learn the balance for that too!

It is a common thing that students learning the body mechanics will protest that the movements 'don't feel natural' but forget that we had to learn to walk at one point and now those movements are so 'natural' we do not even have to think about them.

There is no clearer example of this than in my comrades who lost limbs in conflicts and had to literally re-learn to walk. They told me that the frustration of this was made worse by the fact that they were not used to having to think about the act of walking. Learning to move like a fighter is like this sometimes too. We believe that we should not have to think about how to move and how even to put one foot in front of the other. But fighting is not like walking down the street. When I am strolling in the park thinking about what to have for dinner, I am not moving in a way that allows me to deliver or receive force - nor should I be as this would be ridiculous and exhausting!

We learn to move like a fighter by repetition and by trial and error. This is how the Moving Centre learns. We should not stop our repetitions continually in order to analyse. Rather if we feel we have not done a repetition correctly we should keep going and try to get it right on the next one. Constant stopping is a curse as it allows the Intellectual Centre in to try and do the work of the Moving Centre which it cannot do well.

If we think again of the centres, 'imitation' and 'reflexes' are in the Moving part of the Moving Centre - as Moving Centre as it gets. This means we just need to get on and do it without too much thought. The body will find its way through imitation in many, many repetitions of the action. To help this process it is useful to compare yourself against what you should be doing. This is why dance and martial arts studios have mirrors!

The modern version of this is to take video clips on mobile phones as previously mentioned. This should be done at the end of your training session to see where you are at. I use these short movie clips all the time to aid my memory on what has been trained and to see how I am doing. It gives us all a third eye and helps with our self-observation too.

THE BASIC MECHANICS

SMILE

SMILE
MECHANIC
FROM THE
NEUTRAL
STANCE

THIS DRILL
IS PRACTISED
STANDING
STILL.

THE KEY
WITH ALL
THESE
DRILLS IS TO
PRACTISE
THEM OVER
& OVER TO
THE FULLEST
RANGE OF THE
MOVEMENT.

THE BASIC MECHANICS

SMILE

SMILE MECHANIC FROM LEFT STANCE

NOTICE HOW OUR FIGHTER IS NOT BENDING FROM THE WAIST BUT USING HIS LEGS TO MOVE. IF YOU ARE DOING IT RIGHT, YOUR LEGS SHOULD BE STINGING!

THE BASIC MECHANICS

SMILE

SMILE
MECHANIC
FROM RIGHT
STANCE

TO USE YOUR
LEGS CORRECTLY
YOU NEED TO
'SIT' INTO THE
MOVEMENT, LIKE
SITTING DOWN
ON A BENCH.

THE BASIC MECHANICS

CIRCLE

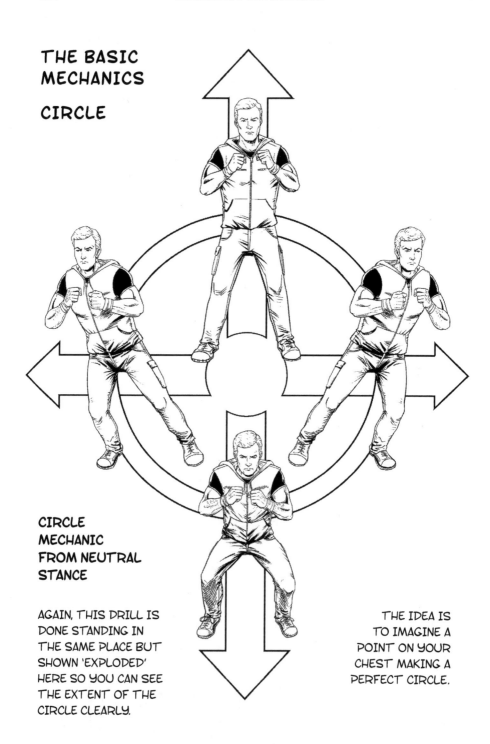

CIRCLE MECHANIC FROM NEUTRAL STANCE

AGAIN, THIS DRILL IS DONE STANDING IN THE SAME PLACE BUT SHOWN 'EXPLODED' HERE SO YOU CAN SEE THE EXTENT OF THE CIRCLE CLEARLY.

THE IDEA IS TO IMAGINE A POINT ON YOUR CHEST MAKING A PERFECT CIRCLE.

THE BASIC MECHANICS

CIRCLE

CIRCLE MECHANIC FROM LEFT STANCE

THE CIRCLE CAN BE PERFORMED 'FORWARDS' OR 'BACKWARDS', OR EVEN 'BROKEN AT THE TOP OR BOTTOM, WITH THE FIGHTER CHANGING DIRECTION.

THE BASIC MECHANICS

CIRCLE

**CIRCLE
MECHANIC
IN RIGHT
STANCE**

NOTICE HOW OUR
FIGHTER'S REAR
HEEL IS UP EXCEPT
WHEN HIS WEIGHT
IS TRANSFERRED
BACKWARDS.

HAVING THE HEEL
UP ALLOWS US TO
EXPLODE FORWARD
TOWARDS OUR
OPPONENT LIKE
A SPRINTER
IN THE BLOCKS.

THE BASIC MECHANICS

ELLIPTICAL

ELLIPTICAL
MECHANIC
FROM THE
NEURTAL STANCE

THIS IS SIMILAR TO
THE CIRCLE MECHANIC
BUT WITH A TWIST,
LITERALLY.

THIS IS NOT AS
EASY AS IT LOOKS
AND WILL REALLY
DEVELOP YOUR
BALANCE. DON'T
WORRY IF YOU FALL
OVER A FEW TIMES
AS YOU LEARN THIS,
IT WILL HELP YOU
FIND YOUR LIMIT.

THE BASIC MECHANICS

ELLIPTICAL

ELLIPTICAL
MECHANIC
FROM LEFT
STANCE

NOTICE AGAIN HOW
OUR FIGHTER'S HEEL
IS UP, EXCEPT WHEN
HIS WEIGHT IS BACK.

THIS MOVEMENT
INVOLVES PIVOTING ON
THE BALLS OF YOUR
FEET AS YOU TWIST.

THE BASIC MECHANICS

ELLIPTICAL

ELLIPTICAL MECHANIC FROM RIGHT STANCE

EACH ONE OF THESE DRILLS INVOLVES TRANSITION – FROM A HIGH STANCE TO A LOW...

...AND OUR WEIGHT THROUGH OUR CENTRE OF GRAVITY.

THE BASIC MECHANICS

FROWN

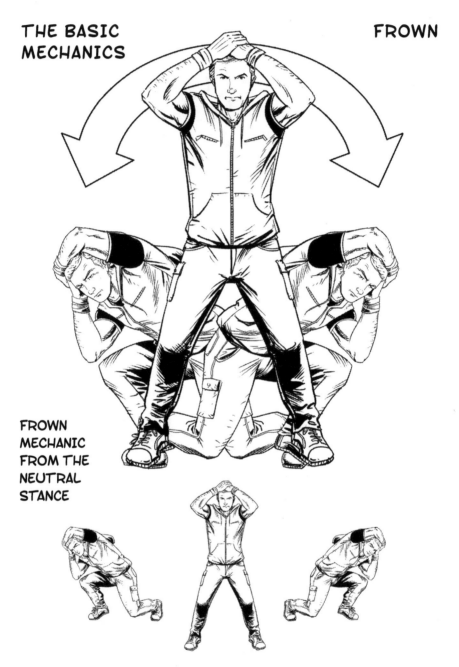

FROWN MECHANIC FROM THE NEUTRAL STANCE

IN THE NEUTRAL POSITION, IN THE CENTRE, THE WEIGHT IS ON THE BALLS OF THE FEET AND THE MOVEMENT SHOULD BE LIGHT AND BOUNCY.

THE BASIC MECHANICS

FROWN

FROWN MECHANIC FROM THE LEFT STANCE

THIS MOVEMENT IS A REAL LEG KILLER! IT CAN BE PERFORMED WITH THE HANDS ON THE HEAD OR WITHOUT. THE KEY IS TO GET YOUR WEIGHT FULLY ON THE LEG YOU ARE MOVING TO.

THE BASIC MECHANICS

FROWN

FROWN MECHANIC
FROM THE
RIGHT STANCE

AS YOU GET USED TO MOVING YOUR BODY WEIGHT WHILST STATIONARY
YOU CAN START TO MOVE AROUND WITH THE 'FREE' LEG AS THE ONE THAT
MOVES. THE ULTIMATE AIM IS TO BE ABLE TO COMBINE ALL THESE
MECHANICS IN A SINGLE DRILL.

THE LEVELS

In addition to training the isolated body mechanics in transition from neutral to left to right we also need to isolate the transitions between the levels, from standing to kneeling, sitting and lying. This is an idea that seems very simple and easy but in practice is far from that. Remember that we always need to be moving in a way that allows us to deliver and receive force, so we always need a base. We cannot simply just 'get up' from the lying position. Try this now. Lay down on the ground on your back and get up into the standing position.

Were you able at every stage in that movement to deliver or receive force? Probably not! You probably looked about as efficient and elegant as a drag queen falling down the stairs. Imagine now being knocked down in the fight, either through being struck, being pushed or falling over a kerb. Think about how vulnerable you are to attack as you struggle to get up.

From the fights I have either witnessed or been a part of, it is clear that an almost natural human reaction is to close in on a downed opponent. It's like a pack of wolves suddenly closing in on a kill. When someone goes to the floor a surge of predatory energy goes through the attacker.

Suddenly they see the weakness of the opponent and sense that they can now strike with impunity. I have seen fights when this happens when guys not even involved in the fight initially have taken the chance to attack the downed man out of the sadistic thrill of being able to assault someone in a weak position. This act then, of getting back to our feet is a critical one for certain.

It is this position in particular - being on the ground with standing opponents striking our head that leads to serious injury including brain damage and death. This is no joke. Neither is this a sports fight that can be waved off by the referee. This is why fights in self-defence are more akin to battle than they are to sport.

In the UK, we are particularly vulnerable in street fights when we fall to the ground. The simple reason for this is that most young boys in this country grow up learning to kick a football. This might sound obvious but in countries that don't play football much you don't find this widespread skill in kicking a round object on the floor to the same extent.

Because football is so ubiquitous we take it for granted that most males (and an increasing number of females) have a trained kick ready to go. The act of kicking a head on the ground with shoes on is no different from kicking a football.

An old training partner of mine was an operating department practitioner at the Salford Royal Hospital. Basically he assisted the surgeon in the operating theatre dealing with brain injuries. Every single weekend he would be in the theatre trying to stop a young man from having permanent brain damage as a result of being kicked in the head whilst lying on the floor on a night out.

When we consider that there might be more than one opponent we understand how critical this skill of getting back to our feet is. The transitions between the levels must therefore be trained over and over until they become our habitual way of moving in the fight. We can say much more about the ways of doing this later, but for now we need to appreciate only the basic format of moving through the levels.

STANCES IN THE STANDING POSITION: NEUTRAL, LEFT AND RIGHT

MOVING FROM THE NEUTRAL INTO RIGHT OR LEFT STANCE CAN BE DONE BY MOVING THE LEADING FOOT BACK OR BY BRINGING THE REAR FOOT FORWARD. EXPERIMENT WITH BOTH.

STANCES IN THE KNEELING POSITION: NEUTRAL, LEFT AND RIGHT

LEARNING TO MOVE WELL IN THESE POSITIONS MAY SEEM STRANGE AS
IT IS NOT OUR INTENTION, BUT IF WE END UP HERE WE MUST BE ABLE
TO MOVE, AND DELIVER AND RECEIVE FORCE NO MATTER HOW BRIEFLY –
IT COULD BE THE DIFFERENCE BETWEEN SURVIVAL OR DISASTER.

STANCES IN THE SITTING POSITION: NEUTRAL, LEFT AND RIGHT

NOTICE HOW THE REAR ARM PROVIDES A FRAME IN LEFT AND RIGHT STANCE. THIS CREATES A MORE STABLE BASE TO DELIVER AND RECEIVE FORCE.

STANCES IN THE LYING POSITION: NEUTRAL, LEFT AND RIGHT

THE FEET ARE BASED ON THE GROUND TO ALLOW THE HIP TO RAISE
UP TO ENABLE MOVEMENT.

STEPS AND MOVEMENT

It seems an obvious thing to say but if we are forced to resolve a situation through violence we need to be able to strike and control an opponent without being hit or controlled ourselves. We need to be the one dominating and overwhelming our opponent. Sport fighting has moments that ebb and flow across the set time period. Fighting in self-defence is, by contrast, one big explosion. Sports fighting is cautious, measured, tentative. The engagements in self-defence I think of as being like medieval knights jousting each other. They gallop in and there is a moment of super violence as the lances connect.

We need to understand how our movement can help us to not be overwhelmed in the moment. For ease of understanding let us first consider a single opponent. To hit them and yet not be hit we can strike them at a range that they cannot strike us at. This is fine if we have much longer limbs for example. But as mentioned before, fights in self-defence are not split into weight and size categories. We cannot know beforehand the physical attributes of our opponent. To hit them and not be hit therefore we are going to need to create an ANGLE.

In the diagram, we can see how the most desirable position to make on our opponent is directly behind them. If we achieve this it is very hard for them to strike us in this moment and easy for us to strike them.

But our opponent will not allow us to run around them at a 'broken distance' i.e. out of striking range of both parties. It is too easy for an opponent to turn towards us in this case to prevent us going around their back. If we can take their back it will be when we are attached to them at close distance and can grapple them around. This will be discussed later.

Therefore, the next most desirable angle will be at their side - the 'T' position. In this position my hips and striking weapons are facing him, yet his hips and striking weapons are facing away from me. It is true that he can shoot out a punch or kick to the side but his body mechanics are not as efficient at delivering power in this angle whilst the hips are facing away. It is possible for us to achieve this angle for an instant but again, the opponent will try and face you by instinct as you try to move round.

What is more likely is that you can achieve a slight angle in the moment. With one opponent we can refer to this as the 'L' position.

ACHIEVING THE 'T' POSITION WITH ONE OPPONENT

HERE THE FIGHTER IS MOVING TO ACHIEVE A HIGHLY DOMINANT ANGLE AT 90° TO THE OPPONENT.

THIS REPRESENTS A FAVOURABLE POSITION FOR OUR FIGHTER, AS IT SEVERELY LIMITS THE OPPONENT'S ABILITY TO DELIVER FORCE, WHILST MAXIMISING THE FIGHTER'S ABILITY TO DO THE SAME.

This gives us an advantage in the exchange as the opponent will have to turn to strike us cleanly. It is difficult for them to generate power in a strike whilst they turn so this gives us a 'beat' in time where we have the upper hand.

When you watch fights break out on the rugby pitch between two big forwards they face off and trade haymakers in a show of who is the toughest. This 'toe to toe' fighting is exactly what we DON'T want. We have no interest in showing who is toughest, this is not our aim. Our aim is to resolve the situation. You can be a prime human specimen, big, strong, agile and quick. But even with all that, if you stand in front of another man punching straight at you, you run the risk of being 'tagged' and knocked out.

ACHIEVING THE
'L' POSITION
WITH ONE
OPPONENT

IN REALITY, THE
'T' POSITION IS DIFFICULT
TO ACHIEVE, AS THE
OPPONENT WILL
INSTINCTIVELY TRY AND
CUT THIS OFF TO KEEP
HIMSELF IN FRONT
OF THE FIGHTER.

THE 'L'
POSITION IS AT
45° FROM OUR
OPPONENT AND
RETAINS SOME
BENEFITS...

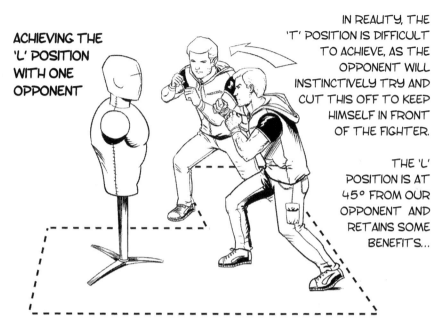

...IN TERMS OF DOMINANCE, WHILST BEING RELATIVELY 'EASIER' TO
ACHIEVE. THESE MOMENTS OF DOMINANCE ARE FLEETING AND ONLY
TRAINING AND SPARRING CAN GIVE US THE ABILITY TO EXPLOIT THEM.

With two opponents, how are we going to do this? The very
worst position to be in is going to be in between two opponents,
with one in front and one at the back, or surrounded on all sides
if there are more than two. How can we fight more than one opponent at once? In truth we can't really. It is always difficult to speak
in absolutes because many strange circumstances come about but
in general, it is sensible to assume we cannot effectively fight two or
more opponents simultaneously.

If I have an opponent facing me I can do everything right but
if I have an opponent at my back as well I am in real trouble. I need
to find a way to prevent both opponents being in range at the same
time.

Movement wise this means I am trying to get into a position
where one opponent shields me from the other - a 'T' position
with two opponents. I need to recognise that my opponents will be
moving as well so this position is a moment in time, a 'beat' in the

fight only. I will need to continuously move in order to maintain this and even then it will only exist for a moment. My opponents will not simply stay still and allow me do this. In fact as explained before the natural instinct will be for them to try and flank me and get behind to surround me.

ACHIEVING THE 'T' POSITION WITH MULTIPLE OPPONENTS

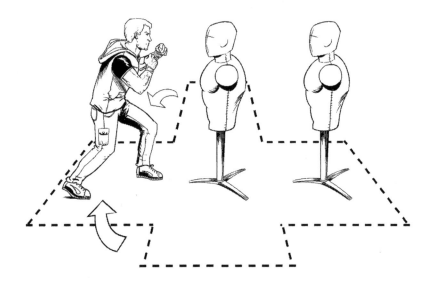

TO TRY AND FIGHT MORE THAN ONE OPPONENT SIMULTANEOUSLY IS A TOTAL DISASTER. HERE OUR FIGHTER MOVES TO POSITION ONE OPPONENT IN FRONT OF THE OTHER. THIS IS ACHIEVED AS A 'MOMENT' IN TIME AS BOTH OPPONENTS WILL MOVE TO ATTACK. BUT IN THIS MOMENT, OUR FIGHTER USES ONE TO SHIELD HIMSELF FROM THE OTHER.

If this sounds like it is difficult, it is. Fighting one opponent is hard enough. But remember we are not looking to WIN as such. We are looking to resolve the situation. This may mean surviving until we can escape for example, or getting into a physical space where we cannot be outflanked or getting to a place where there are people and so on. My default movement position is in a 'V' shape at a broken distance.

ACHIEVING THE 'V' POSITION WITH MULTIPLE OPPONENTS

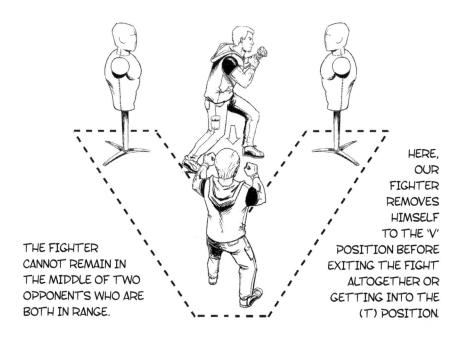

THE FIGHTER CANNOT REMAIN IN THE MIDDLE OF TWO OPPONENTS WHO ARE BOTH IN RANGE.

HERE, OUR FIGHTER REMOVES HIMSELF TO THE 'V' POSITION BEFORE EXITING THE FIGHT ALTOGETHER OR GETTING INTO THE (T) POSITION.

If I suddenly found myself being flanked, this is a position that I can adopt before improving my situation. If I am able to do this and stay at a broken distance this can enable me to prevent being simultaneously attacked by two opponents.

The problems of facing more than one opponent are nothing new. Socrates even comments on this in Plato's The Republic:

> *Do you not believe that one pugilist trained in the most perfect manner to his work would find it easy to fight with two rich and fat men, who do not understand boxing?*
>
> *Not with both at once perhaps.*
>
> *What not if he were able to give ground till one of his assailants was in advance of the other, and then to rally and attack him, repeating these tactics frequently...? Could not such a combatant worst even more than two such antagonists?*
>
> *Indeed, he replied, there would be nothing very surprising in it.*[38]

Let's say I achieve this position. What then? Do I try and constantly move around like how a younger brother might use the kitchen table to prevent his older brother from getting to him? That is all very well but in our case the kitchen table moves as well! These positions are moments in the fight which I can exploit, they are not fixed in any way.

If I am able to achieve the position it will only exist for a fleeting amount of time as the opponents move themselves. In the moment when I am facing one opponent and being shielded from another this is my time to 'resolve' that opponent.

Perhaps in an ideal world we strike that opponent on the chin and he is knocked out or we throw a circular kick at his knee and his knee is destroyed. Certainly with training we can improve the chances of that happening. But we cannot rely on it. The chaos of the fight means that many of our strikes will not be as effective as we would like, some will miss entirely.

When we are facing a moving opponent that does not want to get hit we find out how hard it is to land a clean shot on an opponent. Part of our problem is that we need to get into the range of our own strikes first and many people are simply not aware of how close they need to be to an opponent to strike them. I am sure that you will have witnessed fights, particularly outside pubs where both parties are swinging and missing each other - in some cases by large amounts due to being untrained.

I mentioned that the role of training is to 'recognise yourself'. A big part of this is becoming aware of how long or short your own strikes are. Again this seems simple but it is far from that. Only live sparring will really give you a genuine feel for the range of your strikes. It is likely that when we get into the range of our strikes being able to hit our opponent we are in their range too. It can be a totally valid tactic in a sport fight with one opponent to keep them at range, picking them off with strikes and stepping back or moving off time and time again.

We can guarantee in sport that we have only one opponent. In the street there are no such guarantees and even if we see only one opponent that does not mean that there is not one behind us. This is why training our awareness all around us in drills like the 'black hand' are so important.

With more than one opponent controlling distance like this is exceptionally difficult to do over and over. It may well be that in the first 'beat' of the fight we can move to a better position. But to lose that position and then have to do it over and over? This is not likely as the opponents will read these movements and anticipate them. 'Resolving' the opponent more than likely involves striking and ENTERING. Basically we need a way to hit them without them hitting us and then we need to ENTER into the distance of one opponent, control them and use them like a shield.

Again, we may need to do this for only a few 'beats' in the fight before we can get away or use them to attack, or resolve one opponent and deal with the next. That makes it sound easy. To train this is a serious amount of work, no question. Do we think our opponents are going to just allow us to do this? No way.

All of our movements and actions need to be trained for opponents resisting us with every ounce of strength they can muster. Only then can we find a true ability that may function. I say 'may' function as even with all the training in the world there are no guarantees - just like combat!

What we are training for is the 'worst likely' scenario. It may be that we have only one opponent of course. It might be that we have more than one, but our first strike puts the first opponent straight down. It may be that we can stay on our feet, that we never get hit first and so on. None of these things we can rely on however, so we must train for situations that are less than ideal.

THE FIRST BEAT - GETTING HIT AND HITTING BACK

A key difference between sport fighting and street fighting is that in the street, we may not be expecting an attack. If we go into a sports fighting ring or cage, there is something very badly wrong if we are not ready to fight. If I am attacked in a bar or in the street, the chances are that it is a surprise to me. I may get a fragment of a warning such as catching a punch swinging at me from the corner of my eye. I may get much more warning than this, such as someone pushing me or verbally abusing me as a precursor to an assault. We will deal with anticipation later.

For now let us imagine that we have no warning whatsoever, in fact we do not even see the punch aimed at our head. What happens? Simple, we get hit. If we are not knocked out, we need to react from whatever position we find ourselves in. What if we see the punch coming pretty late? Imagine you are walking through the park and there are guys playing football on the grass.

An overzealous shot at goal sees the ball launched in your direction. A second before the ball hits your head you see a fast object hurtling towards you. You instinctively cover your head with arms and the ball cannons off them, leaving your forearms sore but your head undamaged.

This kind of 'flinch response' is a type of 'startle reflex' and can be a fairly complex one neurologically in contrast to the other reflexes that are primitive. To guard the face and head then is a natural human reaction to an object travelling at speed towards it. We can also see this same instinct to protect the head when someone has fallen down.

The human animal is hardwired to prioritise protecting the brain and the main sensory organs, particularly the eyes. With training, the brain can modify reflexes and make them faster. So it is possible to build a reaction to a strike to the head that provides us a way of avoiding being hit and also a platform from which to hit back.

Depending on what is possible in the moment and how fast your reaction time is, it is also possible to use this shape to attack the strike coming in as well. This involves slightly more anticipation.

If we are able to anticipate the strike more than this, either through reaction time or by provoking the punch, it is possible to attack the strike more directly in a variety of ways. My intention is not to exhaustively go through all the possibilities - they are endless and in any case not best learnt from a book. What can be learnt however is the principle of how this operates.

PROTECTING THE HEAD

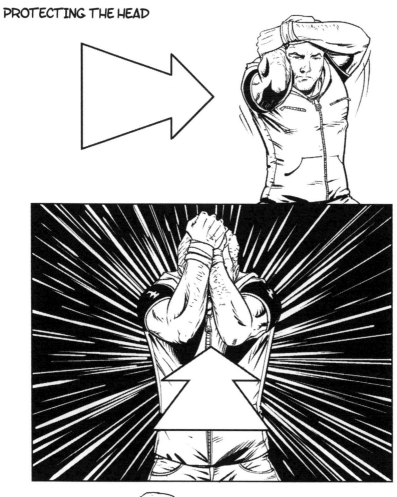

OUR FIGHTER RAPIDLY RESPONDS TO A STRIKE TO THE HEAD FROM THE LEFT, CENTRE AND RIGHT.

THIS CREATES A PLATFORM FOR OUR FIGHTER TO STRIKE BACK.

COUNTERING THE PUNCH TO THE HEAD

A MOMENT'S ANTICIPATION OF THE STRIKE ALLOWS OUR FIGHTER TO MODIFY HIS RESPONSE AND TAKE HIS OPPONENT'S PUNCH ONTO HIS ELBOW, DESTROYING IT IN THE PROCESS.

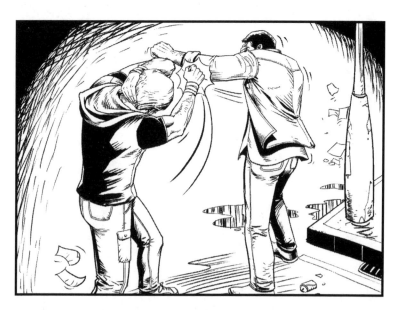

WITH MORE ANTICIPATION OUR FIGHTER HAS BEEN ABLE TO ATTACK HIS OPPONENT'S STRIKE WITH A STRIKE OF HIS OWN.

This principle operates too with a low kick to the legs. We can block at the first instance, block with more power attacking the strike, or attack the strike directly in a variety of ways.

We can refer to these timing beats as 'counter' timing beats. If I am countering an opponent's attack whilst he is in the action of completing it, we can refer to the timing of that counter beat as 'during'. If I counter the strike at the very first instance we can call the timing 'before' and if I counter the action after he has completed it we can call that timing beat 'after'.

In order to get inside my opponents OODA loop it follows that the most desirable timing beat is 'before' and the least desirable 'after'. The one exception to that rule is if we have deliberately provoked an attack that we then counter, having the benefit of anticipating our opponent's action. The result is the same however, we are dominating the decision-action cycle process.

Surprise can be our biggest weapon in the street for that reason. To be able to strike first and strike hard is a huge advantage. But this depends on us being made aware of the threat of an attack beforehand. Suppose that our would-be attacker begins by verbally abusing us then steps forward. To cut the distance and strike this person without prior warning gives us the upper hand. To continue our attack until the situation is resolved is our aim. If the individual is incapacitated we can regard that as resolved.

A common question I am asked is 'How do you know whether to strike first or not?' In other words, how do you know if that person verbally abusing you is actually going to strike? It is a great question and for me personally represents one of the most difficult aspects of self-defence.

I have heard some people say that if you are in any doubt strike first. This sounds good but to me is a thuggish way of living life. It may be that the individual is having a bad day, has a little too much to drink and says a few words to you as you unintentionally bump his shoulder as you squeeze past in a crowded bar. Do we then just attack him as hard as we can? Well, it depends.

Every time we get involved in a fight there is risk. Risk of things not working out for us and getting seriously injured and the risk of

ANTICIPATING THE OPPONENT'S KICK, OUR FIGHTER RAISES HIS REAR LEG WHILST 'BITING' DOWN ON THE OPPONENT'S LEG WITH HIS ELBOW, WITH FORCE BEING APPLIED FROM TOP AND BOTTOM SIMULTANEOUSLY.

THIS TIME OUR FIGHTER'S ANTICIPATION HAS ENABLED HIM TO CATCH HIS OPPONENT'S LEG. DEPENDING ON THE SITUATION AND OUR FIGHTER'S BALANCE IN THE MOMENT, HE CAN KICK THE OPPONENT'S STANDING LEG, ENTER WITH PUNCHES TO THE FACE OR SLIDE IN AND TAKE THEM DOWN – AMONGST OTHER OPTIONS!

COUNTER-STRIKE TO THE KICK

WITH SOME ANTICIPATION OF THE KICK, OUR FIGHTER IS ABLE TO COUNTER-STRIKE WITH A MODIFICATION OF HIS PROTECTIVE SHAPE.

seriously injuring or even killing another person. We live in a world of CCTV and enthusiastic lawyers. We may well be called upon to later justify our actions. Also, we need to live with the consequences of our actions. This person may, for example be a family man of normally good character. If we strike in self-defence it needs to be in self-defence.

This does not mean we need to disadvantage ourselves by allowing the other guy to hit first. We have no obligation, legal or otherwise to do this. It revolves around our genuine belief. Here for me is the answer to the question. I do not claim it to be a scientific or technical answer but it doesn't need to be either. It is an answer that has allowed me to live with the consequences of my actions and to justify them to the authorities when needed as well.

In the UK it is not unusual to be verbally abused either on the roads on in bars - even on the streets of our cities. Some of my female friends in particular can give depressing examples of this as an almost daily occurrence. This is unpleasant for certain. But when that verbal abuse is accompanied by a feeling of fear in my stomach, literally a 'gut reaction', I trust this reaction as being my 'genuine belief' and either strike first or get the hell out of there if this is the better option. The mind can subconsciously pick up on a thousand things we are not consciously aware of and this translates as the feeling of fear in the stomach.

Training can make these feelings more attuned however. Think of the way that a tennis player learns to read an opponent. Think of how a boxer can do the same. Our physical training is designed to recognise ourselves and our opponents both physically and emotionally.

Our self-observation should make us more sensitive to clues as to the intentions of our opponent. This should not be a conscious process as we run the risk of trying to second guess events. Rather train hard and let our gut do the rest.

It is possible to read books on how to interpret body language but I have always found that these bog us down. Better to let our learning be directly from our own experience. This means we need to put ourselves in places where we can observe violent emotions.

You don't have to be facing rioters in Belfast for this! Football matches are a good place to start.

In sparring during training there are often characters that get a little too emotionally charged or 'amped up' as the Americans say. Watch closely! A certain level of detachment is needed to observe the reactions. If we watch ourself watching the reactions via the method of self-observation we can achieve this.

This is another reason why we should compete and spar. As I took up Brazilian jiu-jitsu a large portion of that was spent in sparring or 'rolling' as it is known. As a beginner, you are going to spend a lot of that time being sat on by more advanced students, having the air crushed out of you and generally getting pulled around. Anyone with a strong fighting spirit is going to be tested by this.

It's hard on your body and ego to be dominated in such a physical fashion time after time. But it's a great opportunity to observe yourself. Again, with detachment you can ask about yourself - what is it doing now? Is it getting angry? Is it getting disappointed? Is it throwing its toys out of the pram? (the 'it' being you seen through dispassionate observer's eyes).

You can also observe the emotional state of others from such a close and intimate physical connection. Some people are emotionally super calm, others more agitated, some literally shaking with nervous energy. You can feel all this whilst in an embrace! This is all good training in how to recognise your own emotional state and the state of others.

DISTANCE, TIMING AND ENTRY

Having previously mentioned the concept of ENTRY into the opponent, we now need to expand on this and see it in application. If we consider again being in the middle of two opponents, we can step out into the 'V' shape and look to move into the 'T' position, or we can ENTER in to one opponent and increase the distance from the other opponent.

When we enter into an opponent in this way, we dynamically

cut the distance between us. We are not in the business of 'chasing after' an opponent to do this. If the opponent is backed off, our movement as per previous diagrams is appropriate. If our opponent is coming forward to us, this entry uses that forward pressure against our opponent. Imagine running towards a stationary bull and then the bull suddenly dipping its head and smashing into you as you come in range.

In self-defence, it is more common that the opponents are coming forward to attack you, rather than bobbing in and out in a measured way like in sports. We need to be able to deal with both for sure but we can deal with an opponent at broken distance with movement and coming forward with ENTRY.

When we enter, an opponent will react by bouncing off thus creating distance, or by staying within our range. Our next action is then a result of the awareness of what has happened to our opponent. But we are now dictating the fight. For example, if an opponent reacts by bouncing back off to long range we can continue the attack with a long range strike such as a kick. If short then a short range attack is appropriate and so on.

If the opponent stays connected to us we are in what we refer to as 'trapping' range. If we use the example of entering into an opponent from having been between two opponents then perhaps here we may seek to turn that opponent around to put him in between us and the second opponent, using him as a shield.

From here we can resolve this opponent, drop him to the ground and escape or use him to attack the other opponent all depending on what is possible in the moment. None of these things will be easy as the opponent will resist as hard as he can. Within our training we will have to practice gaining control of the opponent and how to regain control as the opponent resists or counters our attacks.

A common theme of controlling an opponent is the idea of physically taking away the space in which he can move. When we can move but he can't, we stop the action part of his OODA loop whilst continuing our own. A real secret of self-defence however, is how we stop his decision making process too. This comes down to taking away his space - not his physical space this time, but his mental space in which to think.

A perfect example of that is how we use shock and pain to fill his head. Whilst shocked, our opponent has no thinking space - we have taken it all away. There is a way of gripping an opponent called the Monkey Grip. This is where the fighter grips the opponents flesh as hard as he can with just the fingers (not the thumb) of his hand. Its uses are many but a main function is to cause intense pain whilst controlling an opponent. The shock of this pain prevents our opponent from thinking, deciding and acting and gives us space to act.

ENTRY

IN 'GOING THROUGH' AN OPPONENT WE CAN
INCREASE THE DISTANCE BETWEEN US AND
OPPONENTS BEHIND US FOR A MOMENT IN TIME.

ENTRY – THIS METHOD OF ATTACK COUNTERS OUR OPPONENT'S AGGRESSION AND FORWARD PRESSURE WITH EXPLOSIVE FORWARD PRESSURE OF OUR OWN. THIS ENABLES US TO RESOLVE THE SITUATION AS THE INITIATIVE IS NOW OURS.

MONKEY GRIP

OUR FIGHTER IS USING HIS OPPONENT AS A SHIELD. THE OPPONENT
WILL NOT SIMPLY ALLOW THIS TO HAPPEN. OUR FIGHTER CONTROLS
HIS OPPONENT USING HANDFULS OF FLESH AS HANDLES. THE SHOCK OF
PAIN THIS CAUSES KEEPS OUR OPPONENT IN A REACTIVE, RATHER THAN
PROACTIVE, STATE OF MIND.

MONKEY GRIP – IN THE CHAOS OF A FIGHT THE SUREST WAY OF PREVENTING OUR OPPONENT'S ACTION IS VIA OUR OWN SPEED AND AGGRESSION. THE INSTINCT MUST BE TO CAUSE MAXIMUM DAMAGE AS QUICKLY AS POSSIBLE.

IN ANY FIGHT OUR OPPONENT WILL BE DOING EVERYTHING HE CAN
TO RESIST OUR ACTIONS. THE MONKEY GRIP IS USED HERE AS A
'FORCE MULTIPLIER', THE PAIN FROM THE GRIP DISSUADES HIM FROM
ATTEMPTING TO REBASE HIS LEG.

THE BODY AS A HOUSE

We can refer to the body as a house in order to help our understanding. I first came across this metaphor when training with Justo Dieguez. The limbs we can refer to as doors and the spaces in between them as windows. The reason this is useful is because it places the emphasis on us to act decisively and enter into the opponent rather than stay out and become dominated by a number of opponents. The doors prevent my entry into the house but doors can be opened by my opponent striking, by me busting them down and by me opening them myself.

When I try and enter, the opponent may try and close the door - it is up to me to find a way in in order to control my opponent. I can enter through an open door or via a window. Again, it is not useful to exhaustively go through all the possible ways and variations of doing this - there are plenty. But if we understand the concept then we can discover many for ourselves. I may also enter and turn to face another opponent, having my back to the first.

This may seem unwise as it looks like I am giving my back to one opponent. But my back is already facing the other opponent.

The key understanding here is that if I turn my back to an opponent deliberately then I have control of that opponent. For sure, if I do this without controlling the opponent then I have put myself in a weak position. With one opponent, it is hard to imagine ever needing to do this but with more than one I need to constantly mitigate the vulnerability caused by being outnumbered.

When I have control of the opponent on my terms I can strike, takedown, move them around and so forth. This control of my opponent is a moment in the fight. Their resistance means that I cannot expect this control to exist forever. I must take immediate advantage of this control to keep their posture broken and prevent them from gaining back their base.

The phrase 'use it or lose it' springs to mind. In sport the referee may disengage us at this point or we may consensually decide to disengage to prevent a stalemate or because our opponent does not want to risk an offensive move in a certain position. None of this generally applies in self-defence. The onus is on me to act fast and decisively to resolve the situation. Remember that this can also mean running away (call it a tactical withdrawal if you prefer!).

DOORS

WITH THE BODY SEEN AS A HOUSE, THE LIMBS BECOME DOORS. THIS IS USED IN TRAINING AS A WAY OF UNDERSTANDING HOW TO ENTER THE HOUSE AND 'RESOLVE' (CONTROL & DESTROY) THE OPPONENT.

TECHNICAL PRINCIPLES

To maximise my power, I need to use my whole body with every movement. We have established the idea that when we strike we are in a distance that typically means that our opponent can also strike us. We also understand that we make ourselves more vulnerable as we strike as we 'open' our doors to do so.

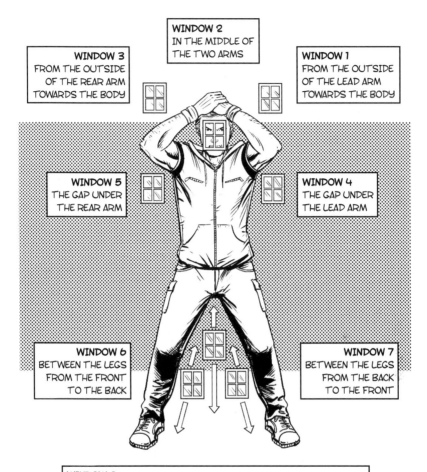

WINDOW 2
IN THE MIDDLE OF THE TWO ARMS

WINDOW 3
FROM THE OUTSIDE OF THE REAR ARM TOWARDS THE BODY

WINDOW 1
FROM THE OUTSIDE OF THE LEAD ARM TOWARDS THE BODY

WINDOW 5
THE GAP UNDER THE REAR ARM

WINDOW 4
THE GAP UNDER THE LEAD ARM

WINDOW 6
BETWEEN THE LEGS FROM THE FRONT TO THE BACK

WINDOW 7
BETWEEN THE LEGS FROM THE BACK TO THE FRONT

WINDOW 8
MOVING ALL THE WAY THROUGH OPPONENT'S LEGS & OUT THE OTHER SIDE, EITHER FROM FRONT TO BACK OR BACK TO FRONT

WINDOWS

WITH THE BODY SEEN AS A HOUSE THESE REPRESENT WAYS WE CAN MOVE INTO OUR OPPONENT OR WITH OUR OWN BODY AS THE REFERENCE, THE UPPER WINDOWS REPRESENT GAPS IN OUR GUARD THAT WE CAN LOOK OUT OF AND OBSERVE. THE BODY IS OF COURSE NOT STATIC - AND NEITHER IS OUR OPPONENT'S, BUT THESE REFERENCES MOVE WITH THE BODY.

CONTROLLING AN OPPONENT AT OUR BACK

WITH MULTIPLE OPPONENTS SOMETIMES IT IS NOT POSSIBLE TO AVOID
HAVING OUR BACK FACING AN OPPONENT. IF WE CAN PREVENT THAT OPPONENT
ESTABLISHING A BASE WE CAN CONTROL THEM IN THAT INSTANT AND FACE THE
OTHER OPPONENTS. NOTHING IN THE FIGHT IS 'IDEAL'.

Let's take the example of a punch directly aimed at an attacker's face. As I strike, I need to lean to one side, off the centre line of my opponent in order to create an angle and avoid the strikes he is throwing to where he thinks my head is. In this approach to self-defence, we need to be constantly moving to make ourselves a hard target. Hitting someone clean in the face is nowhere near as easy as it seems. When that target is moving constantly it's even harder.

In self-defence we do not have the opportunity to learn to read an opponents patterns like you do in a sport over many rounds and many engagements. We move therefore by default. Because we cannot always know where the strike may come from we mitigate this vulnerability by covering up as we strike and move and by moving the body all the time. The secret of how to do this is in training the body mechanic as shown previously.

All of the habitual movement we practice goes into this ability. Can you see how the 'techniques' themselves are not even the most important part of fighting? The important parts remain ATTITUDE and BODY MECHANICS. If, however we practice the techniques in harmony with these elements then we increase the chances of what we are doing functioning well.

The word 'harmony' is a key one in learning this physical skill. In order to deliver force, to move well and to resist force, the body needs to be in harmony. With the punch, the foot turns to allow the knee to turn to allow the hip to turn to generate the force with which the arm will accelerate the fist to strike.

Like the timing gear in a motor car, if these actions occur in harmony, force is delivered to the action - the wheels in the case of a car, the fist in the case of the punch.

In this example of the punch direct to the face, if I am following the first punch with a direct punch from the other side, then I will utilise my body mechanic to transfer my whole body weight into the punch and lean to the other side off the centre line again. Remember that we train these movements in an exaggerated form as the stress of the fight will tighten up our movements. This is not just true of the punch but of the hammerfist as well.

THE PUNCH

THE PUNCH IN THE CHAOS OF A FIGHT DIFFERS FROM THE WAY WE
MIGHT PUNCH IN THE CODIFIED ENVIRONMENT OF A SPORT FIGHT. THE
CHAOS MEANS WE NEED TO DO MANY THINGS ALL AT ONCE. WE MOVE
OFF THE CENTRE LINE TO MITIGATE THE RISK OF RECEIVING A BLOW
FROM OUR OPPONENT. OUR HEAD SINKS AND OUR SHOULDER ROLLS UP
TO PROTECT OUR CHIN. OUR HAND ROTATES AS A CONSEQUENCE OF
OUR SHOULDER COMING UP BUT ALSO TO PROMOTE OUR STRONGEST
KNUCKLES FORWARD. WE ALSO CHANGE LEVEL WHICH GIVES US THE
POSSIBILITY OF 'SHOOTING' IN LOW ON OUR OPPONENT!

ANGLES OF ATTACK

We learn various angles with all of our attacks - punches, kicks, elbows, knees, headbutts, attacks with the shoulder, with the hip, the hand grips and so on. This is because we move and the opponent moves. We need to attack across all our potential ranges and in different angles to control the opponent and to strike them as we or they move, changing their angle to us.

Although I train all these angles separately and consciously in order to give my body the chance to find power in the moment in that angle, in my head I do not 'select' an angle. I let my body do it for me, having trained the hell out of them. In my head, in the fight, every strike angle feels like it's direct and I am just striking whatever I can. In order to let the body flow like this we need to train it hard so it finds the movement when we need it.

To train strikes without the body mechanic is pointless - ineffectual strikes in the street will get walked right through. I once sang *Sitting On The Dock Of The Bay* by Otis Redding with a fellow officer in a run-down pub in Wales on karaoke. When the song was over we could hear a group of Welsh lads hurling abuse at us for being English. Fair enough. Then they took it up a notch threatening violence.

My comrade and I went over to calm them down a bit 'come on lads no need for that' and so on. They turned pretty friendly then and we had a bit of a laugh and a chat. All being full of beer we left the pub at the same time. As I was about to walk out I turned around to check the rest of our lads were coming.

When I turned back I thought I had bumped into a closed door and was confused for a second. My comrade suddenly threw a punch at one of the Welsh lads that connected and the fight spilled into the street. Somehow I had one of the lads in a headlock and my comrade had restrained an opponent over the bonnet of the car and was punching him in the face. Caught in a stalemate for an instant and worried about my exposed head, I flicked my opponents head upwards and headbutted his face. He staggered backwards and his mates pulled him away. My comrade let go of his guy and the Welsh lads made a tactical withdrawal, giving us verbals as they went.

After it was all over I asked my comrade why he had thrown that punch. He looked at me and laughed 'because one of those blokes punched you in the face Rich!'.

What I had thought was me bumping into the door was actually a fist hitting my face with no real power. The lad had obviously been waiting for me to turn round and picked his moment to ambush me pretty well. If he had a decent punch he may well have knocked me clean out. In fact the friendliness of those boys had been a ruse to lure us in and it worked. What let them down was poor body mechanics!

The strikes are thrown with the whole body. The fact that a hand makes contact if it is a punch and a foot makes contact if it is a kick is merely the end result of a whole body movement. It is worth once again comparing fighting in self-defence with sport fighting here. In the history of boxing, the jab in its modern form evolved due to the nature of boxing gloves and the changing rules of boxing with timed rounds and so forth.

The jab is a distance finder, a distance management tool, a points scorer and used to set up power punches. It is ideal for energy efficiency over a series of rounds. For self-defence we have established that an opponent is likely to be going at us 100%. What we need is powerful strikes off both hands.

Rather than a 'jab' and a 'cross' we need a lead punch and a rear punch that both deliver as much power as we can develop. We may not get another chance. There are no rounds and no cautious and measured engagements.

To the eye of the sports fighter, self-defence mechanics look big and over-committed. We need to understand how the principles differ between these two seemingly similar activities. A sports fight is more like the duel we encountered in an earlier chapter. To me, in fact, a modern MMA fight is the ideal of a duel without weapons. It is a civilised and restrained version of a fight with rules and boundaries. The street fight is more like combat. No fixed duration, no rules but a desperate and immediate struggle for survival.

Another analogy that highlights the difference in the skills needed comes from soccer. You may have seen these 'freestyle soccer' guys. They do amazing, unbelievable tricks with a football. Sometimes you look at them and think "why aren't you playing for a top football club earning £200,000 a week? But the skills are different between freestyle soccer and playing team football.

The best and most skilful players like Cristiano Ronaldo can do both however. He can do all the tricks and yet also has the positional and tactical understanding of a different situation with the same basic tools. This is also the case with the more analytical MMA fighters. They understand the sport of mixed martial arts with one opponent and also how the same tools are used of striking, entering and so on in the explosive situation of a street fight with potentially more than one opponent.

Even with no understanding of multiple opponent movement, the individual who has well trained strikes with good power is increasing their chances of achieving the aim of resolving the situation. I make a big deal of the problems of facing more than one opponent but of course it may be that you only ever get into a couple of real fights in your life and they both turn out to be against one opponent only. But if I rely on this always being the case I am making myself more vulnerable to circumstance.

This is the same as someone never training kicks because in the very few fights they might have been in, they never needed them. Who's to say what the future may hold? Maybe I never need to do anything different in my whole life. Maybe I need it tomorrow, we don't know. This is at the heart of what it means to be truly prepared and Battle Ready.

This is also why I train different angles to cover the possibilities I may have to find in the moment. Relate this again to the doors and windows. In the illustrations previously shown and to follow, look at how the different angles that we train can function against an opponent in a range of positions, from standing to lying. These are examples, the possibilities are endless!

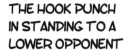

THE HOOK PUNCH
IN STANDING TO A
LOWER OPPONENT

BEING ABLE TO ACCURATELY
STRIKE A MOVING HUMAN
TARGET IS WAY HARDER THAN
MOST PEOPLE REALISE.

ADD FEAR AND
ADRENALINE INTO
THE MIX AND WE
UNDERSTAND WHY SO
MUCH PRACTISE IS NEEDED
- BOTH AGAINST THE
PADS AND IN SPARRING.

THE PUNCH FROM A KNEELING POSITION TO A SUPINE OPPONENT

THE MECHANIC OF THE PUNCH REMAINS THE SAME BUT WE MUST PRACTISE THESE POSITIONS AND NOT ASSUME WE CAN DO IT WELL BECAUSE WE PRACTISE IT STANDING. EVERY POSITION HAS ITS OWN 'FEEL' WE MUST DEVELOP.

DISTANCE AND RANGE

We take as an example now a longer range attack - the kick. Again if we compare this to a sport like Muay Thai we can find a 'teep' -a type of front kick driven into an opponent's midsection to cause winding but mainly to manage distance. This keeps an opponent at range and also can disturb their base to set up a round kick that they cannot block due to being unbalanced. In some ways it operates like a jab in boxing hence its name which means 'foot jab'.

For self-defence however, the reasons to kick are to destroy, to

THE HAMMERFIST UPWARDS FROM THE KNEELING POSITION

WE MAY CATCH THE GROIN, BUT THE INTENTION WITH STRIKES TO THE LOWER BODY IS TO BREAK THE BASE AND POSTURE OF AN OPPONENT TO REGAIN THE INITIATIVE AND PREVENT THEIR ABILITY TO STRIKE IN THAT INSTANT. THEN OUR FIGHTER FILLS THAT SPACE IN TIME WITH HIS OWN ACTION, RUTHLESSLY EXECUTED.

provoke or to connect. If we understand the typical 'one big engage-ment' nature of fighting in self-defence then the reasons become clear. To destroy is perhaps the most obvious, we look for example to strike the head of a downed opponent or perhaps look to destroy the knee or ankle of a standing opponent. It is kind of obvious to state that this limits the capability of our opponent to strike us back but its true nonetheless.

To provoke is a way of getting our opponent to open up his doors by striking him at long distance, allowing him to close the distance and anticipate his attack with a simultaneous counter. To connect is to use the kick to attack but also make use of the foot's ability to hook onto an opponent in order to control him with subse-quent actions. This has the result of moving under dynamic control from the long to short distance.

As always, there are exceptions that prove the rule. Having said that the 'teep' as seen in Muay Thai is not our intention in the street, I can recall an example of its effective use. When I attended Leeds Metropolitan University I lived near the Headingly Cricket ground, as a great many students do. The area was always packed when Pakistan played England because Leeds and nearby Bradford have a high proportion of people of Pakistani origin, first, second and third generation.

They come in big numbers to support Pakistan so the sight of English people waving Pakistani flags around in the streets of Headingly is common on match day. This causes some tension even though I have never seen it reported in the papers. Around the area we lived in were also many families of Indian origin, Muslim, Sikh and Hindu.

I had gone to hang out round the corner from my own shared house at the home of one of my friends on the rugby league team. The noise outside was deafening as the fans streamed through - drunk English fans, singing Pakistani fans and us caught in the middle.

We could hear some fights breaking out and some glass smashing. My friend had his car parked outside which was his pride and joy even though it was a beaten up Ford Fiesta. Not many students could afford cars in those days. We opened the door to look outside and wished we hadn't. All we did was attract attention. In truth we probably should have just closed the door but our attitude was full of the arrogance of youth and we started giving back any abuse that was directed at us. The problem was apparently that we were students.

So, in a fascinating example of mixed up tribalism, English people of Pakistani AND native origin were combining to abuse other English people for going to uni and getting educated. My favourite insult was from a British Pakistani man, supporting Pakistan against England, shouting 'get out of Yorkshire and go home' at us in a thick Bradford accent. My friend, almost by reflex, shouted 'get out of England and go home'.

As soon as the words left his mouth I knew the shit would hit the fan. It was probably the worst and most stupid thing he could have said given the situation. There we were, a right pair of tits standing on the doorstep outside the house. Clearly the only thing to do was get the hell back into the house and shut the door. Like all the houses in that area, every door had a cage that locked over the door to prevent burglaries. If we could get that shut then we should be ok. All the windows had metal grills over them too.

A group of fans came over to us as we started to withdraw into the house. Emboldened by our retreat, one fan jumped into the door way, his hands in the door frames trying to launch himself inside. I was standing directly in front of him in the hall. To shut the door I needed to clear him out of the doorway.

Lifting my leg right up, I gave him the hardest teep I could manage and he flew back off his feet, out of the doorway, his back smashing against my friend's car. In the gap in time that had created, we closed the cage, locked it and slammed the door shut inside it. Breathing hard and with the adrenaline still going strong we disappeared out the back. My friend looked at me and said 'Did you have to kick him into my car?'.

The 'teep' was appropriate in this case as I needed precisely to create distance to resolve the situation. This is a very specific example to this particular incident but the principles remain the same.

The kick angles again are an example of how to find a powerful strike in a given moment in time. We cannot afford in such an explosive encounter to take the time to adopt our most favoured position and launch our favourite strike. Like with so many things that are time critical it is better to go with a good solution right now than a perfect one too late.

We need to 'go with what we've got' and find as much power and function as possible. Different angles with the kick can give us certain opportunities, however, as shown in the illustrations.

Typically for self-defence we tend to keep the kicks pretty low. This may mean that we kick the lower limbs of a standing opponent or use the kick against the head or torso of an opponent that is kneeling, sitting or lying. This is due to the fact that attempting to kick the head of a standing opponent has many risks from over balancing, having our kicks caught and so forth.

It is also true that it is likely that our kicks are a bit more ragged in the street than in the gym. We can watch people kicking beautifully in the gym, on the mats with shorts on and bare feet. When we kick on uneven surfaces with jeans and shoes on perhaps the kicks are not as 'clean'. I say perhaps as there are always those characters who have trained the kick super hard for years and can kick to the head as fast as punch to the face. These individuals are rare though and you will know if you are one of them so low kicks are the general rule.

This is also true even in mixed martial arts where the majority of kicks are low rather than to the head. This is due to the fact that a head kick is vulnerable to being countered and the opponent taken down in a bad position. When fighters do kick to the head in mixed martial arts it is more likely than not that they have set up this attack with feints, strikes and so forth. Or they may be reacting to an opponent that is hurt or fatigued. In any case, the head kick is used most when the opponent's base is compromised in some way.

Taking a different angle of the kick - the oblique kick from standing. Typically this is used as an opponent is rushing in. They may have passed the distance where we can side kick their leading leg. They then enter into the range of a shorter kick which does a similar job. Our front kick can also do this, but with a different range again. This applied with good mechanics and an aggressive attitude to an onrushing leg, on or just above the knee with shoes on, can give us an amazing function.

The fast thrust of this kick can straighten the opponent's leg and hyperextend the knee joint. Maybe this severely damages the leg and maybe it doesn't in the moment. But the opponent is stopped in their tracks allowing us the counter beat to exploit.

The aforementioned 'side kick to the kneecap' (as opposed to the oblique kick) was advocated by Bruce Lee as an opening attack to the attacker coming forward in a street situation. The side kick gives us a longer range than any other kick as in this angle, the leg is longer than if it is straight out in front of us (especially when accompanied with the 'shuffle' step).

This is true anatomically of the punch as well, a punch side on to the body is longer than straight out in front. This does not mean however that we should always punch or kick side on for self-defence as the situation dictates the angle and what is needed.

We have previously covered how stance effects our ability to deliver and receive force and what stance is desirable for self-defence. I can be side on in a given moment but I need to return to a stance where my hips are squared to be able to resist and generate forward pressure.

If I am engaged in a points fighting martial art however, side on is good as I need not worry about generating power. If we look at the strange spectacle of Olympic Taekwondo we can see this in action.

Again the kick should be trained in isolation then in combination with the punches and hammerfists and everything else so that it becomes just another strike which can be found in a given moment. Having to consciously select our strike is something we need to train beyond so we can react with instinct.

CIRCULAR KICK FROM SITTING

OUR INTENTION IS NOT TO END UP ON THE FLOOR, BUT IF WE DO WE MAY NEED TO FIND A FUNCTIONAL STRIKE WHERE WE ARE. HERE, OUR FIGHTER FRAMES OFF HIS HAND AND STRIKES HIS ONCOMING OPPONENT BEFORE THEY CAN CAPITALISE ON THEIR POSITION.

THE FRONT KICK FROM STANDING

WE NEED TO UNDERSTAND HOW OUR FOOTWEAR CAN INCREASE THE FUNCTION OF OUR KICKS AND WHETHER WE AIM TO STRIKE WITH THE HEEL OR TOE OF OUR SHOE. WHAT IF WE ARE WEARING STEEL TOE CAPS? WHAT IF WE ARE WEARING LEATHER SOLED BROGUES? WHAT IF WE ARE WEARING FLIP FLOPS?!

THE SIDE KICK FROM STANDING

THE CHOICE OF WHICH STRIKE IS A CONSEQUENCE OF THE DISTANCE OUR FIGHTER IS FROM HIS OPPONENT, RATHER THAN A 'PREFERENCE' FOR ONE STRIKE OR ANOTHER. THE SIDE KICK IS THE LONGEST RANGE STRIKE AS THE SIDE ON POSITION INCLUDES THE LENGTH OF THE HIP

OBLIQUE KICK FROM THE STANDING POSITION

THE KICK TECHNIQUE USED BY OUR FIGHTER IS DICTATED BY THE DISTANCE TO THE TARGET. HERE OUR FIGHTER USES A SHORT RANGE KICK – THE OBLIQUE – TO DESTROY OUR OPPONENT'S BASE AND THROW HIM DOWN TO THE GROUND.

TRAPPING AND ENTERING

We have previously encountered the concept of 'entering in' to the opponent. Maybe our strikes are so strong, functional and accurate that the opponent drops. We train them as hard as we can to increase the chances of this happening. If so, great. But more likely we need to enter and in doing so may end up in the 'trapping range' (also called the 'clinching range') as a consequence. It is not our intention *per se* to end up here but it happens and if so, we need to deal with it just like anything else.

For me, the most important word when discussing this range is CONTROL. If we have gained some forward pressure from our entry we may already be disturbing our opponent's posture, placing him on the back foot to be able to launch further strikes or destroy his base and take him down, move him around or whatever. If we get our opponent under control in this way then in that moment he is ours until he can regain control and counter. The idea is never to allow him to regain control. Attack must follow attack again and again until the opponent is resolved. Having created our opportunity we need to ruthlessly exploit it.

It is vital to assert again that our aim is to RESOLVE the situation. Therefore, we do not have to take a certain course of action like for example in judo. We may be able to control our opponent in the trapping range and continue with strikes. We may take them down to the ground and strike them whilst we are standing.

We may exit the trapping and disengage with strikes in order to continue attacking from a different range. This may be as a prelude to escaping for example. Our control of the opponent will allow us to use them as a shield in a moment in the fight as well.

Every movement in the trapping should help us control the opponent. We need to break his posture and disturb his base. Rather than placing our hands in position on him therefore, we need to strike and grasp the opponents flesh as hard as we can. Every grip needs to be like this to help our control. As well as giving us a firm handhold to control our opponent it also shocks them with pain and lifts their body weight. This is the previously mentioned 'monkey grip'.

It is key to understand that our control of an opponent lasts throughout the engagement. We are not in the business of 'tussling' with an opponent. If we trap an opponent then we are trapped as well! This is a serious vulnerability when we consider that there may be more than one opponent involved. Even if we are in a neutral position to the opponent who we are connected to we may well be in a weak position with regard to another opponent. Every second that we spend tied up makes us vulnerable.

The trapping range then is a moment in time not an end to aim for. This is very different from seeking to 'restrain' an opponent. If I am in law enforcement for example, it may well be my aim to control and restrain an individual. It may be that a violent person is resisting arrest. In this case my aim is the restraint of the individual in order to arrest them. If I found that I was suddenly outnumbered it may be that my aim would change.

Imagine having to try and restrain an uncooperative and violent person on your own with other individuals attacking you as you did so. What would happen even if you managed to take the person you wanted to arrest down to the ground? Imagine having to put the handcuffs on them as the others surrounded you, aiming kicks at your head! I have seen a lone policeman restraining an uncooperative person many times but never when a group of people were trying to stop him. Policing in this country relies on the cooperation and consent of the general public in order to function.

If I end up in the trapping range and I meet resistance I do not therefore try to fight fire with fire in a simple trial of strength. This may function well if the opponent is significantly smaller and weaker than I but this is never taken for granted! What if my opponent is as strong or at least as strong as me in that moment? It may be that the opponent is simply so strong that I cannot control them in the trapping range. Remember that this is the street and in this chaos we will find some things function and others don't function in a given moment.

An old saying is that 'everything functions and nothing functions, it depends on us'. Maybe in that moment my intention was to take my opponent to the ground whilst remaining standing myself, perhaps controlling them by my knee on their belly or chest as I strike them with punches to the face. Instead when I try and move the opponent, he feels like concrete, rooted to the ground like a great oak tree. He is giving me nothing to work with and is solid. I abort the movement, exit the position and continue the attack with strikes.

If my opponent tries to move towards me, rather than resisting this movement I go with it and pull him forward. If he is pulling himself back, I step beyond him and use his momentum to take him down. If he is in a neutral position, I can twist him down, turning him off his base. These are all just examples of how an opponent can be moved. A great deal of practice is needed for the body to find and feel each mechanic.

TRAPS & TAKEDOWNS

The reason I am taking an opponent down is to put myself in a much more advantageous position so I can destroy the opponent. I use the word 'destroy' to mean resolve the situation by my opponent not being able to hurt me anymore through my use of violence. It is therefore meant in a technical sense, just as the mission verb 'destroy' in the army means 'render combat ineffective'. Again, I don't have to take my opponent down, it is one way that I can move towards resolving the situation.

It would be possible to write an entire book (and many have done) just on how to take an opponent to the ground, Remember here that what we want to grasp are the principles, rather than all the different technical aspects and variations of which there are a seemingly endless variety.

For our purposes, we can split our traps and takedowns into high-line, midline and low-line and further into front and back with each. These refer to where on the opponent we connect to - high-line is around the head and shoulders, midline the waist and low-line the legs. Its right to focus on taking an opponent down as it's a way of resolving a situation that has lots of benefits.

We don't want to stand up and simply trade blows continuously with our opponent or opponents. We know why that is so difficult with more than one opponent but with one even, the longer we trade blows the more likely we get clocked. The opponent is likely going 100% so the chance of getting hit with something big is high, even if the opponent has little skilled training.

Any opponent swinging hard must not be underestimated. This is a good way of getting humbled. Once we are knocked incapable in the street our life is in danger and we have no means of controlling the outcome. This is no place to be. Striking hard, entering and resolving the situation is the way forward.

Basically speaking, what determines whether high-line, midline or low-line is the opportunity that presents itself in the moment. If we think back to the 'doors and windows' we can see that when an opponent strikes, he opens a door. When we strike an opponent likewise, a door or window is open for us to exploit.

Regardless of where the takedown is, the principle remains the same, we need to take away the opponents base and prevent them from re-establishing that base. Timing is crucial. There is a military expression called 'overmatch'. To overmatch an opponent means to bring more force to the fight in that moment in time and overwhelm them.   Concentration of force is key to this principle. Even if the enemy has a larger force than mine, in a specific location, where he cannot bring his numbers to bear I can 'overmatch' part of his force. This means I could break through his lines, establish a 'break in' point and so on. Concentration of force is a key principle in the use of artillery as well. We want to get maximum effect in a focussed area rather than 'penny packet' our artillery - spreading it out too thinly to achieve a significant effect in any one area.

In fighting we overmatch with power and speed of action, exactly the same. My speed gives my opponent no time to counter and my power prevents him from countering once that action is begun. Before he knows it he is in a terrible position if he is still aware of his surroundings at all.

In the gym in which I train and teach we have a young MMA fighter of twenty years of age. His real strength is his low-line leg takedowns. His opponents study his fights and watch him time after time shoot in for this takedown, take his opponent to the floor and submit him with a variety of methods. Even though they know exactly what he is going to do, they can't stop him doing it.

HIGH LINE TAKEDOWN

HAVING GAINED SOME FORWARD PRESSURE AND BROKEN HIS OPPONENT'S POSTURE, OUR FIGHTER CLAMPS TIGHT AROUND HIS OPPONENT'S HEAD AND USES A TWISTING MOTION TO TURN HIM OFF HIS BASE AND ONTO THE GROUND.

ENTERING THE MIDLINE

OUR FIGHTER IS DOMINANT IN THIS SITUATION ONLY IF HE BREAKS
THE POSTURE OF HIS OPPONENT. SEE HOW THE FIGHTER SMASHES
FORWARD WITH HIS SHOULDER AND HEAD WHILST PULLING IN WITH
HIS ARMS. THIS BREAKS THE OPPONENT'S
POSTURE AND DESTROYS HIS BASE.

LOW LINE TAKEDOWN

OUR FIGHTER DRIVES HIS SHOULDER INTO THE OPPONENT TO BREAK
HIS POSTURE AND GRIPS HIS LEGS TO PREVENT THE OPPONENT RE-
ESTABLISHING HIS BASE. HIS INTENTION IS TO PUT HIS OPPONENT
ON THE GROUND WHILST NOT ENDING UP ON THE GROUND HIMSELF.

This is the benefit of developing real speed of action and should not be overlooked. He is so fast on his entry that just as your mind clocks that it is happening he has already done it. So much for their carefully prepared strategy! Of course, as he climbs the ranks his opponents attributes will get better and better too and he will face fighters with equally as fast takedown defences. Then the real fun begins for the spectator!

COUNTERING TRAPPING & TAKEDOWNS

If we are trying to do this to an opponent it is likely that the opponent is trying to do the same as us. The chaos of the fight means that even if we trained super hard, there will be moments when we find that something has been done to us rather than the other way around. We have looked at countering the strikes with blocks and attacks and how this depends on how fast we can act with reference to the before, during and after timing beats of the action.

The trapping and takedown counter-timing is the same. If we are 'trapped' in control of the opponent we need to maintain our base and posture and counter his control with an attack of our own. A key element of this will be how we make space. To control an opponent the opposite is therefore true, for in that moment of control we take space away. Think of how a spanner needs to be tight onto a nut in order to control it. If the spanner is loose, we cannot turn the nut properly.

When we have space we exploit what space we have created. So if I control my opponent I need to take his space away. And if I am controlled by my opponent I need to make space.

Distance and timing are interconnected so that space equals time and vice versa. I can fill the time that I have 'created' by making space with my own actions to regain the initiative. The grips we looked at before are a way of controlling and making space also. A strike in the trapping distance can make space also and cancel my opponent's forward pressure whilst creating my own.

When I have the initiative again, I apply attack after attack to resolve the situation. This involves anything that the situation

COUNTERING THE HIGH-LINE TRAP

IF WE REMEMBER THAT THE OPPONENT IS TRYING TO CONTROL US BY TAKING AWAY OUR SPACE, OUR FIGHTER USES THE MONKEY GRIP TO COUNTER THE FORWARD PRESSURE OF OUR OPPONENT, BREAK HIS POSTURE AND CREATE SPACE, PRIOR TO FURTHER ATTACKS.

demands, whether using the opponent as a shield, taking them down, striking and escaping or whatever. The point is that the outcome is in my control now rather than my opponents.

This tells the story technically, but my attitude must be one of total aggression. It is not the case that the attitude should be zen-like calm. That attitude may be appropriate for some sports fighting competitions where positions can be relaxed into and so on. For the street we cannot allow our opponent anything at all. Every beat may be our undoing with serious injury or worse being the consequence.

COUNTERING THE LOW-LINE TAKEDOWN

OUR FIGHTER MUST PUSH HIS HIPS FORWARD IN ORDER TO COUNTER THE FORWARD PRESSURE OF HIS OPPONENT. IF THIS IS NOT DONE IN TIME, THE NEXT CHANCE TO COUNTER MIGHT BE ON THE GROUND – NOT IDEAL!

The attitude must be always explosive to take the initiative and overmatch the opponent. This is particularly true when we are being attacked and must counter the opponent's actions. Often if we have the right attitude, the 'technique' itself is of less importance.

Even with sheer aggression alone we can find a solution that works. I wasted a lot of time looking for the zen-like calm approach, the movie star unruffled persona. This is a dead end. The approach we follow is more like turning on a switch that unleashes fury and violence and then turns off when the situation is resolved.

People often say to me "what should I be thinking about before the fight or during the fight?' or 'if I am walking down the street and see a suspicious character what should I be thinking about if we get into a fight?' The answer is not to think of anything. The training you have been doing will be reflected in what you do if you have been training properly, without you needing to think about it.

If you have to think about it, it is held in the wrong centre. If the fight occurs, allow your attitude of aggression to emerge and guide your Moving Centre. When you look back and recall that your body seemed to just do something of its own accord you will know your training was good.

GROUND

We know that we are not seeking to get involved in the street with a fight on the ground. The street is no place to be lying on with an opponent either on top of you or underneath you with others standing anywhere in your vicinity. To advocate the approach of fighting the opponent on the ground is not to understand correctly our dangers and vulnerabilities in the street rather than sport. Even the surface of the street itself is a danger to us.

If I think of where my gyms are, in Liverpool and Manchester, I can bring to mind many incidents over the last year where individuals have been killed in fights from hitting their heads on the pavement. Often they have not died instantly but several days later. When we are on the ground we are fixed in a location and even if we are in a position on top of an opponent we are in a very vulnerable position to others standing.

If I am fighting a 'challenge match' or a duel-like fight this matters little. If we are in a dominant position on the ground to our opponent then we can control the fight. We do not need in this case to worry about who is coming up behind us. But in a bar or in the street there is no guarantee whatsoever that we will face one opponent only. The fight may begin one on one but once we are on the ground we have little control over our movement and no control over who then can join the fight.

If I am in a very dominant position astride an opponent on the ground I may be able to control the opponent beneath me but my head is up and exposed to everyone else like a golf ball on a tee. If I am the one underneath then this vulnerability is compounded by the difficulty I will now have efficiently striking and moving. I will have to contend with an opponent or opponents raining down strikes on me. It is absolutely true that I may be able to fight the opponent on the ground and if the fight remains one on one throughout. M a n y people have done just this and 'got away with it'. But we are dealing here with possibilities and vulnerabilities. In a risk versus reward analysis it makes sense to stay on my feet and anticipate another assailant. Of course it is possible to come up with scenarios where we may only have one opponent and can safely predict this. In these cases you need to use your discretion. As a general rule, the ground is no place to be.

Just because we do not intend to get involved in a fight on the ground does not mean we will not end up there. In every fight, the opponents have a vote - meaning that we alone do not always dictate events. If we end up in the ground in any position, our aim is the same: to get back to our feet. If we have landed in a position on top of our opponent then we may need to control them to prevent them holding us down and then continue our attack from our feet, or from for example, 'knee on belly'. The opponent will instinctively want to hold onto us to prevent us posturing up and being able to strike down onto him. If we ourselves are on the bottom therefore, we need to control our opponent and get up.

The ground is a very technical area, meaning that detailed technique in movement and understanding is needed to get good function. On the ground, leverage and body mechanics work by 'feel' rather than by sight as it is hard to see what you are doing and likewise hard to see what the opponent is doing.

We need to develop the ability to feel through our bodies what the opponent is doing and to know in a moment where our own limbs are and what the opportunities and possibilities are in any given moment. All while we are involved in a struggle for survival.

Ability on the ground does not come easy. Of all the areas we can train in, it's the one that takes the most time. This is because, as adults, moving around on the ground is unfamiliar. We almost have to relearn how to move. It is amusing to watch toddlers play at any time, but particularly when they are moving in and out of the cardboard boxes we discard from our household goods.

There we can see that they have a very natural way of moving on the ground that we soon lose when we stop doing it. This is what we need to relearn. It can feel particularly hard on the body as normally we only have the soles of our feet in contact with the hard surface of the ground.

We can find ourselves involved in a fight on the ground for a number of reasons. We can be pushed over, we can trip, we can stumble and lose our balance, we can be taken to the ground by an opponent or we can get pulled onto the ground as we ourselves are taking an opponent down. The sooner we can recognise this and act, the less vulnerable we are. But perhaps we get pulled in on top of the opponent. We need to control the opponent so that they cannot continue to hold us in a fixed position or to damage us with strikes or with bites or with thrusting their fingers in our eyes.

Our intention is then to keep our attack going and get back to a less vulnerable position on our feet. We can fall in a number of ways and positions onto an opponent - but we should instantly make them pay for this by striking as we fall into the ground. The principle here is to control on the earliest timing beat we can to control and get up. We do not want to get into the chaos and danger of the ground.

When we control, we will often have to expose our head for an instant, but this is all it should be - an instant. To minimise the risk to us from other opponents we should only be exposed for a moment in time, like 'breaking cover' on the battlefield. Getting up whilst continuing to control the opponent needs serious practice as it's like a game of stepping stones.

When we control the opponent, we need to deny him the space to move. Whilst he is free to move, he is able to get control of us. If he can touch our face with his hands then he can gouge our eyes, whilst he can move his neck he can bite our ears and so on. This control must be gained with the urgency of desperation. We cannot allow any opportunity for our opponent to get us mixed up in this battle. Although of course this may happen in the chaos of the fight, we cannot acquiesce and allow it to happen thinking that we can simply deal with it on the ground. Our vulnerability is such that this could be the last thing we ever do.

At no point in the fight should we be allowing our opponent anything. This is different in the sport where for reasons of strategy we may even encourage an opponent to set up a position which we then aim to counter. There is a distinction here to make between allowing an opponent a position and provoking a strike which we can predict

SIDE CONTROL FROM THE SITTING POSITION

NOTICE HOW THE FIGHTER IS CRANKING THE NECK OF THE OPPONENT IN ORDER TO PREVENT HIS MOVEMENT. IN ADDITION, THE FIGHTER'S WEIGHT IS TRANSFERRED ONTO HIS OPPONENT AND HIS HIPS ARE OFF THE FLOOR TO MAXIMISE THIS.

SIDE CONTROL FROM THE KNEELING POSITION

HAVING ENDED UP ON THE GROUND, OUR FIGHTER IMMEDIATELY GAINS CONTROL OF THE OPPONENT'S MOVEMENT VIA THE FORCE EXERTED ON THE OPPONENT'S HEAD. BECAUSE THE OPPONENT CANNOT MOVE HIS NECK, THIS MAKES MOVEMENT WITH HIS SHOULDERS OR HIPS EXTREMELY LIMITED.

BECAUSE OF HIS VULNERABILITY TO OTHER OPPONENTS, OUR FIGHTER NEEDS TO EXIT THIS POSITION WITH A SENSE OF URGENCY. HE DOES THIS VIA THE 'STEPPING STONE' METHOD; WHILST KEEPING THE ELBOW CONTROL ON THE FACE, HIS LEFT KNEE IS PLACED ON THE OPPONENT'S BODY. THIS ALLOWS HIM TO REPLACE THE ELBOW CONTROL WITH HIS RIGHT KNEE AND THEN STAND UP, CONTROLLING THE HEAD OF THE OPPONENT THROUGHOUT.

and counter. The difference is this: provoking a strike does not make us vulnerable to other opponents in the way that allowing a position does.

Any situation in which we are trapped by an opponent is a red light danger signal. Although we can work hard at countering these positions, nothing can be taken for granted as we play for the highest stakes. The consequences of not being able to counter are dire. Far better not to have to.

COUNTERING THE GROUND CONTROLS

Let us say though that this has happened despite our best efforts not to allow it. We have lost the initiative, missed the timing beats that would allow us to counter in the standing or at any other point and we find ourselves on the ground fighting with our opponent. The aim again is to return to our feet. The method of doing this is simple to state but hard to do. We need to make or maintain space in order to move.

A great deal is talked about in self-defence about the things you can't do in sport such as grabbing testicles, gouging eyes, gripping the flesh, fish hooking our opponents face and so on. These are not magic techniques though, they still must conform to the principles of what we are trying to achieve. In terms of countering being controlled on the ground, they are ways of making space. For example, try not moving your head back from having fingers in your eyes. These may be particularly effective techniques if we are able to reach the eyes or other parts. But even if not, we need to go to where the opportunity is and keep going until we find the function.

Relentless and desperate perseverance is what is required to get the function. The attitude here is a world away from that of sport grappling where we are taught to relax in a bad position to be efficient with our energy. We may even hold an opponent down and wait for them to have to move and create their own space in doing so. I have no doubt that if we put our collective minds together we could think of a scenario in self-defence were we could be sure that there is no chance another opponent could get involved. There are always exceptions if we think hard enough. But a fight in a bar or on the street carries this risk even if the fight begins one on one. On the ground now we are a sitting duck so to speak!

Making space comes from all these things; our body mechanic itself (for example 'hipping out' or 'shrimping'), strikes, grips, gouges and so on. When space is made we can now counter and get up. If we have not yet arrived at the 'after' beat, in other words if our opponent is in the process of trying to control us rather than already having done so, clearly we have more time and distance in order to deny the opponent his control of space.

The 'best' timing beat is simple to understand - the sooner the better. There is so much nonsense surrounding the martial arts that it can seem like there is a solution to everything, no matter how bad it seems. But this is not the reason that we do not give up in the street. Everybody that does sport grappling for example knows that you can be put in situations from which you can't escape if you leave it too late. If any of the guys in the gym get a choke in deep on me I'm going to sleep. This is why people 'tap out' or submit. In the street we can never surrender like this because our opponent will not stop like they do in sport. For us, we need to keep going whatever.

I remember well a friend of mine recounting how he had been badly beaten up in his teens by a group of lads. He had an opponent

MONKEY GRIP FROM THE LYING POSITION

OUR FIGHTER USES HIS FREE ARM TO GET HIS MONKEY GRIP ON THE OPPONENT'S FACE. RIPPING THE OPPONENT'S HEAD AWAY FROM HIM BREAKS THEIR POSTURE AND OUR FIGHTER TURNS THEIR BODY OVER HIS OWN, ESTABLISHING HIS OWN TOP POSITION.

on top of him and was being beaten on all sides but he continued to move, block and try and fight back regardless. Just as he felt everything starting to go black the lad on top of him was dragged off violently. An old lady had seen the fight and called the police. The policeman who saved him also got an ambulance there quickly. He had broken ribs and his jaw still clicks when he talks but he lived to tell the tale. We can never know when something will change that can save us or an opportunity open that we can exploit.

EYE GOUGE FROM THE LYING POSITION

THIS IS ANOTHER WAY OF MAKING SPACE. AS OUR FIGHTER FORCES HIS THUMBS INTO THE EYES OF HIS OPPONENT, THE OPPONENT DRAWS HIS HEAD AWAY, LIFTING HIS WEIGHT OFF OUR FIGHTER. IF OUR FIGHTER IS STILL UNABLE TO MOVE HIS HIPS AWAY FROM THE OPPONENT, HE CAN TURN THE OPPONENT OVER HIS BODY IN THE DIRECTION SHOWN.

CHOKES AND WRENCHES

When it comes to chokes, strangles and joint locks for ground fighting or at any level we need to ask ourselves if what we are doing conforms to our principles. Typically if we are looking to attack the joints then we are looking to wrench rather than lock, unless we are using that opponent as a shield and use the lock to force them to move in the direction we want them to go.

This is due to the fact that locking a joint up also involves locking ourselves in one position. Imagine the 'arm bar' in ground fighting - applying pressure to the elbow joint with our hips whilst preventing the arm escaping. Whilst we are in the action of doing this, our head is exposed on the ground. With a guaranteed single opponent this is no issue, but with the chance of more a great deal of risk is involved here. This does not mean that it will not function nor that it shouldn't ever be done, just that it should be applied as a wrench rather than a lock in order for us to regain some protection and get back up. Following this fight logic forward, the same applies to chokes or strangles.

It can take many moments for an opponent to be unconscious from a choke and even with a strangle, we may need to spend time to get the strangle on properly. This may be time we don't have. We cannot say 'never', but I hope that you can see that there is always this weighing up of risk versus reward with whatever we are trying to do in the fight.

Maybe we are a guy that is a super cool demon master of applying chokes and can do them faster than you can believe. Maybe we are so good that all our attempts at chokes come off without fail and the opponent is unconscious in seconds. After the fight we leave a trail of unconscious bodies like breadcrumbs leading back to whatever hole the bad guys crawled out from. Again, if that's you then awesome.

But for the rest of us we need to understand the risk versus the reward of being tied up trying to apply a choke. Perhaps more likely for us is to go on hard with the neck crank as a wrench and continue the attack.

In training, these wrenches of the arm, leg, hip and particularly the neck need to be done with serious care and attention as not to hurt our training partner who has been kind enough to allow us to use his body to train on. With a live body, training a crank or wrench is a 'mime' rather than a proper action. We do it with space in between rather than taking the space away as we would do for full function. You can still train the full function, but with inanimate grappling dummies rather than your friend!

ARM WRENCH FROM THE KNEELING POSITION (RIGHT)

THE INTENT HERE IS TO DYNAMICALLY 'SNAP' THE ARM RATHER THAN THE MORE CONTROLLED PRESSURE WE MAY APPLY AS AN 'ARM BAR' IN BRAZILIAN JIU-JITSU. THIS IS DUE TO THE FACT THAT WHILST OUR FIGHTER IS FIXED IN THIS POSITION, HE REMAINS VULNERABLE TO ATTACKS FROM OTHER OPPONENTS. OUR FIGHTER SNAPS THIS WRENCH ON TO LIMIT THE TIME HE IS EXPOSED TO A MINIMUM, WHILST DOING MAXIMUM DAMAGE TO HIS OPPONENT.

ARM WRENCH FROM THE KNEELING POSITION

CHAPTER 8
TRAINING THE PRINCIPLES

I find that quotes from the great jazz musicians describe the process of learning fighting better than many who are fighters. Perhaps this is because musicians are skilled at expressing themselves, I don't know. But the process of learning can be likened to a becoming a great jazz player.

This is because what we do in the fight is fundamentally an improvisation. Far more so in self-defence than it is in sport fighting as there are so many variables of location, time, opponents and so on. We are never fully prepared and we have to do what we can in the moment. We could try and train for every scenario we might face and, whilst it is necessary to train in loads of different scenarios we could never cover them all. Far better to learn how to improvise.

The jazz greats began as all musicians do by learning how to play a note. Then they learn scales then chords, then chord progressions and so on. For the piano players they learn scales with one hand then with two hands and move onto simple songs and more. There needs to be a serious level of competency with the basics in order to even think about improvising. Never mind the melody to start with, can we actually find a note? The process begins formal and structured, but as time and ability progress, ever more freedom is given to express and improvise.

> You've got to learn your instrument. Then you practice, practice, practice. And then, when you finally get up on the bandstand, forget all that and just wail."
>
> Charlie Parker

Charlie Parker could just have easily been talking about learning to fight as playing jazz. It's the same process exactly of learning Moving Centre skills.

"Sometimes you have to play a long time to be able to play like yourself."

Miles Davis

Have you ever watched a child trying to communicate who has not yet learnt to speak properly? You can see the frustration as the child wishes to say something but has only a few words to use. What they want to express is already in there, inside them. But you need skill to channel it out and make it something real.

Music is like a language, fighting is like a language. We can see ourselves in our minds eye defeating opponents left, right and centre, our strikes powerful and accurate, our movements swift and sure. But we can only do that for real if our bodies have the skill to channel this expression. In music, we call those that can truly play out their expressions 'virtuoso' performers. This ability is what we are going for!

"Anyone can make the simple complicated. Creativity is making the complicated simple."

John Coltrane

So many people come to train in fighting skills and end up getting worse - suddenly they are hesitant and uncertain because they have had their instinct knocked out of them trying to learn complex strategies and movements. We humans have a terrible habit of over complicating things because we can. Often it is because we think it looks more impressive or has more value in complexity.

We love moving things into the Intellectual Centre where we can sit and talk endlessly in arguments over this or that style or whether something would or wouldn't work. All this talk is ultimately pointless. We need to find the simple solution and learn how to execute it with the right timing. We can build this ability on our natural fighting instincts because we do not have to think too much about them under pressure. Anything that comes naturally should be exploited as this is likely to continue to function during stress.

There is no doubt that a powerful and well-placed punch is potentially devastating in the fight. But what makes the punch so valuable is that fact that hands will naturally ball into fists under pressure. Again, the example of small children is relevant here. You can watch them ball up their little hands as they feel threatened or angry. If it's an instinct, then we want to follow that instinct and build skill around it to make it more effective. The instinct will remain under pressure and guide our actions.

People will sometimes comment that punching with a bare fist in a fight is dangerous as you might break your hand. Actually, every time you hit another person with part of your body you have a chance you might hurt that part. You get a headbutt wrong you can seriously damage your neck or knock yourself out.

The first two knuckles of your hand are pretty strong (the index and middle finger knuckles) whilst the last two (the ring finger and pinky finger knuckles) are relatively weak. This means we need to practice hard to mitigate the risk of damaging our hand. If we are punching over and over for an extended period of time we will certainly increase the chances of damaging our hands. But the street is often a short engagement where good punches can resolve the situation quickly.

"You can read all the textbooks and listen to all the records but you have to play with musicians that are better than you."
Stan Getz

Learning is not easy and it takes time and hard work. There are no shortcuts other than putting in as many hours as possible in a given period. Often the people we think of as making fast progress have been practising in their own time and therefore only appear to be learning more quickly.

So many of the businessmen I train are disheartened by not being as good as me at a particular skill even though they have only been doing it for five minutes! They say 'I'm no good at this' and 'you make it look so easy'. I make it look easy because I have done it thousands of times. That's it. No talent or mystical ability needed.

They often regard the things they are good at - like buying and selling - as their 'natural' gifts when they, in fact, forget that it took them years to build up their businesses, making mistake after mistake before getting it right. This can be no different. The more exposure you can get to training with good people the better you will get, even if you feel like you are making no progress.

We certainly believe that we should be 'good' at things right away, especially if we have done well at school. This is never the reality with skills that are worth having. We forget that we had to learn to walk early in our lives. A baby doesn't give up trying to walk because it falls over time after time. The baby doesn't try it for five minutes, decide it's 'no good at this' and give up!

I spend most of the time rolling in Brazilian jiu-jitsu against people a lot better than me with many years more training. That was a big reason that I took up a new martial art, rather than stay in my own bubble. At the end of a session I feel like I've been in a car crash. It isn't until someone says to you that it is getting a lot harder to beat you that you know you are improving.

Likewise we need to have an instructor as we are unable to recognise our own habitual behaviour. This is a weakness in humans. We must get the views and guidance of people who are better than us at a certain skill.

The understanding that we lack the ability to recognise our habitual behaviour is important. When we accept this weakness in ourselves we can do something about it. Getting a trusted individual to help us is vital in all human endeavours. The human is a creature of habit. When those habits are positive then we reap the benefits but when they work against our aim we need to change them.

When we think of 'habits' we may think of addictions, which after all, are simply very powerfully ingrained habits. We talk of people having 'addictive' personalities. But we ALL have addictive personalities - personalities that build and follow habits. They might not be quite as obviously destructive as chemical addictions but humans are basically a collection of habitual behaviours.

If they work for our benefit then we may not even recognise them as habits. But habits they are nonetheless. We may think of the bodies' dependency on chemical substances exclusively through alcohol or drug addictions, but what of the 'people pleaser' whose habitual behaviour is driven by chasing after the warm glow of endorphins that flood the system from helping people? What of the gym junkie who craves the natural chemical high from exercise? Or the adrenalin junkie who cannot help themselves doing dangerous activities? We all have our triggers, some which are positive and some which aren't, but they are there regardless and take many different forms.

The job of any good instructor in any field is to help an individual acquire 'good' habits. 'Good' in this context means any habits that enable us to achieve our aim.

RHYTHM

When it comes to different martial art expressions, for example the street versus sport we will find that everything has its own rhythm. People say to me 'why do you also spend the hours learning a sport martial art when your interest is in 'the street?'. Well, my interest is in the skill and art of fighting. It is true that that for me means fighting in self-defence but do you remember the quote from *The Hagakure* that talks about "...he should be able to hear about all Ways and be more and more in accord with his own."?

When you train in a sport martial art you are able to get a new perspective and that perspective allows you to reflect on your own training and have a deeper insight on why certain things are done in a certain way. From outside of the method, you can see the principles that underpin it.

Going back to the musical analogy, someone I greatly admire is Nigel Kennedy. A true virtuoso violinist, I have watched and listened to him at his concerts overwhelm the audience with his skill and expression. Sometimes he plays classical music during the first half and then jazz in the second, exchanging his wooden acoustic violin and plugging in his electric violin.

The rhythms of Vivaldi or Bach are quite different from the rhythms of jazz but such is Mr Kennedy's understanding of music, he can play anything. He even played some Jimi Hendrix at the end of the concert. It is said that Mozart had the skill to be able to play in the style of anyone else and that he could play with his hands reversed and so on. Jimi Hendrix himself is said to have been able to get up on stage at someone else's gig by invitation and play a guitar strung for a right hander left handed, merely playing everything reversed.

This is a good example to follow in our own training. With some sport martial arts we can get away with being proficient in only one side as we have one reference point (our single opponent). In self-defence fighting we must be able to fight off any side and in any stance.

The human is designed for this after all as we have evolved bi-lateral symmetry - the ability to go and attack prey and to be able to take an opportunity off either side. It would be going against nature not to use it!! Unfortunately we grow up mostly only developing skill in one side which starts with learning to write with one hand only. It need not be like this of course.

Any decent footballer can play off both sides as it gives them an advantage. The skilled footballer can take the ball early on his 'other' side rather than having to wait for it to cross his body. A story is often told about the tennis player Rafael Nadal, that he learnt to play with both hands from a very early age and elected to play with his left hand because opponents had less practice against left handers. We may always have a stronger side or a preferred side but we need to be able to use both well.

Breaking down the process of learning as we did for the jazz musician, we need to first orientate ourselves to the thing we need to learn. A would-be jazz musician can simply listen to records of Miles Davis, Thelonious Monk, John Coltrane and so on. The would-be fighter should watch footage of fights, particularly fights captured on CCTV. At this stage to read a little on fighting and to watch some real fights is all that is needed.

This is a continuous process as is listening and appreciating new music to the musician. The physical process begins with learning an element - a direct punch for example in isolation. The punch can be trained first by imitation. This allows the body to feel what it should be doing. Over and over with many repetitions is the way to do this. Then we can train that punch with a reference - a partner holding up a pad to hit. The punch now is trained developing power so the body can feel how it should transfer body weight though your centre of gravity.

We can evolve that training now with movement, our pad feeder moving around and demanding a punch at irregular intervals. The body has to 'find' the action each time. We can progress to training this same punch as an action and reaction drill. The pad feeder attacks us with a direct punch, we cover and throw back our own punch. This is now a kind of fighting dialogue that allows us to pick up a rhythm, meaning that the body can now act without thought but just by recognising the rhythm, over and over.

Once we have a basic function with the punch, we can move to training it with two opponents. As an example training drill we can have one designated 'driver' and one designated 'chaser'. The chaser's job is to try and get round our back. Once there he can unload some strikes with the pads onto our back.

Our job is to try and keep the driver in between us and the chaser so he cannot get to our back. Meanwhile the driver will hit us with a pad, we cover and hit back - and move and continue moving all the time. This is an exhausting drill but it practices what might be only one beat in the fight but over and over. It adds limited chaos to the drill to place us under pressure.

As we get better, our opponents can turn up the pace. We can add pressure by training in low light, training with distractions of flashing lights and so forth. Sometimes we introduce a fourth person whose only job is to periodically push us to disturb our balance.

We can train any isolated element like this - a round kick, a hook punch, entry and so forth. We can add combinations of elements as we improve. This is one example of a drill we can do to train elements with pressure that can be increased or decreased depending on the ability of the person being trained.

There are other elements that we will need to continuously train to keep fresh and sharp - isolated steps and movement drills for example. As we develop though our shadow fighting should get more fluid and natural. Shadow fighting is a way of visualising opponents and improvising actions and reactions.

With this kind of improvisation we can go through countless scenarios without too much pressure - like improvising music without an audience. This is something that should be done daily. As the ability builds the mind can experience many, many different movements and find connections between them.

We can also improvise with a partner or partners with 'freeplay'. This adds some feedback to your movements by doing them on a live person. This is still consensual as we allow our partner to train and improvise on us as part of the back and forth of the training.

Finally we have sparring. This is where our training partner will resist and make a game of the fighting. We can limit sparring to punches, to kicks, to punches and kicks only, to adding takedowns and so on. Or we can have just takedowns or have one partner defend only and one attack only. We can do two on one sparring or every man for himself and so on. We need not necessarily go 100% - we should be able to control the intensity depending on what we are doing.

For training striking we may well want to wear mixed martial arts sparring gloves or light boxing gloves. The idea with sparring is not to replicate a real street fight but to practice technique with a moving resisting opponent. This gives us a much better way of learning the distance and timing required to get function than pad work alone.

Pressure does strange and important things to us. It can also be our ally and make our reactions sharper and our movements quicker.

When travelling back to my house late at night, I stopped off at a local petrol station to get some food. As I went through the automatic doors I could hear people shouting and things being thrown. My adrenaline shot up and I thought maybe a gang was fighting inside. Worried for the girls who worked in there whom I knew, I cautiously went inside. A man ran towards me down the aisle I was facing. He had a mask on and had an axe in his hand held upright. He was carrying something in his other hand that I noticed but didn't register.

People I couldn't see were shouting at him. I instinctively moved to one side to keep the end of the aisle in between him and I. I certainly did not want to tangle with a man carrying an axe, training or no training, the odds are not good. Not something to get involved with if you don't have to.

A huge man appeared in the doorway, blocking the axeman's path out of the door. All at once it became clear that the axeman had robbed the till and was trying to escape. I couldn't believe that this huge but unarmed man was going to deliberately take on a desperate guy with an axe. The big man rushed him and the axe came down. Except at that point I saw that it wasn't in fact an axe but the broken off end of a garden rake! Now I understood the big man's courage and jumped in to help him wrestle the 'rakeman' onto the floor and wait for the police to arrive.

What had been in his other hand that my eyes saw but did not register was £10,000 in cash. My eyes in survival mode had clocked the weapon but ignored the non-relevant (to my survival) details. Because he was running with the rake side on, my brain had played safe and interpreted it as an axe making sure I got the hell out of the way!

We can add to our training the use of weapons, from impro- vised weapons such as pens, keys and rings to weapons such as sticks and knives. What we need to find is the reality of facing them and using them and the principles that guide their use. A good deal of falsehood has come into martial arts and self-defence training around these weapons. This is perhaps due in part to martial arts movies but also due to training with practice blades for example.

Many martial arts sell themselves on the promise that you can face an opponent with a knife and through training, deal with him easily. Nothing could be further from the truth. With or without training, facing a knife unarmed is likely to end up very badly for you. All you need is one mistake and it's over. When we train to face the knife we are forced to begin by being 'fed' a prearranged angle that we identify and then counter. With training we should make the angle more and more unpredictable.

In doing this, we will soon see how hard it is to pick out the angle. With a real knife you can imagine the consequences. Often when people train the knife they forget the fact that they are being given an angle and never get beyond this phase, leaving training in the mistaken belief that they are good to go when facing a knife.

If we do a simple training exercise we can see the difficulty. Give your training partner a big felt tip marker pen and put a white t-shirt on. Now get him to attack you, trying to mark you anywhere on your body. Try not to get marked. Each mark is a cut. It shouldn't take long to realise that the tactical withdrawal is the best option against the knife.

When we train to defend against the knife we must train with this understanding. People carry knives for a good reason, they give the wielder a huge advantage over the unarmed opponent. The reality is that facing them is a disaster waiting to happen. This does not mean defence is not possible, but know from the beginning where the advantage lies. To enter into the fight with these odds should never be by choice.

With training knives and training sticks we can spar as well and this has value but again we must recognise that this is not the same as using real weapons in a real situation. This does not mean it is pointless - far from it. If that was the case then infantry training with blanks would be pointless too which it certainly isn't, but we must know that this is a training drill. The same is true of sport fighting.

Sport fighting also gives us an opportunity to practice one element of fighting. In terms of supercharging your progress, it makes sense to spar and practice mixed martial arts as well too. You may also find it very useful to compete in mixed martial arts at whatever level. We are not talking here about becoming the next UFC world champion, it may just be an inter-club competition with limited contact or a local amateur fight. The reason is that competition adds a significant level of intensity and pressure.

If our focus is self-defence then we need not pursue this necessarily to the point where it is taking up all our training time. But without doubt competing gives us an extra edge. If you happen to be a bit more mature a good solution is to compete in, for example, Brazilian jiu-jitsu in a mature age category. Of course, this is not the street where our opponent can be of any size or weight but remember that sport is not the street and in sport we need to play an agreed game.

The key in the street is not to play our opponents game! But there is still great value in this to experience some adrenaline and need to perform. Perhaps the perfect mix for the street is to train self-defence and also spar and compete in mixed martial arts. The self-defence training needs to build body mechanics and attitude, of which the attitude part must focus on awareness and aggression. It is imperative to understand movement and principles with multiple opponents.

The mixed martial arts training gives us the best opportunity to train distance and timing against a range of training partners and opponents. It is best if some of these training partners are not the same guys you train self-defence with if possible. You need to be tested against people who will not fall into a familiar rhythm with you.

We have to use the physical body to absorb these principles. During our training, we will experience things and understand things that we could not have foreseen at the beginning when we weren't aware of what we didn't know. We can use this as the blueprint for learning any physical skill and by extension, learn about all kinds of possibilities for our development throughout our life.

TRAINING ATTITUDE AND BODY MECHANICS

Do you remember what we said about the army training developing a sense of urgency? To do this, the environment that we train in needs to reflect our training goals. This starts with the instructor. If I want to train a sense of urgency in my students, I can't turn up late myself. If my demeanor is so laid back it's horizontal, the students will be too. If I wish to create an attitude of awareness, I need to instil it in the training session from the very beginning. A typical example of this is to shout 'ready?' before the training drill begins, to which everyone must reply 'yes!' and then immediately start the drill. If the reply is not fast enough or some students don't reply at all, everyone does 2 press-ups including the instructor.

It is remarkable how a simple thing like this can lift everybody's sense of urgency, alertness and awareness. In reality, you can't lose as press-ups are a good exercise anyway! But people will do anything to avoid what they see as a failure. Rituals are important too. Here I'm not talking about elaborate bowing to the master but we need an acknowledgement that the session is beginning, such as a communal salute, in whatever way you do it. We also need a similar ritual for the end.

If you are training hard, sometimes emotions can threaten to get the better of you and you can get wound up by others or through frustration. Having a formal acknowledgment that the lesson is ended and a show of respect to the instructor and fellow training partners allows you to dissolve this and continue with the right attitude. Half-assed training will quickly creep in unless we create the ethos that we need to train well.

Some of the very best instructors I trained under in the army were Scottish. I'm not sure why that is but they were able to break down complex subjects into clearly understandable pieces. The environment they created was disciplined and everybody stayed switched on for sure. But they tempered that with humour and made the experience enjoyable as well as hard work. They never added complexity unless it was unavoidable and even then, the clarity with which they explained it allowed your understanding to develop. To teach people well, you must be sure not to give the student all the answers. The best approach is to give the student only what they need right now in the moment and then let them absorb it and make it their own.

Techniques and body mechanics are 'what' we train - they form the content of our sessions. But attitude is trained by 'how' we train and the environment we create.

DOING IT FOR REAL

It is an unavoidable truth that to have a clearer understanding of self-defence, we must be in a self-defence situation for real. This is true of a soldier training for conflict as well. When I look back on my army career, I can recognise that there was a progression of understanding that was linked to the intensity of my experience. At first I was in training, then on operations in Northern Ireland, then Iraq, then Afghanistan.

As fate would have it, each operational deployment chronologically raised in intensity. I now understand armed conflict on a far more profound level than if I had never been deployed on operations at all. But does this mean I am now an 'expert' on all types of warfare, historical, present-day and future? Of course not! But my knowledge of some of it is at least first hand. Specifically I can talk with some experience of patrolling and patrol commanding, public order, base security, running brigade operations rooms, battle management and so on.

I can talk with knowledge about certain other aspects such as clearing compounds or bridge demolitions without actually having done it myself first hand. But my understanding is of a lesser order than those things I directly experienced.

Clearly the more direct and varied my experience is, the more likely it is that my understanding is deep. I say varied because some have experience of only one aspect but again and again. This is a trap we can get into when we sometimes give too much credence to self-appointed experts. It may be that they have great experience but perhaps that experience is in a very narrow field or even out of date.

An individual may try to impress us by stating that they have 'twenty five years of experience'. But is that perhaps merely one years' experience repeated twenty five times?! Just because someone has been in the game a long time does not guarantee that their growth and learning was constant.

We need then to show discernment in who we give credence to. No-one can claim to be an expert in an area of life where each new experience is unique and chaotic by nature. There is no doubt however that you can get an understanding by experiencing fighting at first hand that you cannot get in any other way.

This does not mean that you have to abandon all common sense to get it. I had been involved in some fights before I started training seriously on account of being in the same place as groups of hot headed young men. After I started to train properly I found, as many people do, that the idea of fighting outside of training was something to be well avoided. Hanging out in those places was no longer appealing.

But I felt very strongly that my training needed to be tested. It may have been that I could wait to be attacked and see what happened - but this may never happen, especially as I was much better at recognising warning signs and removing myself from situations.

My solution was to go back to the kind of places where I had experienced fights before. If you live in the industrial north of England this is not hard to do. There still exists a culture of drinking and fighting in certain places. This culture is not knife wielding or gun carrying but more a legacy of the hard working, hard drinking lifestyle of the past. Mining towns are now ex-mining towns but this aspect of recent history remains in part. If you go out with friends in the wrong places you need not look for fights but merely don't back down when they come to you.

Knowing that I was going to be an instructor in self-defence, how could I stand up with credibility, look into the eyes of students and know that the training we were doing had value? Clearly I had no intention of coming to serious harm or injury, which was a distinct possibility. So the friends I decided to go with were guys that could handle themselves and back me up if needed.

Sure enough the lessons were proved. Striking hard and fast and continuing to strike hard and fast was the key - to which I would add making your exit hard and fast as well. Constant forward pressure to resolve the opponent. No strike selection as such but whatever strike is available at the time and at that distance be it hand, elbow, shoulder or head.

Once those lessons were tested, there was no need to keep repeating this dangerous experiment. It should be noted too that even this type of testing does not replicate the exact circumstances of an attack out of the blue. After all, I was expecting it and therefore not too drunk or otherwise to deal with it. But it's pretty close. Close enough.

Whether or not this is something that you decide to do I leave entirely to you. It is, of course dangerous and carries the possibility of very serious injury or worse. To some, this may seem ridiculous and irresponsible. But I have friends who downhill mountain bike, base jump and all kinds of crazy stuff that I wouldn't do. When I train in Spain I often walk past the Valencia bull ring and I definitely wouldn't go and stand in front of a bull. But if I wanted to really understand any of these things I would have to do them. And be prepared to take the dire consequences if things went wrong. There is a Spanish saying that translates as 'if you play with the bull, you get the horns'. Be warned!

OUR LEARNING POTENTIAL

"The secret to happiness is freedom...And the secret to freedom is courage".

Thucydides

Our focus has been to improve the knowledge in the Moving Centre because that is what we lack more than any other. Our Intellectual Centre is very well looked after by our countless, abundant information, but we need to find a foundation of truth in our lives to make our thoughts real, rather than fantasies. The Moving Centre can provide that foundation. This is only a beginning. To follow the building analogy, the wise man builds his house upon the rock. You can start to build that rock by following this book.

You may wonder why it is that our schooling does not give us a better beginning. The reason is that we have an unfortunate academic snobbery in this country, a legacy of the time when not everybody went to school past fourteen years of age. Think of the employment that most of us have. We mainly have jobs that involve us doing something be it sales or administration or whatever. It is more likely than not to be a commercial pursuit. Why is it then that our schools overwhelmingly focus on academic subjects? These are the least useful subjects to the majority of students as preparation for life.

The truth is that our academic system is a self-licking lollipop. We study at school to get the academic grades for more academic study at university. A bachelor's degree is an academic preparation for a master's degree. A master's degree for an MPhil and an MPhil for a PhD. Then, when all common sense has been slowly grinded out of you, perhaps you can get a professorship back at a university! We have met a good professor in a previous chapter, so this is not true in every case but as a critique of our system it holds true.

The university was only ever designed for certain people who required genuine academic study. These were research scientists and archaeologists, theoretical mathematicians and anthropologists. It wasn't meant to be a passport to a higher grade job which contains little academic work.

If we are honest, if we leave aside the access to graduate jobs for a moment, that time - three or four years when we are young and vigorous could be better spent learning something more useful. That is not to say that there is NO value in the university system. We meet with people from all over the country and the world and broaden our horizons.

There are some occupations that require the theoretical study that you need, including the occupations identified above. But for most of us, three more years of academic study is a gear change down rather than up. How much theory do you need? We do it to get a better job and time and time again, it does not build the kind of skills employers want.

Taking it back to our school system, which has become a preparation for university, what skills should we be teaching? Some academic study is needed certainly. We need to be able to read and write well. We need a working and practical level of application in mathematics. We can argue the toss of how much we need to know about science and other subjects. But look at the way they are taught.

It hasn't changed much in decades of teaching. We still have classrooms with children sitting in rows with a teacher in front boring the hell out of everyone.

I hated History at school. Absolutely hated it. The teacher was shocking and just talked and talked about boring dates. We were expected to take notes and then write essays for exams. I even managed to get a score of 3% in a History exam at the end of the year. When I left school, I started to read and became fascinated by history, a fascination that continues to this day. But my fascination with history is always tied to something - what can we learn about the process of war? What can we learn about product design or fashion or technology? The study of history for the sake of the study history is boring and pointless.

It is by doing something that we then need the theoretical underpinnings rather than just learning theory that floats around in the air never sticking to anything. We need to start with the application and grow from there.

If we had learned something useful at school then perhaps such a book as this would not be required. But... this is the situation we are in. There are things that we should have learned at school, for example how to sell. There are schemes to do just this, like Young Enterprise. But they are done not to learn well but to bulk out applications for university and we are in the same problem again. If we forget about going to university unless we actually want to be an academic then this frees us up to learn how to sell properly.

Selling is a skill that everybody needs, whether they go into sales or not. We need to sell products, sell ideas, convince others to back us, to employ us and so on. It is also a huge advantage to be able to drive. Why isn't this taught at school?

The level of sports played at state schools varies greatly with location and whatever policies are currently in place. The reason that independent schools have a disproportionately high level of sporting achievement is because they spend more time doing it. Being well coached and putting in the hours is the biggest factor in success. The same is true of acting. The kids that go on to make it in sports and acting if not nourished at school, find local clubs and societies that fill that void. This relies on their parents to take them however and the availability of good ones locally.

Now onto the subject of this book being Battle Ready. Do we have any current methods in schools of teaching this? What methods do we use to encourage young people to learn how to deal with crisis and pressure? Do we teach leadership and team-working?
This is something that the Duke of Edinburgh's award scheme is designed for. But what is it actually for? Bulking up an application for university again! It is not even a compulsory subject so only those that aspire to university are doing it.

So why aren't we learning what's in this book? Why aren't we learning fighting skills as well as a vehicle for creating a strong foundation in every student? We are unfortunately overshadowed by our perception of what that means. It conjures up images of 'fagging' and sadistic 'character building' activities originally designed to create leaders for Empire. This is the perception and it has some truth in it. There was a time when the British public school was a cold and forbidding place, full of sanctioned violence of master to pupil and pupil to pupil.[39]

Undoubtably this system produced some tough, independent and extraordinary men and it also gave others a painful memory for life that made them think of their childhood as a time of strife rather than growth. It was an education sometimes lacking in development of the Emotional Centre.

The idea of the Englishman as having a 'stiff upper lip' comes from this time. It is an important distinction to make as being robust and ready is often confused with being a blunt instrument and being insensitive. This needs to be addressed as we need sensitivity in all centres in order to read situations and other people correctly.

This has nothing to do with the fact that it is 'nice to be nice' and everything to do with increasing our ability to make good decisions. There may be times when we need to display anger to get things moving or compassion in order to keep people onside. To have this flexibility means we cannot be brutish. Dunderheaded brutes are the bane of operational environments. They only have one response whatever the needs of the situation.

If we look back in history, to Shakespeare's time and on into the 18th century and beyond, we find a very different Englishman. The times were different and the world was slower and much less populated. The whole population of England in 1700 was just over five million.

One of the striking things from this period was the way that people spoke and addressed each other. There is an example from a letter that Issac Newton wrote to a companion of his that was sick. In it, he expresses his affection for him and signs the letter off with 'Your very loving friend'.[40]

To our emotionally unsophisticated minds we suspect that perhaps there is a homosexual relationship between them. There isn't at all, that assumption demonstrates how clumsy and constipated our expressions of affection from one man to another are. It wasn't just men either. If you read the letters from a lady to another they are similar in their expressions of love towards their female friends.

Perhaps this emotional sincerity was partly due to the harsh times they lived in. Newton lived through bouts of the plague and bouts of the English Civil War. Relationships were precious and if you needed to say something to someone, it was imperative you took the chance when you could as nothing could be taken for granted.

I had the great fortune to serve with a true gentleman. During the time when I felt most under pressure in Afghanistan he seemed to magically appear. Having not only the outward charm of a cavalry officer but also the genuine compassion of a caring human being, his simple words of encouragement made a huge difference to me. It is things like that that you remember when the memory of other events have long faded.

The 18th century, the time of the great duels, was certainly a time when men and woman took life in both hands as well. One of the striking things about this period was that it lacks the puritanical elements that we have inherited. When you read the lives of people then, they seem rawer and less sterilised, both metaphorically and literally.

Their sexual attitudes seem less prudish and repressed. London was called the 'city of whores' and it is estimated that one in five women in the city was a prostitute and it was seriously big business, along with the theft and criminality that went with it. This is not to somehow romanticise this period - William Hogarth painted the seedy and squalid reality of London then. But cultural attitudes to prostitution were not as they are now in England. This was the era of the libertines and famous mistresses.

Somehow this emotional honesty, sincerity and acceptance of human behaviour became lost as we enter the modern era. Perhaps it is merely a reaction against the preceding times and these things are cyclical. But we must understand that we modern people are masters of the 'veneer' and raw emotion and raw living are ever more masked. We get our kick for violence from movies, our kick for sex from the internet - all through screens. The screen is what? A veneer, a mask, a shield. We are one step removed from everything, from where our clothes are made to how our food is killed and prepared. This makes us wholly unprepared for when that shield is dropped due to economic collapse, terrorist attack, riots, breakdowns of law and order and so on. And there we lie, helpless and useless, complaining about how things aren't fair.

It is also true that our greater specialisation makes us understand less about the whole rather than more. The sheer size and complexities of companies makes it possible to have little idea of what other people working for the same company actually do. There are a whole host of long winded job titles of which the actual meaning is opaque. This is never truer than in any occupation that already deals with an abstraction - money being the obvious example.

People working in financial services desperately need some solid ground or anything like what we might call 'simple morality' disappears very quickly!

What we need is a modern system that produces men and women that are Battle Ready. How else will we best prepare for the uncertain times ahead? This however is a fight for another day. We need only to recognise now why it is necessary to do this outside of the current system and that the system does not help us. The educational system is, if anything, anti creating robust and independent individuals ready for hard times. Rather what they create are dependents.

Don't fight the bully back, tell the teacher instead. Don't learn by doing it for yourself, learn what you are fed. This is another aspect of the focus on theory and academia. When you learn by doing something, you learn independently from the teacher or instructor, you actually learn it for yourself rather than having to rely on the words or theories of others.

LEARNING FROM PLAY

When you look at baby lions you can see that they learn from play. In fact, all animals learn by playing. Perhaps this is partly due to the fact that without sophisticated language, they have to learn from doing rather than being taught theory. When they are taught it is by demonstration and imitation. This is exactly the way I teach students learning to fight in the beginning.

The theory comes after the experience when the student can relate it to something they have done. The play element is important as it allows the learner, whether animal or human to fail and to get things right without pressure to begin with, other than the motivation to enjoy and perhaps compete in a spirit of fun with a sibling or friend.

When I worked in army recruiting I went into a school and a teacher sent a pupil to talk to me. The teacher explained that this was a disruptive boy with ADHD who was a real challenge to teach. It was likely that he would not get any GCSEs of any grade. This lad came up to me with a swagger. I thought 'here we go, another kid they can't do anything with but they think he is alright to join a sophisticated and testing environment like modern combat training'.

This kid looked me up and down and said 'do you use the SA80 A2 rifle? I said 'yes we do' he said '5.56mm standard NATO round?' I replied 'yeah that's right'. 'Do you use the Minimi as well?' I said 'we call it the LMG, the Americans call it the SAW'. He said 'that's 5.56mm as well isn't it? Belt fed?' 'yep it is'. We then went into a question and answer session about various firearms of the world both historic and modern. It rapidly became clear that he knew a lot more than me.

The calibre of the World War 2 M1 Garand was not something I knew off the top of my head (.30 the kid told me). This was a boy that the teacher said could not learn anything! I asked him 'how do you know all this'. He said 'because I'm a gamer', then listed a load of computer games I have never heard of. He learned all these facts and figures from playing.

It is unbelievable given how many children love to play computer games that we do not have excellent, exciting games that you can learn all sorts of things by playing. We are blessed with some of the best games designers in the world in this country who could do a fabulous job.

The games would be better created independent of the system as well. If the system tried to do it they would tone down the fun and not make it competitive enough! No-one would want to play it then.

Think of the games that kids love to play - football games, war games, even games where you steal cars! This is the best and most engaging of all and the competition makes progress much faster. This is making the best use of the 'screen' to learn from. If we cannot change the tide entirely from doing things on screens then we can at least embrace it properly for positive learning.

LEARNING FROM FIGHTING

It is obvious to me that we should be teaching mixed martial arts in schools as well. This can be done at a variety of intensity levels from very soft to much harder. You can imagine the resistance however from the state.

It is easier to imagine it (if anything) being embraced by a school like Eton than it is by the state school sector and that's a great shame if our goal is to improve everybody's ability.

Learning mixed martial arts would take the individual back to the reality and away from the detachment of experiencing life, but in a controlled environment. This is not to say that every pupil should be forced to be involved at the same level. Like anything, if the pupil does not enjoy the activity at all, little good learning will take place.

We need to make a distinction here however between 'can't be bothered' and 'taking no value from'. There are aspects of all worthwhile activities that are difficult. Sometimes the best in any field don't enjoy aspects of their training. What I am talking about is a type of disinterest that means that no results are possible. With such a thing as mixed martial arts however, it is my experience that everyone can enjoy it to a level. For example, it maybe that an individual wants to go the whole hog, or to strike pads without competing or sparring, or to grapple only with no striking and so on.

This is also true for you in your own progress. The best mix as stated is for you to learn self-defence and also a sport martial art, with mixed martial arts being the most appropriate. You may want to compete however, as I do, in a purely grappling event or whatever. This will form the core of your Moving Centre training via fighting arts in the same way it did for Plato, Pythagoras, Shakespeare, Voltaire, Caravaggio and Churchill.

In my student group is a Rastafari. He has referred to our training as a physical 'reasoning'. In the religion of Rastafari, one of the ceremonies is 'reasoning', where Rastafari will get together to discuss things and find the truth. The spirit of finding the truth is at work in play, in training and in life if it is our intention to make it so.

LEARNING FROM ENEMIES AND RIVALS

Something that the military can teach us is to learn from enemies and rivals. Remember that the warrior has respect for his enemies and that respect stops him making the error in thinking he is naturally superior by right. Often the other people engaged in trying to succeed will have developed good solutions.

It is common in military circles to examine the tactics, organisation and leadership of the enemy forces. In many conflicts in fact, the enemy turns out to be the best teacher!

The Germans in WW2 were very quick to seize on the concept

of the all-arms battlefield and grouped units together of different combat, combat support and combat service support arms to create a self-supporting unit, usually brought together for a specific mission. This potentially produces a faster and more efficient way of operating and it effectively devolves and decentralises command for supporting units to the battlegroup commander.

So the engineers attached to the battlegroup become the battlegroup commanders troops to command as he sees fit. This tactic was widely adopted. A key innovation was to have the battlegroup operating on the same radio net, so the commander could rapidly coordinate their actions.

So too, in the world of sports do we see one team adopt a certain successful tactic and then soon everybody is doing it. Often the urge to adopt it comes when you have been defeated by it! This is the great benefit of competition, it is not possible to hide. Your defeats are out there for all to see.

Finding the truth, finding the best way involves opening our mind to whatever is successful regardless of the moral status or otherwise of the individual or group doing it.

PROGRAMMING

It is easy to see the analogy between the processes of our ubiquitous digital technologies and our method of learning. We have created computers in our own image, and the idea of 'programming' is a useful way of seeing what we are doing with our training. We are 'programming' the Moving Centre when we are physically training for example. One of the most powerful ways to speed up this programming is using visualisation and hypnosis.

We have covered the idea of visualisation in shadow fighting and this can be taken further with hypnosis. Hypnosis is really only a way of limiting our attention to internal, rather than external things. We get a slice of this when we daydream. It's the same thing but more focussed. This means that we can get into our internal processes more effectively. Some call this going straight into the 'subconscious' mind.

We need to be aware that the simplistic view of us as having a 'conscious' and 'subconscious' mind is only a theory and one way of describing our mental framework. There are of course many processes that take place below the level of our conscious awareness.

But perhaps a better understanding is that the mind has many, many layers of awareness and that our mind moves daily and frequently between many 'states' of awareness. States of awareness vary between the deepest levels of sleep, dreaming sleep, light sleep, daydreaming, partial awareness and full sensory awareness - such as during moments of high danger. There are plenty of states in between these and beyond.

It is easy to get concerned when we hear the term 'hypnosis' and imagine being in a theatre being forced to act like a chicken. This is, in fact, suggestion rather than hypnosis and only functions on those who are suggestible. Normally the stage hypnotist will ask the audience to do a 'suggestibility' test beforehand, typically asking them to close their eyes and imagine a helium balloon in one hand and a lead weight in the other.

Most peoples hands don't move, some will move a little and some will move a whole lot! It is the last category of people who will be invited to the stage. Coupled with the expectation of the audience and the slick performance of the showman, the chosen few will put on quite a performance if suggested to do it.

Hypnosis is quite different in that we are talking about a normal but internally focussed brain state. People experience states of hypnosis every day. A typical experience is driving home from work and not really remembering much about the journey when you arrive home. This is typical as often the Moving Centre can perform the familiar task of driving home with little conscious attention needed. The mind is then free to day-dream about all kinds of things.

States of hypnosis are common too when being immersed in a film or computer game or listening to music or reading a book. You will know when that's the case if you are disturbed and feel like you have 'snapped out' of your state of trance. It can be quite a shock to be pulled back into the real world when you have been in Narnia or Middle Earth or the land of Oz or whatever!

We can use this process however as way of establishing a positive thought process. This is done most powerfully by visualisation. The use of visualisation is now well established, particularly in sporting endeavours. We need to make sure that we have habitual positive visualisations, rather than negative visualisations.

To put this in a very simple example, we can imagine the football penalty shoot-out. If I go on the long walk from the half way line to the penalty spot to take my kick thinking "I hope I don't miss, I hope I don't miss", the chances are my visualisation is of me missing the penalty. Sure enough, like a faithful servant my mind then runs through that programme and I miss the penalty.

Instead, if a walk up visualising the ball going into the net my mind and body will do everything they can to make it happen.

The rugby player Lee Briers was famous for last minute drop goals for the Warrington Wolves and was asked once how it did it. His answer was instructive. He said that ever since he was a little kid he had been practising successful drop goals and would actually speak the commentary at the same time "..and it's Briers, in the last minute to win the game...YES!!!!"

When we think that this programming was happening without design, what things do we programme into ourselves without our awareness?

We are also programmed by our upbringing and by our culture. This is why we find it so difficult to gain a different perspective. We can be programmed in any of the centres. For example, military training is a great way to program the centres. Even now, people will observe me walking into a room and ask if I had been in the army. They do this because I still march purposefully as I walk with a straight back even all these years later.

This is an example of a Moving Centre programme that I am happy to keep as a good posture is useful. However, when I left the army, I became aware of other types of programming that are limiting, rather than useful. The nature of the teamwork in the army means that blatant self-promotion is seriously looked down upon. This is part of the culture and something you don't even know you believe. When you go into industry, where self-promotion is essential for the market to be aware of what you offer this lack of desire to push yourself forward at the expense of others is a disadvantage.

Clearly re-programming is what you need. This begins with knowing what your programming is in the first place. I was institutionalised in many ways from my army experience - for better and worse. It was not possible to see that when I was surrounded by other individuals with the same programming. Do you remember that we described where this programming is held in the Formatory Apparatus?

The solution to this is to constantly expose yourself to different environments and ways of thinking. To challenge yourself with 'work' such as learning fighting arts and being tested will act as a way of becoming aware through self-observation of your programming. We can use hypnosis, either with a partner, group, or self-hypnosis to aid the process of establishing good habits, whether in the Moving Centre or any other. An example of this is that you may often find yourself in the thrall of an Emotional Centre sub-routine when you keep being submitted in grappling training.

Depending on who you are, it may be of anger, of depression, of frustration or whatever. The most useful response is to use the occasion as an opportunity to find out what you need to improve. But going through the training in the first place is the key to finding the programming at all.

At the end of my training sessions, I always leave time for a few minutes of visualisation. During this visualisation, students sit down, relax and visualise themselves using the training successfully. For the sake of a few minutes of time, we can supercharge the learning process by programming in our desired aim.

AWAKENING THE WARRIOR

Now we are ready need to put all those elements together to awaken the WARRIOR.

The training that we have done and the understanding that comes from it need to activate this character that lives within us. The Warrior is relentless in chasing the aim, whatever that aim is. The Warriors strength comes from the fact that he/she is resolved to die to achieve that aim. All of the characteristics of the Warrior exist to achieve the aim.

The skills of the Warrior are perishable and must be kept alive via challenge, particularly by the facing of new challenges that force us to find new ways to solve new problems.

THE WARRIOR IN ACTION - WARGAMING

Now that you are building the skills of the Warrior, it is necessary to 'wargame' scenarios. This is in essence, a rehearsal which forces you to visualise and find a successful outcome. When we think through possible scenarios like this, we build a resource that the mind can draw from in real times of crisis. It should also allow us to identify gaps in our knowledge and take practical steps to do something about this.

It does not matter if our scenarios are extreme or fantastic - the more vivid the better as this will challenge your thinking. You will have observed people who can make super-fast decisions even though it appears to be the first time they have encountered a particular problem. Often this is because they have thought through similar situations a thousand times. The spirit of curiosity sustains this. Everything is within the Warrior's scope to try and understand.

SCENARIO 1 - TERRORIST INCIDENT.

POSSIBILITY 1

What if terrorists tried to take over the Arndale Shopping centre in Manchester, in a similar fashion to the incident in Kenya?

This is an interesting wargame for me as I walk through this shopping centre most days. Thinking about what factors are important is not useful just in case it happens for real, but it gets me thinking about the PRINCIPLES involved and how to deal with them.

Because I use a real place that I know well, I can run through a possible scenario. I imagine that I am in the Arndale Centre having a coffee. I hear shots being fired. Instinctively everybody takes cover and we hit the deck. We hear shouts and screams of alarm from all over. Glass is shattered. An armed man runs into the coffee shop and demands that everybody kneel against the wall. He is carrying an AK series rifle and a radio - a walkie talkie type - in his hand.

What are the factors I need to think about? Is there something I can achieve or isn't there? I don't know what this individual has in mind. Will he execute us all or is he here for something else. I take in all the details I can despite my fear. He is Arabic in appearance and shouts 'Allahu akbar'. Based on my previous knowledge I assume he is not afraid to die. I assume a terrorist motive. This is all I can do from my Observation and Orientation at this stage.

On the balance of risk, I weigh up rushing him to try and disarm him. I understand that this will get harder to do the more settled in he becomes. Now there is chaos around and it presents possibly the best chance I will have to surprise him. If I do nothing, I risk having my future and perhaps the manner of my death decided by others.

I make my decision and take my action. As I rush the terrorist he manages to fire his weapon. I die and that's the end of this chapter of my existence.

POSSIBILITY 2

When I rush the terrorist I manage to get close enough to control his weapon away from him. Others then rush into help and we wrestle his weapon from him. I shoot him in the chest in case he has a suicide vest.

In my wargame in my head now I imagine the court after the incident asking me why I felt it necessary to shoot rather than restrain the terrorist. The best I can come up with is that he might have had a vest on.

Whilst this is true, mulling the thoughts around in my head I wonder how you can effectively restrain a terrorist that is uninjured and not afraid to die? The simplest solution, divorced from legal constraints is to shoot him dead. Morally I deal with this conundrum now so it won't slow my thinking down later.

Do I have a moral problem with shooting an unarmed terrorist during his act of terror? I decide I don't (you may decide otherwise) and instead think again of the best solution. I hear the shouts of the terrorist's comrades from other parts of the shopping centre. What do I do know? Taking his radio I listen in and decide to press down and hold the pressel switch to jam the terrorist communications. I collect the terrorists rifle. Is my best course of action to try and get the people in the coffee shop out? What is my priority? The preservation of life (ours, not the terrorists).

This priority will guide my actions. Can the people get themselves out? Do I try to take on the terrorists by myself? I don't even know how many there are. Do I need to get more information (the Observation phase of the OODA loop)?

The above is just an example of how I can run a situation through. The main thing I get from the exercise above is that my priority is that my actions should try to preserve life. In the event, maybe there is nothing I can do to help this but who knows?

But by wargaming things I can practice good thinking about difficult challenges. It is necessary as well to do the unthinkable and put yourself in the mind of the terrorist as well. What is my priority now? Maybe maximum publicity/loss of life whatever. I run these things through trying to extract the principles that should govern my actions, exactly as my physical training and sparring does for physical principles.

SCENARIO 2 - DEATH OF A LOVED ONE.

This is a scenario that no-one likes to think about very much. But the Warrior engages with this to be of use to the rest of the family that remain when the time comes. He engages with it to take away his own fear and so that his grief when the moment comes does not completely overwhelm his ability to function.

When running through the scenario in your head perhaps you

discover that you know nothing about how to arrange funerals, deal with wills and estates, even what to do if you discover your loved one has died in their sleep. You find, in fact that you cannot even do a proper mental rehearsal without more information and so you resolve to find out the things you need to know.

When you find these out and run it through again, you find more about what you don't know and so on. Finally you get to the point where you can start to look at how the essential mechanics of your actions can ADD something to the situation beyond mere functionality. Can you bring a dignity to the occasion worthy of the life that has been lived? By preparing for the event, the Warrior can ensure that the necessities of the times do not overwhelm the occasion for lack of foresight.

The eventual solution may not be exactly like the ones you have rehearsed but you have created a working plan, something to bounce off, in order to create the best outcome in the circumstances.

The Warrior has a contingency for everything he can think of and he is always thinking of more. It is like a game within his mind:

What would happen if I woke up in a hedgerow at 8am with no money and needed to get back to home 300 miles away by 8am the next day?

What if someone starts a malicious rumour about me at work? What are the best actions to take? What are my priorities?

What if I return home to find my house has burnt down?

What if I discover my partner is having an affair?

What if my car is stolen?

What if my card declines?

What if an alien spaceship lands in my garden??!!!!!!
What if.......and so on.

The Warrior can build contingency plans because he knows that everything runs on principles and through his training has activated the necessary parts of his centres to have sufficient vision and skill in execution to deal with anything.

In military parlance, these contingency plans are referred to as 'actions on'. What are the 'actions on' seeing the enemy? What are the 'actions on' receiving mortar fire?, what are the 'actions on' taking casualties from enemy fire?

Again the key element is to describe the action you will take. Focussing our response upon a known action allows us to see through the uncertainty that would otherwise threaten to overwhelm us. One of my favourite 'actions on' was for encountering an improvised explosive device in Northern Ireland. The response is the four C's - Confirm, Clear, Cordon, Control. The commander's actions to make that happen is the three P's - Pause, Plot, Plan.

We can reduce even seemingly super complex situations into simple actions to take if we understand the principles we need to follow. When you see someone controlling a situation with confidence and certainty you can often wonder how it is that they can do this despite the panic going on around them. Have you ever watched the paramedics operate at a serious car crash? They know the priorities and principles they need to follow. They may ignore the screaming victim to get to the silent one who isn't breathing.

All of their training has been towards being able to unravel the situation into manageable chunks. The 'art' of the job is then being able to cope with the reality over the training. Good training will be realistic enough that this is not too big a chasm to jump. But even then, experience counts for a great deal and the old hands who have seen it all are rarely knocked out of their stride.

To the onlooker, the paramedics can seem super-human, working with decisiveness and urgency without panic amid the blood and gore. What we don't see is the training and experience that have lead them to this point. Although every situation is unique, the principles of how to act have been wargamed countless times by these professionals.

BRINGING IT ALL TOGETHER

In every one of these wargames, in every one of these visualisations, you are programming into yourself the role of the Warrior. It is YOU who have the will to act in these circumstances and YOU that is taking control. You take control because every situation needs a leader.

Every situation needs somebody who can create order out of chaos. There have been moments in my life when I have looked around for someone to deal with the situation and then realised that person is me. This is not because I am some kind of superman, far from it, but I have accepted responsibility for myself and for others.

If someone else in a situation has stepped up to the plate and is doing a good job, the role of the warrior is then to help in any way possible. More than likely though, if you have followed the principles in this book, it will be you that finds yourself in that position. Why? Because you will have built your Warrior and are Battle Ready.

During the course of the development of yourself, it will be necessary to involve others who are like minded to your team. You will need training partners and sparring partners, both in the literal and metaphorical sense. As you grow in any one area, your role is to help your partners in anyway you can, as they help you also. You may find that this bond of common purpose is far stronger than our differences of gender, race, religion, politics and so on. In truth, none of us exist alone but to be of service to others we must first have skills to serve them.

It is fortunate that one of the great joys of life is working with others towards a common goal. You will find that helping others to develop will further develop your own skills as well, as you are forced to articulate and demonstrate what you have learned.

Kind Alfred the Great, one of the greatest examples of the Warrior *par excellence*, said that 'every man must speak as he can speak and do as he can do'. He was a man that encountered huge obstacles in his life, tasted defeat on many occasions but ultimately achieved something remarkable by creating a nation called England.

It is up to all of us, regardless of who we are, to carry that banner forward and speak as we can speak and do as we can do.

THE ROADMAP

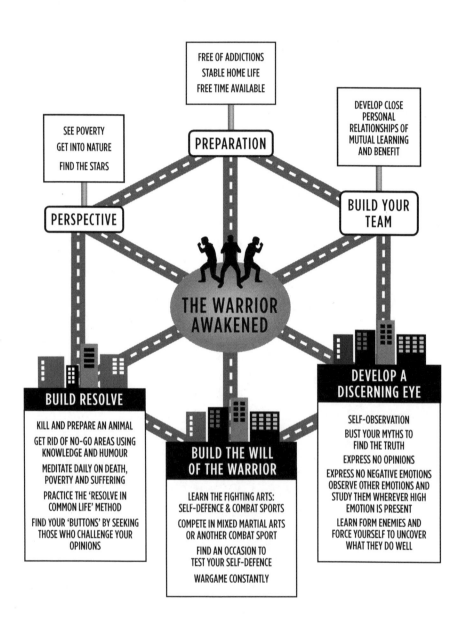

FREE OF ADDICTIONS
STABLE HOME LIFE
FREE TIME AVAILABLE

DEVELOP CLOSE PERSONAL RELATIONSHIPS OF MUTUAL LEARNING AND BENEFIT

SEE POVERTY
GET INTO NATURE
FIND THE STARS

PREPARATION

BUILD YOUR TEAM

PERSPECTIVE

THE WARRIOR AWAKENED

BUILD RESOLVE

KILL AND PREPARE AN ANIMAL

GET RID OF NO-GO AREAS USING KNOWLEDGE AND HUMOUR

MEDITATE DAILY ON DEATH, POVERTY AND SUFFERING

PRACTICE THE 'RESOLVE IN COMMON LIFE' METHOD

FIND YOUR 'BUTTONS' BY SEEKING THOSE WHO CHALLENGE YOUR OPINIONS

BUILD THE WILL OF THE WARRIOR

LEARN THE FIGHTING ARTS: SELF-DEFENCE & COMBAT SPORTS

COMPETE IN MIXED MARTIAL ARTS OR ANOTHER COMBAT SPORT

FIND AN OCCASION TO TEST YOUR SELF-DEFENCE

WARGAME CONSTANTLY

DEVELOP A DISCERNING EYE

SELF-OBSERVATION

BUST YOUR MYTHS TO FIND THE TRUTH

EXPRESS NO OPINIONS

EXPRESS NO NEGATIVE EMOTIONS OBSERVE OTHER EMOTIONS AND STUDY THEM WHEREVER HIGH EMOTION IS PRESENT

LEARN FORM ENEMIES AND FORCE YOURSELF TO UNCOVER WHAT THEY DO WELL

EPILOGUE
BEYOND THE WARRIOR

Awakening the Warrior is a serious and difficult task but it is one that is worthy of your best efforts. With the Warrior in you active and prepared to step up whenever needed you have built a capability that will unlock your potential.

But this is not all there is. Awakening the Warrior begins the process of linking the Moving, Emotional and Intellectual Centres together. To recap, let us look once again at our table of what activities take place in which centre.

INSTINCTIVE CENTRE		
MOVING Habitual sensations	EMOTIONAL Animal love and hate	INTELLECTUAL Intuitions
MOVING CENTRE		
MOVING Reflexes, imitation	EMOTIONAL Acting, love of activity	INTELLECTUAL Inventiveness
EMOTIONAL CENTRE		
MOVING Like and dislike	EMOTIONAL Aesthetic and Religious	INTELLECTUAL Higher creation
INTELLECTUAL CENTRE		
MOVING Knowledge gathering	EMOTIONAL Desire for knowledge	INTELLECTUAL Creative thinking (or fantasy)

Remember that the Instinctive Centre is activated in us all and cannot be developed, being complete already. The act of awakening the Warrior activates and develops the entire Moving Centre and links us into the other two centres via their 'moving' parts. Specifically this means controlling and developing 'like and dislike' in the Emotional Centre and 'knowledge gathering' in the Intellectual Centre.

Remember also that all of us come into this word with 'inclinations' towards one centre more than the others. These can be called our talents or our proclivities. By working on yourself you can achieve a greater balance in the centres which raises your vision and ultimately your level of wisdom.

What is wisdom but your ability to discern 'truth'? The quest for truth may seem like an abstract one, but its one that many of us are on without even realising it. Without doubt, it is this quest that lead you to reading this book! It is also the quest that people are on when they take up learning martial arts, or a craft skill, or start to write novels or create art or try to master any skill whatsoever.

It is my experience that this innate quest for truth does not exist within everyone to the same extent. But then those who are not interested in this would not have spent the time to read this book anyway, nor seek to learn new skills!

We can say that the task of awakening the Warrior is the best way to begin for the times we live in but that quest does not end there. If we consider the life of Miyamoto Musashi we can see this quest laid out. He lived the life of the warrior and found elements of the truth within the art of fighting which he later went on to write down in *The Book Of Five Rings*.

In order to explore and develop wisdom further he became a master of the art of painting in ink. In doing so, he found how the principles of fighting are linked to artistic expression. It is crucial to recognise that this was achieved by the actual process of painting, rather than by reading about it or merely thinking about it.

Musashi learnt how to express the principles of aesthetics in his work, which not only added to his wisdom but gave him a new perspective on those skills that he had already developed to a high level. He was in fact adding the understanding of the emotional and intellectual parts of the Emotional Centre to his knowledge in the Moving Centre. It should be no surprise to us that Musashi was consciously deepening his understanding of Zen Buddhism as he was painting, as both aesthetic and religious considerations occur within the emotional part of the Emotional Centre.

If wisdom is what we are seeking to have, then we should not be frightened to move into an investigation of these areas. If we have sufficiently awakened our Warrior, then our discerning eye will prevent us from getting lost too far down the 'rabbit hole'. So too will it ensure we maintain our practicality when broadening our quest again into the area of creative thinking.

These areas are beyond the scope of this book but as we go through one door, we can, at least, allow ourselves to look out of the window into what lies further. Whatever route in life your journey takes, I wish you the very best of luck.

NOTES & CITATIONS

CHAPTER ONE

1. Miyamoto, M., Yagyū, M., & Cleary, T. F., (1993). *The Book of Five Rings*. Boston; London: Shambhala.
2. Helft, M. (2014). *How Music Education Influenced Larry Page*. [online] Available at: http://fortune.com/2014/11/18/larry-page-music-education/
3. Mitchell, Sally (1998) *Victorian Britain Encyclopedia*. New York: Garland Publishing

CHAPTER TWO

4. Joseph Campbell, *On Becoming An Adult*. Campbell Foundation, 2010, {https://www.youtube.com/watch?v=aGx4IlppSgU&t=203s}

CHAPTER THREE

5. Johnson, B. (2014). *The Churchill Factor: How One Man Made History*. London: Hodder.
6. Diamond, J. (2005). *Guns, Germs & Steel: A Short History of Everybody for the Last 13,000 Years*. London: Vintage.
7. Cohen, R. (2010). *By The Sword*. Sydney: Pocket Books.
8. Hopton,R. (2011). *Pistols at Dawn: a history of duelling*. London: Piatkus.
9. Ibid, p.214.
10. Ibid, p.80-85.
11. (1974) Boxing. *Encyclopedia Britannia*. London: Helen Hemingway Benton.

CHAPTER FOUR

12. Campbell, J. (1991). *The Power of Myth*. New York: Anchor Books, p.95.
13. Yamamoto, T, Wilson, W.S. (2000) *Hakakure: The Book of the Samurai*. Tokyo: Kodansha.
14. Ibid.
15. Machiavelli, N. (1961). *The Prince*. Harmondsworth: Penguin Books, p.97.
16. *The Bible, New International Version*. London: Hodder Classics, 1 Timothy 6:10.
17. Plutarch, Talbert, R. (2005). *On Sparta*. London: Penguin.
18. Hibbert, C. (1994). *Nelson: A Personal History*. London: Basic Books, p.261

CHAPTER FIVE

19. Plato, Davies, J.W and Vaughn, D.J. (1935). *The Republic*. London: Macmillian & Co, Book I. 329.
20. Herbert, F. (2006) *Dune*. London: Hodder.
21. SunTzu and Giles, L. (1989) *Sun Tzu on the Art of War*. Singapore: Graham Brash, p.xi-xii.
22. Plato, Davies, J.W and Vaughn, D.J. (1935). *The Republic*. London: Macmillian & Co, Book IV.
23. Wilson, J (2016). *Up The Micks!: An Illustrated History of the Irish Guards*. Barnsley: Pen and Sword, p. 274.
24. Aurelius, M, Farquharson, A.S.L and Rees, D.A. (1992) *Book VII, Article LXIV*. New York: Knopf.
25. Poliakoff, M.B. (1987). *Combat Sports in the Ancient World*. New Haven: Yale University Press, p. 102-103
26. Ibid, p. 101. A quotation from the Spartan war poet, Tyrtaios.
27. Ibid.
28. Ibid. p.109.
29. Yamamoto, T, Wilson, W.S. (2000) *Hakakure: The Book of the Samurai*. Tokyo: Kodansha.

30. Hadot, P and Chase, M. (1995) *Philosophy as a way of life*. Malden: Blackwell Publishing, p.185
31. Ibid. p. 188.

CHAPTER SIX

32. Church, N.B.E. (2014). *Wack: Addicted to Internet Porn*. Bvrning Qvestions.
33. Ting, L. (2002). *Skills of the Vagabonds*. Hong Kong: Leung's Publications. p. 40.
34. Cummins, A. (2015) *Samurai and Ninja*. Tokyo: Tuttle.
35. Cohen, R. (2010) *By The Sword*. London: Pocket Books, p. xxiv.

CHAPTER SEVEN

36. Miller, R. (2008). *Meditations on Violence: A Comparison of Martial Arts Training and Real World Violence*. Wolfboro: YMAA.
37. Machiavelli, N. (1961). *The Prince*. Harmondsworth: Penguin Books, Chapter 13, p.86.
38. Plato, Davies, J.W and Vaughn, D.J. (1935). *The Republic*. London: Macmillian & Co, Book IV, 422.

CHAPTER EIGHT

39. Note for my American friends: the term 'public school' in the UK refers to a private school. Confusing isn't it?
40. White, M. (1998), *Isaac Newton: The Last Sorcerer*. London: Fourth Estate, p.50

INDEX

88829717R00207

Made in the USA
Columbia, SC
12 February 2018